MIX
Papier aus verantwortungsvollen Quellen
Paper from responsible sources
FSC® C105338

500 BREAD RECIPES
Fine Old Recipes

Title: Baked Cheddar Toast
Categories: Breads, Cheese, Eggs, Main dish
Servings: 6
1 c Heavy Or Whipping Cream 1 c Cheddar Cheese; Md, Shredded
1/2 ts Nutmeg 1/4 ts White Pepper
4 Eggs; Lg, Well Beaten 12 Bread Slices; White
In the top of a double boiler, combine the cream, cheddar, white pepper, and nutmeg. Stir over hot water until the cheese melts and the mixture is well blended. Remove from the heat and cool to lukewarm. Generously butter a large baking sheet and set aside. Cut the bread slices diagonally and dip each triangle into the cheddar mixture. Place 1/2-inch apart on the baking sheet and bake until browned and bubbly, about 15 minutes. Serve hot.

Title: French Toast Cheddar Sandwiches
Categories: Breads, Cheese, Eggs, Main dish, Sandwiches
Servings: 4
2 Eggs; Lg 1/3 c Milk Or Light Cream
1/2 ts Salt 8 White Bread; Slices
Mustard; Prepared 4 Cheddar Cheese; Thick, Slices
3 tb Butter
Set out a heavy skillet or cast iron griddle. Beat the eggs

slightly in a pie tin or shallow bowl and add the milk or cream and salt, set aside. Spread the bread slices out on a flat working surface. Spread one side of four slices of bread lightly with the prepared mustard. Top each with a slice of cheddar cheese. Butter the remaining four slices of bread and top each cheese slice with bread, butter side down. Heat the butter in the skillet or on the griddle. Carefully dip each sandwich into the egg mixture, coating both sides. Allow the excess egg mixture to drain back into the bowl. Dip only as many sandwiches as will lie flat in the skillet or griddle. Cook over low heat until browned. Turn and brown the other sides. Repeat for the remaining sandwiches and if necessary, add more butter to the skillet or griddle to prevent sticking. Or you can place the sandwiches, after dipping, on a well greased baking sheet and brown in the oven at 450 degrees F. for 8 to 10 minutes. Serve hot.

Title: Stuffed Rolls

Categories: Breads, Cheese, Main dish, Sandwiches, Vegetables
Servings: 6

16 oz Cheddar; Sharp, Shredded 8 oz Green Olives; Stuffed, ,,
2 Green Bell Peppers; Md 12 French Rolls; Large
6 oz Tomato Sauce; ,,1 Onion; Md.

,,These are approximate sizes. Recipe called for 1 small jar of stuffed olives and 1 can of tomato sauce. It should be to your taste.

Cut the tops off of the rolls and hollow them out leaving a thin shell. Grind all of the ingredients and bread in a meat grinder or food processor and stuff back into the rolls. Place the tops back on the rolls and secure with tooth picks. Bake on an ungreased cookie sheet at 350 degrees F. for about 45 minutes. Serve Hot.

Title: Poppin' Fresh Barbe Cups
Categories: Breads, Cheese, Main dish, Meats, Sandwiches
Servings: 6
3/4 lb Ground Beef; Lean 1 tb Onion; Minced
2 tb Brown Sugar 12 Biscuits; ,,
1/2 c Barbecue Sauce; ,,,,3/4 c Cheddar; Sharp, Shredded
,,Use 1 8-oz tube of store bought biscuits, or your favorite 12 biscuit recipe. ,,,,Use store bought sauce or your favorite recipe.

In a skillet brown the ground beef and then drain off the excess fat. Add the bbq sauce, onion and brown sugar and set aside. Separate the biscuit dough into 12 pieces and place one in each of 12 ungreased muffin cups,pressing the dough up the sides to the edge of the cup. Spoon the mixture into the cups and sprinkle with the shredded Cheddar Cheese. Bake in a preheated 400 degrees F. oven for 12 minutes. Serve hot.
VARIATIONS: Use 1
13-oz can of chili beans in place of the meat mixture (or 1 13-oz can of baked beans, and frankfurters or hot dogs that have been cut into pieces) in place of the meat mixture. You can also add green bell pepper or a hot pepper to the above recipe with good results.

Title: Cheddar Crackers
Categories: Breads, Crackers, Cheese
Servings: 6
1/2 c Butter Or Margarine 1 1/2 c Unbleached Flour; Sifted
1/2 ts Salt 1 ts Baking Powder
1 ds Cayenne Pepper 2 c Cheddar; Extra Sharp, ,,

„The Extra Sharp Cheddar Cheese should be finely grated.

Stir the dry ingredients into a bowl and then cut in the butter to resemble cornmeal. Blend in the cheddar cheese with a fork until well blended. Mix in the remaining ingredients and shape into 1 1/2 to 2-inch rolls. Chill for 30 to 40 minutes in the refrigerator and then slice each roll into slices about 1/4-inch thick. Bake on an ungreased cookie sheet at 400 degrees F for about 10 minutes. Remove from cookie sheet and let cool. Store the cooled crackers in airtight containers in a cool place. They will keep for several weeks this way and if you freeze them, they will last indefinitely.

Title: Cheddar-Olive Bread
Categories: Breads, Cheese, Vegetables
Servings: 6
3 c Cheddar; Sharp, Grated 3 oz Pimento-StuffedOlives;Sliced
1 c Mayonnaise 1 French Bread; Loaf, Unsliced
Mix the cheese, olives, and mayonnaise together. Spread on the cut surface of the French Bread, which has been sliced horizontally. Bake at 350 degrees F for 20 to 30 minutes, then slice into thick slices and serve hot.

Title: Chili-Cheese Bread
Categories: Breads, Vegetables
Servings: 6
3 c Monterey Jack Cheese; Grated 4 oz Chiles; Chopped, „
1 c Mayonnaise 1 French Bread; Loaf, Unsliced
„You can use one can of sweet green chiles or jalapenos that have been chopped.

Mix the cheese, peppers, and mayonnaise, blending well. Spread on the cut surface of the French bread, which has been sliced in half horizontally. Bake at 350 degrees F for 20 to 30 minutes and cut into thick slices and serve hot.

Title: Cheddar Fans
Categories: Breads, Cheese, Quickbreads
Servings: 4
5 oz Cheddar; Sharp, Grated 2 c Unbleached Flour; Sifted
1 tb Baking Powder 1 ts Salt
1/2 c Butter Or Shortening 1/2 c Milk
Butter; Softened Butter; Melted

Grease the bottoms of 12 muffin pan cups. Grate the cheese into a bowl, if not already grated and set aside. Sift the flour, baking powder and salt into a bowl. Cut in the shortening with a pastry blender or two knives, until the mixture resembles coarse corn meal. Make a well in the center of the mixture and add the milk all at once. Stir with a fork until the dough forms a ball. Gently form the dough into a ball and put on a lightly floured surface. Knead it lightly with the fingertips 10 or 15 times. Roll the dough into a 12 X 10-inch rectangle about 1/4-inch thick. Cut into 5 strips and spread with the softened butter. Sprinkle four strips with the grated cheddar cheese and stack the four on top of one another and top with the fifth strip. Cut into 12 equal pieces and place on end in the muffin cups. Brush the tops of the rolls with the melted butter. Bake at 450 degrees F. for 10 to 15 minutes or until the biscuits are golden brown. Serve hot with butter. Makes 1 dozen Cheddar Fans.

Title: Little Cheddar Biscuits
Categories: Breads, Cheese, Quickbreads
Servings: 8
2 c Unbleached Flour 1 ts Mustard; Dry
1 ts Paprika 1/4 ts Baking Powder
1 c Butter; Room Temperature 10 oz Cheddar; Sharp,

Grated
1 ts Worcestershire Sauce

Combine the flour, dry mustard, paprika and baking powder in a medium bowl.Beat the butter, either by hand or with an electric mixer at medium speed, until light and fluffy. Slowly beat in the cheddar cheese and Worcestershire sauce. Gradually add the flour mixture, stirring with a fork, until well blended. On a lightly floured surface, shape the dough into a long roll about 1 3/4-inches in diameter. Wrap in plastic wrap or foil. Place on a platter and refrigerate for at least 2 hours, better overnight. Preheat the oven to 325 degrees F. Slice the dough about 1/3 inch thick. With your hands, roll each slice into a ball. Flatten slightly and place on an ungreased baking sheet about 2 inches apart. Bake 8 minutes in the preheated oven. Biscuits will only brown slightly on the bottom.

Title: Cheddar Biscuits

Categories: Breads, Cheese, Quickbreads
Servings: 8

2 c Unbleached Flour; Sifted 4 ts Baking Powder
1/2 ts Salt 1 c Cheddar; Sharp, Grated
1/4 c Butter 2/3 c Milk

Sift the flour, baking powder, and salt together and mix with the grated cheddar cheese. Cut the butter into the dry ingredients, add the milk and mix quickly but thoroughly. The dough should be soft. Turn onto a floured board and knead lightly for a few seconds. Pat to a 3/8-inch thickness and cut. Bake on a baking sheet in a hot-oven (450 degrees F.) about 30 minutes or until lightly browned. Serve hot.

Title: Cheddar Pinwheels

Categories: Breads, Cheese, Quickbreads
Servings: 6

2 c Unbleached Flour; Sifted 1/2 ts Salt
1 tb Baking Powder 1/4 c Butter
2/3 c Milk 1 c Cheddar; Extra Sharp, Grated

Sift the flour, salt, and baking powder together in a mixing bowl and then cut into the butter. Add the milk and stir together quickly but thoroughly. Turn out on a floured board and knead for 30 seconds then roll out to a 1/8-inch thickness. Spread with the grated cheese and roll up tightly like cinnamon rolls. Cut into 3/4-inch slices and transfer to baking sheets and bake in a moderate oven (375 degrees F.) for 20 minutes or until delicately browned.

Title: Cheddar Bread Ring

Categories: Cheese, Breads, Yeast bread
Servings: 4

2 3/4 c Bread Flour 2 tb Sugar; Granulated
1 pk Active Dry Yeast; OR 1 tb Active Dry Yeast; Bulk
3/4 ts Salt 1 c Milk
2 tb Butter 1 1/2 c Cheddar; Sharp, Shredded
Butter

NOTE: You can use Unbleached All-Purpose flour in this recipe and up to 3 cups total.

Combine 1 1/2 cups of the flour, the sugar, undissolved yeast and salt thoroughly in a large bowl. Heat the milk and butter together until very warm (115-125 degrees F.). Gradually add to the dry ingredients and beat at medium speed on an electric mixer for 2 minutes, scraping the bowl occasionally. Add 1/2 cup of the flour and the cheese. Beat fir 2 minutes on high speed on the mixer, scraping the bowl occasionally. Stir in enough additional flour to make a stiff but light dough. Turn the dough out onto a lightly floured surface and knead until smooth and elastic, 5 to 8 minutes. Place in a greased bowl, turning once to grease the top.

Cover with a dishtowel that has been soaked in hot water and then wrung out until almost dry. Let rise in a warm place until doubled in bulk, about 1 hour. Punch the dough down and turn out on a lightly floured surface and shape into a 20-inch rope. Place seam side down in a buttered 6 1/2 cup ring mold, pinching the ends together. Cover and let rise in warm place until nearly doubled in bulk, about 35 to 40 minutes. Bake in a preheated 350 degree F. oven for 25 to 30 minutes. Remove from the ring mold. NOTE: For a softer crust, brush with melted butter while still hot. Crust will become crisp when cool if you do not.

Title: Golden Spoon Bread
Categories: Breads, Cheese, Quickbreads
Servings: 6
10 oz Cheddar; Sharp, Grated 2 c Milk
4 Egg Yolks; Lg 1 c Corn Meal; Yellow
1/4 c Butter 1 ts Sugar
1/2 ts Salt 4 Egg Whites; Lg

Thoroughly grease a 1 1/2-quart casserole dish. Place the cheddar in a small bowl and set aside. Scald the milk in the top of a double boiler. Meanwhile beat the egg yolks until thick and lemon-colored then set them aside. When the milk is scalded, add the corn meal very gradually, stirring constantly. Stir until the mixture thickens and becomes smooth. Remove the top of the double boiler from the simmering water and gradually add the beaten egg yolks, stirring constantly. Mix in the grated cheese, butter, sugar and salt. Beat the egg whites, in a small bowl, until round peaks are formed. Gently spread the beaten egg whites over the corn meal mixture then carefully fold together until just blended. Turn the mixture into the greased casserole dish. Bake at 375 degrees F. for 35 to 40 minutes or until a wooden pick or cake tester comes out clean when inserted in the center of the dish. Serve piping hot with butter and maple syrup or honey.

Title: Cheddar Dumplings
Categories: Breads, Cheese, Main dish, Quickbreads
Servings: 4
16 oz Cheddar; Md, Shredded 2 Eggs; Lg
1 c Unbleached Flour 1 ts Salt
3 qt Boiling Water 1/2 c Butter
1/2 pt Sour Cream
---------------GARNISHES--------------------------------
Paprika Parsley
Mash the cheddar cheese and add the eggs mixing well. Stir in the flour and salt. Drop by TBLS into the rapidly boiling water then cover and boil for 15 minutes. Drain and serve with melted butter and sour cream.Sprinkle with chopped parsley or paprika, if desired.

Title: Golden Cheddar Corn Bread
Categories: Breads, Cheese, Side dishes, Quickbreads
Servings: 6
1 c Corn Meal; White If Poss. 1 c Unbleached Flour
1 tb Baking Powder 1 1/2 ts Salt
10 oz Cheddar; Sharp, Shredded 1 c Milk
1/4 c Butter, Melted 1 Egg; Lg, Beaten
Combine the dry ingredients and then stir in the cheddar cheese. Combine the milk, butter and egg then add them to the dry ingredients, mixing until just moistened. Pour into a greased 8-inch square baking pan and bake at 425 degrees F for 35 minutes. Serve hot.

Title: Apple-Cheddar Muffins

Categories: Breads, Cheese, Fruits, Quickbreads
Servings: 4

1/2 c Shortening 1/2 c Sugar; Granulated
2 Eggs; Lg 1 1/2 c Unbleached Flour
1 ts Baking Soda 1 ts Baking Powder
1/2 ts Salt 3/4 c Oats; Quick Cooking
1 c Apples; Finely Chopped 2/3 c Cheddar; Sharp Coarse Grate
1/2 c Pecans; Chopped 3/4 c Milk
Apple Slices; „Butter; Melted Cinnamon-Sugar Mixture
„You should have 12 to 15 thin slices of unpeeled red apple for this recipe.

Preheat the oven to 400 degrees F. Cream the shortening and sugar together and add the eggs, one at a time, beating well after each addition. Combine the flour, baking powder, baking soda, and salt in a mixing bowl, mix lightly. Gradually stir the flour mixture into the shortening mixture. In this order, add the oats cheddar and pecans, mixing well after each addition. Gradually add the milk, stirring until all the ingredients are just moistened. Grease the muffin pans and fill each cup 2/3rds full of batter. Dip the apple slices in the melted butter and then into the cinnamon-sugar. Press 1 apple slice into the top of each muffin. Sprinkle lightly with cinnamon-sugar and bake for 25 minutes in the preheated oven, or until golden brown.

Title: Quick Cheddar Bread

Categories: Breads, Cheese, Quickbreads
Servings: 4

3 3/4 c Unbleached Flour 5 ts Baking Powder
1/2 ts Salt 1/3 c Butter
2 1/2 c Cheddar; Sharp 1 1/2 c Milk
2 Eggs; Lg, Slightly Beaten

Combine the dry ingredients, then cut the butter into the flour until the mixture resembles coarse crumbs, then add the cheddar cheese. Combine the milk and eggs then add the mixture to the cheddar mixture. Stir until just moistened, then spoon into a greased 9 X 5-inch loaf pan. Bake at 375 degrees F. hour. Remove from the pan immediately and let cool on a wire rack.

Title: Cheesy Corn Bread
Categories: Breads, Cheese, Quickbreads
Servings: 6
1 c Unbleached Flour 1 c Corn Meal; White Or Yellow
2 tb Sugar 1 tb Baking Powder
1 ts Salt 1/4 ts Mustard; Dry
2 c Cheddar; Sharp, Shredded 1 Egg; Lg, Slightly Beaten
1 c Milk 1/4 c Vegetable Oil
Combine the dry ingredients, then stir in the cheddar cheese. Combine the egg with the milk and oil. Stir into the cheddar mixture, mixing until just moistened. Pour the mixture into a greased 9-inch square baking pan. Bake at 425 degrees F. for 20 minutes. Cool slightly and cut into squares, then serve warm.

Title: Cheddar Squares
Categories: Breads, Cheese, Quickbreads, Vegetables
Servings: 6
2 c Unbleached Flour 1 tb Baking Powder
1 ts Salt 1/3 c Butter
1 c Cheddar; Sharp, Shredded 1/2 c Onion; Chopped
2 tb Pimento; Chopped 2/3 c Milk
Combine the dry ingredients, then cut the butter into the dry mixture until it resembles coarse crumbs. Add the cheddar, onion, and pimento, mixing well. Add the milk, mixing until just moistened. Spread the dough in a 9-inch square baking

pan and bake at 450 degrees F. for 25 to 30 minutes or until a wooden pick inserted in the center comes out clean. Cool slightly and cut into squares. Serve warm.

Title: Cheddar Date Nut Loaf

Categories: Breads, Cheese, Fruits, Quickbreads
Servings: 4
8 oz Dates; Finely Chopped 2 tb Butter
3/4 c Water; Boiling 1 3/4 c Unbleached Flour; Sifted
1/4 ts Salt 1 ts Baking Soda
1/2 c Sugar; Granulated 1 Egg; Lg, Well Beaten
4 oz Cheddar Md, Shredded 1 c Walnuts; Chopped

Preheat the oven to 325 degrees F. Place the dates and butter in a small bowl and pour the boiling water over them. Let stand for 5 minutes. Stir the dry ingredients together in a large bowl. Add the date mixture, egg, cheddar and nuts. Mix until just blended and spoon the mixture into a well greased 9 X 5-inch loaf pan. Let stand for 20 minutes. Bake for 50 to 60 minutes in the preheated oven or until a wooden pick inserted in the center of the loaf comes out clean. Turn out onto a rack and cool before slicing.
NOTE: The flavor improves is the bread stands overnight before serving.

Title: No-Knead Cheddar Rolls

Categories: Breads, Cheese, Yeast bread
Servings: 8
1 1/2 c Unbleached Flour; Unsifted 1 pk Active Dry Yeast; OR
1 tb Active Dry Yeast; Bulk 3 tb Sugar
1 ts Salt 3/4 c Milk

1/2 c Water 3 tb Butter
1 c Unbleached Flour; Unsifted 1 c Cheddar; Sharp, Grated
1/4 c Butter 1 Egg Yolk; Lg
1 tb Milk

Place the grated cheese in a small bowl and cover to prevent drying then set aside. Combine 1 1/2 cups unsifted flour, yeast, sugar, and salt in a large mixer bowl, blending thoroughly. Measure 3/4 c of milk, water, and butter into a saucepan and heat until the liquids are warm, 115 to 120 degrees F.. Gradually add the liquids to the dry ingredients in the mixer bowl, beating for 2 minutes at medium speed of the electric mixer, scraping the bowl occasionally. Add and beat in 1 cup of unsifted flour at high speed. Beat for 2 minutes, scraping the bowl occasionally. Mix in enough additional flour (1/2 to 1 cup unsifted) to make a soft dough. (Dough will be slightly sticky.) Put the dough into a greased deep bowl. Cover with waxed paper and a clean towel and let stand in a warm place until the dough has doubled, 45 to 60 minutes. Generously grease several baking sheets. Melt the butter and set aside. Punch the dough down wit a fist and turn the dough out onto a lightly floured surface. Divide the dough into two equal portions. Set one portion aside. Roll the dough into a rectangle 16 X 8-inches. Brush with about one-half of the melted butter. Sprinkle with about one half of the grated cheddar cheese. Cut crosswise into 8 equal portions. Cut into halves lengthwise. Fold each strip into thirds, lapping each side portion over the center third. Place the rolls on a baking sheet. Repeat for the other half of the dough. Beat the egg yolk with the tbls of milk, slightly. Brush the tops of the rolls with the egg yolk mixture. Let rise until doubled, about 30 minutes. Bake at 425 degrees F. for about 8 minutes or until rolls are golden brown. Serve rolls hot.

Title: Panhandle Cornbread

Categories: Breads, Cheese, Quickbreads, Vegetables
Servings: 4

1 c Corn Meal; Yellow 1 tb Baking Powder
1 c Cheddar; Sharp, Shredded 2 Eggs; Lg, Beaten
1/2 c Vegetable Oil 1 c Dairy Sour Cream
8 oz Corn; Cream Style, 1 Cn 4 oz Green Chile Peppers; Chopped

Preheat the oven to 400 degrees F. and generously grease a 12 cup bundt or 9-inch tube pan; set aside. In a large bowl, combine the cornmeal and baking powder. Stir in the cheddar. In a medium bowl, beat the eggs, oil, sour cream, corn and chiles together. Add to the cornmeal mixture. Stir until just moistened and then spoon the batter into the prepared pan. Bake for 40 to 50 minutes in the preheated oven until a wooden pick inserted in the center comes out clean. Cool on a rack for 10 minutes then invert over a serving plate.

Title: Hearthside Cheddar Bread

Categories: Breads, Cheese, Fruits, Quickbreads
Servings: 4

2 1/2 c Unbleached Flour 1/2 c Sugar
2 ts Baking Powder 1 ts Salt
1/2 ts Cinnamon; Ground 3/4 c Milk
1/4 c Vegetable Oil 2 Eggs; Lg
1 1/2 c Apples; Cooking, „2 c Cheddar; Sharp, Shredded
3/4 c Walnuts Or Pecans; Chopped

„Apples should be the cooking type (sour not sweet eating apples).They should be peeled, cored, and chopped.

Preheat the oven to 350 degrees F. and grease and flour a 9 X 5-inch loaf pan. In a large bowl, combine the flour, sugar, baking powder, salt and cinnamon. Make a well in the center of the dry ingredients and add the milk, oil, and eggs. Stir until thoroughly combined. Gently stir in the chopped apples, cheddar cheese, and nuts. Bake for 1 hour and 15 minutes in the preheated oven until loaf is browned and sounds hollow when tapped on the bottom. Cool in the pan on a rack for 5 minutes. Remove from the pan and cool to room temperature, on a wire rack, before slicing.

Title: Sunrise Popovers
Categories: Breads, Cheese, Quickbreads
Servings: 8
4 tb Vegetable Shortening 1 1/3 c Unbleached Flour
1/2 ts Salt 2/3 c Milk
2/3 c Water 4 Eggs; Lg
1/2 c Cheddar; Sharp, Shredded

Preheat the oven to 375 degrees F. Place eight 6-oz custard cups on a large baking sheet. Spoon 1 1/2 tsp of shortening into the bottom of each custard cup and set aside. Combine the flour and salt in a large bowl, then gradually stir in the milk and water until well blended. Beat in the eggs, 1 at a time, beating until smooth after each addition. Fold in the cheddar cheese. Place the baking sheet with the custard cups in the preheated oven for 3 to 5 minutes until the shortening melts and the custard cups are hot. Fill the custard cups 1/2 to 2/3rds full with the batter. Bake for 45 minutes in the preheated oven, without opening the oven door until the popovers rise and turn golden brown. If not golden brown after 45 minutes, bake for an additional 5 minutes. Serve piping hot.

Title: Polka Dot Quick Bread
Categories: Breads, Cheese, Quickbreads, Fruits
Servings: 4
2 c Cranberries; Fresh Or Frozen 1 c Milk

1 Egg; Lg, Slightly Beaten 1/4 c Butter; Melted
1 tb Orange Peel; Grated 2 c Unbleached Flour
1 c Sugar 1 tb Baking Powder
1/2 ts Salt 1 1/2 c Cheddar; Md, Shredded
1/2 c Walnuts; Coarsely Chopped

Preheat the oven to 350 degrees F. then grease a 9 X 5-inch loaf pan; set aside. Cut the cranberries in half and set aside in a small bowl. In a medium bowl, combine the milk, egg, butter, and orange peel and set aside. Sift the flour, sugar, baking powder, and salt into a large bowl. Add the halved cranberries, cheese and nuts. Toss with a fork to distribute. Add the milk mixture all at once and stir the flour mixture until just moistened. Turn into the prepared loaf pan and bake for 1 hour and 15 minutes in the preheated oven or until a wooden pick inserted in the center comes out clean. Cool in the pan on a rack for 10 minutes, then remove from the pan. Cool to room temperature on the wire rack before slicing.

Title: Cheddar Braids

Categories: Breads, Cheese, Yeast bread
Servings: 8

1 c Water; Warm, 110-115 Deg. F. 1 pk Active Dry Yeast; OR
1 tb Active Dry Yeast; Bulk 3 1/2 c Unbleached Flour; „
1 ts Sugar 1 1/2 ts Salt
3/4 c Butter; Room Temperature 4 Eggs; Lg, Room Temperature
6 oz Cheddar; Extra Sharp, Diced 1 Egg; Lg
1 tb Milk 2 tb Celery Seeds

„You can use up to 4 1/2 cups of flour in this recipe depending on theweather.

Pour the warm water into a warm bowl and add the yeast. Stir to dissolve then let stand until light and puffed, about 5 minutes. Add 1 1/2 cups of the flour, sugar and salt. Beat with an electric mixer on the lowest speed for 1 minute. Beat on medium speed for 2 minutes longer. Add the butter to the yeast mixture and beat for another 1 minute. On the lowest speed on the mixer, beat in 1 egg and 1/2 cup of flour until well blended, repeating until the 4 eggs are used up and enough flour has been added to make a soft sticky dough. Continue to beat with the mixer or by hand, until the dough is glossy and elastic and pulls away from the side of the bowl. Stir in the cheddar cheese by hand. Cover and let rise in a warm place free from drafts until doubled in bulk, about 2 1/2 to 3 hours. When the dough has doubled in bulk, punch down and place in the refrigerator for at least 5 hours or better, overnight. Remove the dough from the refrigerator. Divide in half and cover and refrigerate the second ball of dough. Knead the remaining ball of dough on a lightly floured surface until soft and pliable. Divide the dough into 3 equal parts and roll each piece into a rope 12 to 16-inches long. Braid the ropes, starting in the middle and working toward each end. Pinch the ends together so seal them. Grease a large baking sheet and place the finished braid on one side of the sheet.Repeat with the refrigerated dough. In a small bowl beat the egg and milk together. Brush the braids with the egg mixture and let the braids rise in a warm place, free from drafts, until dough in bulk, about 1 1/2 to 2 hours. Do not cover. Midway through the rising time, brush with the egg mixture again. Preheat the oven to 400 degrees F. When fully risen, brush with the egg mixture for a final time and sprinkle evenly with the celery seeds. Bake for 40 minutes in the preheated oven until a wooden skewer or pick inserted in the braid comes out dry. Remove from the oven and from the baking sheet. Cool to room temperature, on wire racks, before slicing.

Title: Crusty Cheddar Bread

Categories: Breads, Cheese, Yeast bread
Servings: 4
1 pk Active Dry Yeast; OR 1 tb Active Dry Yeast; Bulk
1/4 c Water; Warm, 110-115 Deg. F. 1 c Cottage Cheese; ,,
1 tb Sugar 1 1/4 ts Salt
1 Egg; Lg. 2 1/4 c Unbleached Flour; Unsifted,,,
1 tb Butter; Room Temperature 1 c Cheddar; Sharp, Grated
,,The cottage cheese should be the small curd kind at room temperature. ,,,,You can use up to an extra 1/4 cup of flour in this recipe depending onthe weather.

Sprinkle the yeast over the warm water and let stand 5 minutes. Gently stir to completely dissolve. With an electric mixer, blend the softened yeast into the cottage cheese, sugar, salt and egg. Add the flour in ½ cup portions to form a stiff but light dough and let rise in a warm place until doubled in bulk. Butter a 1 1/2 quart casserole dish and stir the dough down, then add 1 cup of the grated cheddar cheese. Turn into the buttered dish. Let rise 30 to 40 minutes longer or until almost doubled in size. Preheat the oven to 350 degrees F. and bake for 40 to 50 minutes or until golden brown. Brush the top with butter.

Title: Sourdough Starter #1

Categories: Breads
Servings: 1
2 c Unbleached Flour 1 pk Active Dry Yeast
Water To Make Thick Batter Mix Flour with yeast. Add enough water to make a thick batter. Set in warm place for 24 hours or until house is filled with a delectable yeasty smell.

Title: Sourdough Starter #2
Categories: Breads
Servings: 1
2 c Unbleached Flour Water To Make Thick Batter
Mix flour and water to make a thick batter. Let stand uncovered for four or five days, or until it begins working. This basic recipe requires a carefully scalded container.

Title: Sourdough Starter #3
Categories: Breads
Servings: 1
2 c Unbleached Flour Warm Milk To Make Thick Bat.
This starter is the same as starter #2 but uses warm Milk instead of water. Use the same instructions.

Title: Sourdough Starter #4
Categories: Breads
Servings: 1
Unbleached Flour Potato Water Boil some potatoes for supper, save the potato water, and use it lukewarm with enough unbleached flour to make a thick batter. without yeast. This is a good way to make it in camp, where you have no yeast available and want fast results. This is also the way most farm girls made it in the olden days. Let stand a day or so, or until it smells right.

Title: Sourdough Starter #5
Categories: Breads
Servings: 1
4 c Unbleached Flour 2 tb Salt

2 tb Sugar 4 c Lukewarm Potato Water
Put all ingredients in a crock or large jar and let stand in a warm place uncovered several days.

Title: Sourdough Starter #6
Categories: Breads
Servings: 1
1 c Milk 1 c Unbleached Flour
Let milk stand for a day or so in an uncovered container at room temperature. Add flour to milk and let stand for another couple of days. When it starts working well and smells right, it is ready to use. NOTE: All containers for starters not using yeast, must be carefully scalded before use. If you are carless or do not scald them the starter will fail.

Title: Sourdough Pancakes #4
Categories: Breads
Servings: 4
1 c Buttermilk Pancake Mix 1/2 c Active Starter
1/2 c Milk 1 Large Egg
1 tb Cooking Oil 1/2 ts Baking Powder
Mix well and let stand a few moments. Drop by large spoonsful on hot griddle.

Title: Sourdough Pancakes #5
Categories: Breads
Servings: 6
3 Large Eggs, Well Beaten 1 c Sweet Milk
2 c Active Starter 1 3/4 c Unbleached Flour
1 ts Baking Soda 2 ts Baking Powder
1 1/2 ts Salt 1/4 c Sugar

Beat eggs. Add milk and starter. Sift together the flour, soda, baking powder, salt, and sugar. Mix together. Drop onto hot griddle by large spoonsful. NOTE: If ungreased griddle is used add 1/4 c Melted Fat to the above recipe. Bacon fat give a great taste.

Title: Sourdough French Bread
Categories: Breads
Servings: 18
1 pk Active Dry Yeast 1/4 c Warm Water (110 to 115 F)
4 1/2 c Unbleached Flour, Unsifted 2 tb Sugar
2 ts Salt 1 c Warm Water
1/2 c Milk 2 tb Vegetable Oil
1/4 c Sourdough Starter

Dissolve yeast in warm water. Add the rest of the ingredients. Mix and knead lightly and return to the bowl to rise until double. Turn out onto floured board and divide dough into two parts. Shape dough parts into oblongs and then roll them up tightly, beginning with one side. Seal the outside edge by pinching and shape into size wanted. Place loaves on greased baking sheet and let rise until double again. Make diagonal cuts on top of loaves with razor blade or VERY SHARP knife and brush lightly water for crisp crust. Bake at 400 degrees F for about 25 minutes, or until brown and done. NOTE: Makes 2 loaves at 18 slices each. Also note the the serving sizes in all of these recipes is guesstamate. It all depends on the serving size you select.

Title: The Doctor's Sourdough Bread
Categories: Breads
Servings: 18
1 c Sourdough Starter 2 c Warm Water
2 c Warm Milk 1 tb Butter
1 pk Active Dry Yeast 1/4 c Honey

7 c Unbleached Flour 1/4 c Wheat Germ
2 tb Sugar 2 ts Salt
2 ts Baking Soda

Mix the starter and 2 1/2 Cups of the flour and all the water the night before you want to bake. Let stand in warm place overnight. Next morning mix in the butter with warm milk and stir in yeast until until dissolved.Add honey and when thoroughly mixed, add 2 more cups of flour, and stir in the wheat germ. Sprinkle sugar, salt, and baking soda over the mixture. Gentlypress into dough and mix lightly. Allow to stand from 30 to 50 minutes until mixture is bubbly. Add enough flour until the dough cleans the sides of the bowl. Then place the dough on a lightly floured board and kead 100 times or until silky mixture is developed. Form into 4 1-lb loaves, place in well-greased loaf pans 9 x 3 size. Let rise until double, about 2 to 3 hours in a warm room. Then bake in hot oven, 400 degrees F, for 20 minutes. Reduce oven temp. to 325 degrees F. and bake 20 minutes longer or until thoroughly baked. Remove from pans and place loaves on rack to cool. Butter tops of loaves to prevent hard crustyness. Makes 4 1-lb Loaves

Title: Honeymoon Sourdoughs

Categories: Breads
Servings: 4

1 c Active Starter 1 1/4 c Prepared Biscuit Mix
1/2 ts Baking Powder 1 tb Cooking Oil

Mix all ingredients thoroughly and turn out onto a floured board, knead lightly and then roll out gently and cut into biscuits. Brush lightly with melted butter or margarine. Place of greased cookie sheet and bake at 450 degrees for about 15 minutes. Makes 9 Large biscuits.

Title: Aunt Cora's Biscuits

Categories: Breads
Servings: 4
1 1/2 c Sifted Unbleached Flour 3 ts Baking Powder
1 ts Salt 1 1/2 ts Baking Soda „
2 tb Sugar 1/4 c Shortening, Melted
1 1/2 c Sourdough Starter

„More Baking Soda may be added if the starter if very sour. Place flour in bowl, add starter in a well, then add melted shortening and dry ingredients. Mix lightly and turn out onto a lightly floured board and knead until the consistency of bread dough, or of a satiny finish. Pat or roll out dough to 1/2 inch thickness, cut and put on a greased pan. Coat all sides of biscuits with melted butter. Let rise over boiling water for 1/2 hour. Bake at 425 degrees F for 15 to 20 minutes.

Title: Sourdough Biscuits

Categories: Breads
Servings: 4
1/2 c Active Starter 1 c Milk
2 1/2 c Flour 1/3 c Lard or Shortening
1 tb Sugar 3/4 ts Salt
2 ts Baking Powder 1/2 ts Baking Soda
1/4 ts Cream Of Tartar

At bedtime make a batter of the half cup of starter, cup of milk, and 1 cup of the flour. Let set overnight if the biscuits are wanted for breakfast. If wanted for noon, the batter maybe mixed in the morning and set in a warm place to rise. However, unless the weather is real warm, it is always all right to let it ferment overnight. It will get very light and bubbly. When ready to mix the biscuits, sift together the remaining cup and a half of flour and all other dry ingredients except the baking soda. Work in the lard or shortening with your fingers or a fork. Add baking soda dissolved in a little warm water to the sponge and then add the flour mixture. Mix into a soft dough. Knead lightly a few times to get in shape. Roll out to about 1/2 inch thickness or a little thicker, and cut with a biscuit cutter. Place close together in a 9 x 13-inch pan, turning to grease tops. Cover and set in a warm place to rise for about 45 minutes. Bake in a 375 degree oven for about 30 to 35 minutes. Leftovers are good split and toasted in a sandwich toaster.

Title: Sheepherder Bread

Categories: Breads
Servings: 18
1 1/2 c Active Sourdough Starter 4 c Unbleached Flour
2 tb Sugar 2 tb Shortening, Melted
1 ts Salt 1/4 ts Baking Soda
Into a large bowl, sift the dry ingredients, and dig a well in the center of the sourdough starter. Blend the dry mix into the starter from the edges with enough flour to knead until smooth and shiny. Place in greased bowl and let rise until almost double. Shape into 2 loaves and place in greased bread pans. Bake at 375 degrees F until done.

Title: Sourdough Sams

Categories: Breads
Servings: 4
1/2 c Active Sourdough Starter 1/2 c Sugar
2 tb Shortening 2 c Unbleached Flour
1 ts Baking Powder 1 Large Egg
1/2 ts Nutmeg 1/4 ts Cinnamon
1/2 ts Baking Soda 1/2 ts Salt
1/3 c Buttermilk or Sour Milk
Sift dry ingredients, stir into liquid, roll out and cut with

regular donut cutter. Then heat some oil in a deep fryer to 390 degrees F and fry. Makes about 17 Doughnuts with holes. Just before serving dust with powdered or cinnamon sugar. NOTE: These doughnuts are virtually greasless. And if you want you can make several batches at a time and freeze. They keep well and to me taste after a while in the freezer. Take out as many as needed and thaw and put sugar on or eat plain.

Title: 100% Whole Wheat Bread
Categories: Breads, Yeast
Servings: 6
2/3 c Water 3 pk Yeast
1 tb Sugar 8 c Scalded milk
2/3 c Shortening 1 c Sugar
1/2 c Molasses 2 tb Salt
12 c Whole wheat flour

Dissolve yeast in 2/3 c water while your milk is cooling. Dissolve 1 cup sugar in the hot milk. Stir all ingredients in large bowl, turn out and knead about 5 minutes, adding flour if needed. Knead about 5 minutes. Let rise until doubled in bulk, about 1 1/2 to 2 hours. Knead down and shape into 6 loaves, let rise until doubled in pans. Bake at 375 degrees F. for 40 minutes. Turn out on wire rack and let cool to cold before slicing, if you can. NOTE: Raisins and/or walnuts can be added for a change. Also this bread freezes well.

Title: Bacon, Cheese, And Tomato Sandwiches
Categories: Vegetables, Breads
Servings: 3
3 Slices bacon 3 Slices rye bread, toasted
2 tb Mayo. or salad dressing 1/2 ts Dried dill weed

1 Large tomato, sliced 3 Slices swiss cheese
Place bacon on microwave rack in glass dish. Cover loosely and microwave until crisp, 2 1/2 to 3 1/2 minutes. Spread toast with mayonnaise; sprinkle with dill. Place toast slices on serving plate; top with tomato and cheese slices. Crumble bacon and sprinkle over top. Microwave uncovered on high (100%) until cheese begins to melt, 1 to 1 1/2 minutes.

Title: Corn Bread

Categories: Penndutch, Breads
Servings: 1
1 c Cornmeal, yellow ,,or:
1 c Cornmeal, white 4 tb Sugar
1 ts Salt 1 Egg, well beaten
1 c Milk, skim 1 c Flour
4 ts Baking powder 2 tb Butter, melted

Add the sugar and salt to the cornmeal. Beat the egg well and pour into the milk; stir this mixture into the meal, beating thoroughly. Sift the flour and baking powder into the meal, add the melted butter and beat hard. Pour the mixture into a greased pan and bake at 400-F until brown. To make a thin crisp Johnny Cake, use an oblong pan and spread batter thinly. For a soft loaf, spread batter thickly.
Pennsylvania Dutch Fine Old Recipes, Culinary Arts Press, 1936.

Title: Ham And Cheese With Coleslaw

Categories: Main dish, Vegetables, Breads
Servings: 4
2 tb Margarine or butter 1/2 ts Prepared mustard
4 Slices rye bread, toasted 4 Slices cooked ham
1 Large tomato, sliced 4 Slices cheese
1 c Coleslaw

Microwave margarine uncovered in custard cup on high (100%0 until softened, 15 to 30 seconds. Blend in mustard. Spread margarine on one side of each toast lsice. Place slices buttered sides up on serving plate; top with ham tomato and cheese slices. Microwave uncovered until cheese begins to melt,1 1/2 to 2 minutes. Top each sandwich with a spoonful of coleslaw.

Title: High-Protein Muffins
Categories: Muffins, Breads, Breakfast
Servings: 10
1 1/2 c Raisins 1 3/4 c Milk
1 c Stirred whole wheat flour 1 c Soy flour
1 c Toasted wheat germ 4 ts Baking powder
1 1/2 ts Ground nutmeg 3/4 ts Salt
4 Large eggs, slightly beaten 2/3 c Honey
2/3 c Vegetable oil 1/4 c Dark molasses
Combine Bran Flakes, raisins and milk in large mixing bowl. Stir together whole wheat flour, soy flour, wheat germ, baking powder, nutmeg and salt; set aside. Combine eggs, honey, oil and molasses in small bowl; blend well. Add egg mixture to soaked bran flakes; mix well. Add dry ingredients all at once to bran mixture, stirring just enough to moisten. Spoon batter into paper-lined 3-inch muffin-pan cups, filling 2/3rds full. Bake in 350 degrees F. oven 25 minutes or until golden brown. Serve hot with butter and homemade jelly or jam.

Title: Nifty Hamburgers On A Bun
Categories: Breads, Hamburgers, Meats
Servings: 4
8 Hamburger buns; ,,Prepared mustard or catsup
1 lb Lean ground beef 1/4 c Onion; chopped, 1 small

1 ts Salt 1/4 ts Pepper

„Hamburger buns should be the small ones or use 6 slices of bread. Heat oven to 500 degrees F. Spread cut sides of hamburgers buns or one side of each bread slice with mustard. Mix meat, onion, salt and pepper. Spread mixture over the mustard, being careful to bring it to the edges of the buns. Place meat sides up on an ungreased baking sheet. Bake until desired doneness is reached, about 5 minutes. NOTE: If you like, you can have these burgers ready and waiting in the freezer for last-minute cooking. After spreading the meat mixture over the buns, wrap each securely in heavy-duty or double thickness of regular aluminum foil and label; freeze no longer than 2 months. To serve, unwrap desired number of hamburgers and bake about 10 minutes.

Title: Apple Strudel (Apfelstrudel)

Categories: Penndutch, Breads, Fruits
Servings: 1

2 1/2 c Flour 1 ts Salt
2 tb Shortening 2 Egg, slightly beaten
1/2 c Water, warm 5 c Apple, sliced
1 c Brown sugar 1/2 c Raisins
1/2 c Nuts, chopped 3 tb Butter, melted
1/2 ts Cinnamon 1 Lemon, grated rind of

Sift the flour and salt together. Cut in the 2 Tbsp shortening and add the eggs and water. Knead well, then throw or beat dough against board until it blisters. Stand it in a warm place under a cloth for 20 minutes. Cover the kitchen table with a small white cloth and flour it. Put dough on it. Pull out with hands very carefully to thickness of tissue paper. Spread with mixture made of the sliced apples, melted butter, raisins, nuts, brown sugar, cinnamon and grated lemon rind. Fold in outer edges and roll about 4 inches wide. Bake at 450-F for

10 minutes, reduce heat to 400-F and continue to bake about 20 minutes. Let cool. Cut in slices about 2 inches wide. Pennsylvania - Fine Old Recipes, 1936.

Title: Cinnamon Buns (The Famous Dutch Sticky Buns)

Categories: Penndutch, Breads
Servings: 1
1 c Milk, scalded 1/2 c Raisins, chopped
2 tb Currants 1/2 ts Cinnamon
Brown sugar 2 tb Citron, finely chopped
1/2 c Yeast ,,dissolved in:
1/4 c Water, warm 3 c Flour
1/2 ts Salt 3 tb Butter

Dissolve yeast in warm water and add to milk which has been allowed to become lukewarm. Add sugar (about 3 Tbsp), salt and flour, and knead thoroughly until it becomes a soft dough. Place the dough in a buttered bowl and butter the top of the dough. Cover bowl and put in a warm place. Permit it to stand until the dough becomes three times its original size. Roll until it is one fourth of an inch in thickness, brush with butter and spread with the raisins, currants, citron, brown sugar and cinnamon. Roll as a jelly roll and cut into slices 3/4 inch thick. Place slices in buttered pans, spread well with brown sugar, and bake at 400-F for 20 minutes. Pennsylvania- Fine Old Recipes, 1936.

Title: Coffee Cake (Kaffee Kuchen)

Categories: Penndutch, Breads
Servings: 1
1/2 c Butter 1 Egg, separated
1 c Sugar 2 c Milk
6 1/2 c Flour 1 c Yeast

„dissolved in: 1/3 c Water, lukewarm
Butter, melted Brown sugar

Scald the milk and set aside to cool. Cream the sugar, butter and egg yolk. Add to this the lukewarm milk, alternately with the flour and the dissolved yeast cake. Beat lightly and add the stiffly beaten egg white. Allow this mixture to rise over night. Flour a bake-board and take out large spoonfuls of the dough to which just enough flour has been added to permit it to be rolled into flat cakes. Spread on well-greased pie tins and when light (about 1-1/2 hours) brush melted butter over the top and strew thickly with brown sugar. If preferred, spread "rivels" on top by combining 1/2 cup sugar, 1/2 cup flour, and 2 Tbsp butter. Crumble together and sprinkle on top of cakes. Bake at 400-F about 20 minutes. Pennsylvania- Fine Old Recipes, 1936.

Title: Dutch Schnecken

Categories: Penndutch, Breads
Servings: 1

1 c Yeast „dissolved in:
1 c Water, warm 5 tb Sugar
1/2 ts Salt 2 c Milk, warm
2 Egg, well beaten 1/2 c Butter, melted
Flour „topping:
4 tb Sugar 4 tb Butter
1 1/2 ts Cinnamon

Dissolve the yeast cake and add one Tbsp of the sugar and the salt and enough flour to stiffen to a sponge. Let rise for one hour, then add the rest of the ingredients, using enough sifted flour to make a soft sponge. Let rise again, then roll out dough on a floured board and cover with a mixture of 4 Tbsp sugar, 4 Tbsp butter and 1 1/2 tsp cinnamon. Roll like a jelly roll and cut in 2 inch pieces. Place on well-greased pans and let rise for a third time, then bake at 400-F for 20 minutes. Pennsylvania - Fine Old Recipes,1936.

Title: Fastnacht Potato Cake
Categories: Penndutch, Breads
Servings: 1
2 Potato 2 Egg
1 c Sugar 1 ts Salt
1/4 ts Nutmeg 1/2 c Lard
„or: 1/2 c Other shortening
1 c Yeast „dissolved in:
1/2 c Water, warm Flour

Boil the pared potatoes in enough water to cover them. Drain off the potato water and save. Mash the potatoes and beat lightly. Measure the potato water and add more water, if necessary, to make 1 1/2 pints. Combine with the rest of the ingredients, using enough flour to make a rather stiff batter. Cover and let rise in a warm place until morning. Knead in the morning, adding as much flour as is necessary. Let rise again. Spread on well-greased tins and when light (about 1-1/4 hours) brush melted butter over top. Strew with "rivels" made by combining 1/2 cup sugar, 1/2 cup flour, and 2 Tbsp butter. Pennsylvania - Fine Old Recipes, , 1936.

Title: German Bread
Categories: Penndutch, Breads
Servings: 1
1/2 c Butter 3/4 c Sugar
1 c Yeast „dissolved in:
1/4 c Water, lukewarm 1 c Milk, scalded
2 Egg, well beaten 2 1/2 c Flour, bread
„to: 3 c Flour, bread
1 1/4 c Bread crumbs, soft 3 tb Brown sugar, light
1 ts Cinnamon 1/4 ts Salt

2 tb Butter, melted

Cream together the butter and sugar, add the scalded milk and mix thoroughly. When lukewarm, stir in the dissolved yeast, eggs and flour (using more flour if necessary to make a stiff batter). Beat mixture thoroughly, cover and let rise in a warm place about 1-1/2 hours or until double in bulk. When light, beat again thoroughly. Grease deep pie pan and sprinkle lightly with flour. With a spoon, fill the pie pans with the dough. Sprinkle top of cakes with the following mixture: combine the soft bread crumbs with the melted butter, sugar, salt and cinnamon and mix well.Let cakes rise about 20 minutes and bake at 400-F about 20 minutes.
Pennsylvania - Fine Old Recipes, 1936.

Title: German Strickle Sheets

Categories: Penndutch, Breads
Servings: 1
2 c Sugar 4 Egg, well beaten
4 tb Butter 1 c Yeast
,,dissolved in: 1/2 c Water, lukewarm
4 c Milk 1 ts Salt

Flour Scald milk and add the eggs and butter. When cool, add the dissolved yeast,salt, sugar and enough flour to form a thin batter. Beat all together about 7 minutes, cover well and set bowl containing mixture in warm place for 7 or 8 hours. After time has elapsed, add enough flour to make a soft dough, knead lightly and set to rise again. When well-raised, roll dough to one inch thickness and cut in biscuit shapes. Allow to rise a second time.Before placing in oven, spread with the following mixture: Mix 2 cups sugar with 4 Tbsp flour and add 1/2 cup butter and cream well; add 4 Tbsp boiling water and beat mixture into a sauce. Bake at 400-F about 20 minutes.
Pennsylvania - Fine Old Recipes,1936.

Title: Moravian Christmas Loaf
Categories: Penndutch, Breads
Servings: 1
3 c Milk 1 c Butter
1 c Sugar 1/2 c Yeast
„dissolved in: 1/4 c Water, warm
6 c Flour 1 ts Salt
1/2 lb Raisins, chopped 1/2 lb Currants
1/4 lb Citron, chopped 1/2 c Almond, blanched, sliced

Scald 2 cups of the milk and let cool. Add the dissolved yeast cake, 3 cups of flour and the salt. Mix well. Cover and set aside to rise in a warm place, over night. In the morning, scald the other cup of milk and add the butter and stir until melted. Combine with the yeast mixture and add the sugar and the balance of the flour, kneading the dough well, until it is no longer sticky. Use more flour if necessary. Combine the fruit and sprinkle with some flour and add to the dough, mixing well. Cover and let rise again until double in bulk. Shape in small loaves, place in small pans, and sprinkle with the sliced almonds. Let rise for 2 hours. Bake at 400-F for 40 minutes. Pennsylvania - Fine Old Recipes, 1936.

Title: Potato Sponge Bread
Categories: Penndutch, Breads
Servings: 1
4 Med Potato 2 tb Sugar
1 tb Salt 1 c Yeast
„dissolved in: 1/2 c Water, lukewarm
4 c Flour, bread

Pare and boil the potatoes and while hot, mash finely and rub through a sieve or colander. Add the sugar, salt and dissolved yeast cake. Stir flour into the mixture, beating well.

Add more flour to form soft dough. Turn onto a floured board and knead. Return to bowl, cover and let rise over night. In the morning, form into loaves, let rise until light and bake at 350-F for 45 to 50 minutes.
Pennsylvania - Fine Old Recipes, , 1936.

Title: Raisin Bread
Categories: Penndutch, Breads
Servings: 1
1 Med Potato 1 qt Water
1 c Yeast 1 c Water, lukewarm
2 ts Cinnamon 1/2 ts Cloves
1 c Sugar 1 lb Raisins
1 tb Butter Flour
Pare and boil the potato in the quart of water, mash and mix sufficient flour with the water to form a smooth batter. Dissolve the yeast in 1 cup of lukewarm water and combine with the batter. Cover and set in a warm place and let rise for 4 hours. Add the rest of the ingredients and knead, adding flour as needed. Be careful not to get dough too stiff. Let stand for 2 hours, then form into loaves, place in bread pans and let rise until light. Bake at 400-F for 30 to 40 minutes. Pennsylvania Dutch Fine Old Recipes, 1936.

Title: Small Coffee Cakes (Kleina Kaffee Kuchen)
Categories: Penndutch, Breads
Servings: 1
1/2 c Butter and other shortening, 2 Egg
2 Egg yolk 3 tb Sugar
1/2 c Cream 2 c Flour, sifted
1 c Yeast ,,dissolved in:
1 c Milk, lukewarm 1/2 ts Salt
Cream the butter, sugar and salt and add the eggs and egg

yolks one at a time, beating well after each addition. To the dissolved yeast, add 3 Tbsp of the flour and mix well. Combine with the first mixture. Add the remaining flour and cream alternately. Grease and flour muffin tins and fill 2/3 full of the dough. Set pans in a warm place until dough has risen to the tops of the pans. Bake at 400-F about 25 minutes.

Pennsylvania - Fine Old Recipes, 1936.

Title: Streusel Kuchen

Categories: Penndutch, Breads
Servings: 1

1/2 c Potato, mashed 1/2 c Potato water
1/2 c Butter and other shortening, 1/2 c Sugar
3 1/2 c Flour 1 c Yeast
„dissolved in: 1/2 c Water, lukewarm
2 Egg, well beaten 1/2 c Sugar
1 1/2 c Flour „topping:
1 c Flour 1/2 c Sugar
1 Egg yolk, well beaten

Mix together the mashed potatoes, potato water, shortening and sugar. Add to this about 3 1/2 cups flour and the dissolved yeast. Set this dough aside to rise in a warm place over night. The following morning add the eggs, 1/2 cup sugar and 1 1/2 cups flour. Allow this mixture to stand in a warm place until light. Then roll out pieces 6 by 8 by 1 inch thick and place in greased oblong pans. When cakes are ready to be put into the oven, brush top of cake with melted butter. Strew over the tops of the cakes the topping mixture. This mixture should be rubbed through a coarse sieve. Bake at 400-F about 20 minutes. Pennsylvania Fine Old Recipes, 1936.

Title: Apple Crunch Muffins

Categories: Breakfast, Muffins, Breads
Servings: 4

1 1/2 c Unbleached flour, sifted 1/2 c Sugar
2 ts Baking powder 1/2 ts Salt
1 1/2 ts Ground cinnamon 1/4 c Vegetable shortening
1 Large egg, slightly beaten 1/2 c Milk
1 c Tart apples „Nut crunch topping

„Apples are to be washed and cored. Shred the unpeeled apples for recipe.Sift together flour, sugar, baking powder, salt and cinnamon into mixing bowl. Cut in shortening with pastry blender until fine crumbs form. Combine egg and milk. Add to dry ingredinets all at once, stirring just enough to moisten. Stir in apples. Spoon batter into paper-lined 2 1/2-inch muffin-pan cups, filling 2/3rds full. Sprinkle with nut crunch topping. Bake in 375 degree oven 25 minutes or until golden brown. Serve hot with butter and homemade jelly or jam. NUT CRUNCH TOPPING: Mix together 1/4 c brown sugar (packed), 1/4 c chopped pecans and 1/2 t ground cinnamon in small bowl.

Title: Bara Brith (Currant Bread) Welsh

Categories: Breads
Servings: 16

1/4 lb Dried fruit 4 oz Candied peel
1 pt Warm water 1/2 ts Mixed spice
2 lb Plain flour 2 ts Salt
6 oz Lard 1 oz Fresh yeast
1/2 lb Demerara sugar 2 Eggs

Oven: 450F, Gas Mark 8 for 15 minutes: 375F, Gas Mark 5 for 45 minutes. Soak the fruit and candied peel in the water with the spice. Leave to steep in a warm place and use the warm spicy, strained water to mix the dough. Sift the flour and salt and rub in the lard; cream the yeast with the sugar and a little of the spiced water; mix this into the flour, together with the eggs and use enough of the water to give a firm, yet elastic dough. Knead well, leave to rise and knock back; blend in the drained fruit and knead again. Shape the dough into loaves and set into greased 1 lb tins in a warm place to prove; bake, reducing the temperature after the first 15 minutes. Originally, in some recipies, the fruit content would have been fresh currants or blackberries. Bara Brith is often served as part of the traditional Welsh tea. It can also be purchased at many of the small bakeries found throughout Wales. British Cookery

Title: Beer Biscuits
Categories: Breads
Servings: 4
2 c Unbleached flour 3 ts Baking powder
1 ts Salt 1/4 c Shortening
3/4 c Beer
Preheat Oven to 450 degrees F. Sift dry ingredients together. Cut in shortening until it has cornmeal consistanch. Stir in beer, knead lightly, roll out to 1/2-inch thickness. Bake 10 - 12 minutes or until golden brown. Makes 12 to 15 biscuits.

Title: Bran Date Bread
Categories: Breads
Servings: 12
1 1/4 c Unbleached flour, sifted 1 1/2 ts Baking powder
1 ts Salt 1/2 c Active sourdough starter
3/4 c Buttermilk or sour milk 1 c Finely chopped pitted dates
1 c All bran 1 ts Grated lemon peel (zestonly)

2 Large eggs, beaten 1/4 c Vegetable oil
3/4 c Firmly packed. brown sugar
Sift dry ingredients together. Dust dates with 1 T flour mixture, then add to the bowl. Then add the brown sugar, all bran, and grated lemon peel.Combine 3/4 cu buttermilk, 2 beaten eggs, 1/4 cup vegetable oil.Add all once to flour mixture with the sourdough starter, stirring until well moistened. Pour into greased or waxpaper lined loaf pan about 9 x 5-inches. Bake at 350 degrees for 1 hour. Allow to stand 10 minutes in pan and then remove from pan and cool until cold. Wrap in plastic wrap or foil and place in Refrigerator. Use cream cheese or home made butter on this bread for an out of this world taste.

Title: Bran Muffins-in-waiting
Categories: Muffins, Breads, Breakfast
Servings: 6
1 c Warm water 3 1/2 c Wheat/oat bran cereal
2 1/2 c Unbleached all-purpose flour 2 1/2 ts Baking soda
1/2 c Butter/margarine, room temp. 1 1/2 c Granulated sugar
2 Large eggs 2 c Butter/sour milk.
Mix water with 1 cup cereal. Sift flour with baking soda. In a large bowl, beat butter until creamy. Add sugar 1/2 cup at a time, beating after each addition. Blend in eggs, one at a time, beating well after each addition.Scrape sides of bowl often. Stir in flour mixture 1/2 cup at a time, alternating with butter/sour milk, added 1/2 cup at a time also. Stir in soaked bran and the remaining bran cereal. Cover and store in refrigerator at least 6 hours before baking. To bake muffins, heat oven to 400 degrees F. Grease 2 1/2-inch Muffin Cups. Stir batter gently. Fill each muffin cup with about 1/4 c batter. Bake about 20 minutes, or until

nicely browned. Remove from pan and serve hot with butter. Makes 6 cups batter or about 24 2 1/2-inch muffins.

Title: Candied Orange Rind Bread

Categories: Breads, Fruits, Quick
Servings: 10
4 Oranges; md 1 c Water
1 c Sugar 4 c Unbleached flour
6 ts Baking powder 1/2 ts Salt
1/4 c Butter or regular margarine 1/2 c Sugar
2 Eggs; lg 2 c Milk

Thinly peel the oranges, using a vegetable peeler. Cut the orange rind into thin slivers. (Reserve the oranges for another use, or eat them and enjoy.) Combine the orange rind and 1 cup of water in a 2 quart saucepan and bring to a boil, then reduce the heat, cover, and simmer for 15 minutes or until the rind is tender. Add the 1 cup of sugar and continue cooking, uncovered, until the mixture is syrupy, about 15 minutes. Cool to room temperature. Meanwhile, sift the flour, baking powder and salt together in a bowl and set aside. Cream the butter and 1/2 cup of sugar together until light and fluffy, using a electric mixer set on medium. Add the eggs and blend well. Blend in the cooled orange rind mixture. Add the dry ingredients alternately with the milk to the creamed mixture, beating well after each addition. Pour the batter into 2 greased 9 X 5 X 3-inch loaf pans. Bake in a preheated 350 degree F. oven for 50 minutes or until a cake tester or wooden pick inserted in the center comes out clean. Cool in the pans for 10 minutes before removing to wire racks to finish cooling. Wrap in aluminum foil and let stand overnight before slicing. This bread slices better when it has cooled for 24 hours.

Title: Cardamom Coffee Cakes

Categories: Breads, Christmas
Servings: 2

1 1/2 c Milk   1 pk Cake yeast
3/4 c Sugar   6 1/4 c Sifted all-purpose flour
1/2 c Butter   1/4 ts Salt
3 Egg yolks   1 ts Cardamom
----------topping----------- 2 tb Milk
6 tb Sugar

1. Scald milk and cool to lukewarm. Crumble yeast into bowl, add 1 Tsp
sugar and lukewarm milk. 2. Beat in 3 cups flour; beat until smooth. Cover well and let rise until light and double in bulk, 1 - 1-1/2 hours. 3. Add soft butter, remaining sugar, salt, egg yolks, cardamom and 3 cups flour. Mix thoroughly. Place remaining 1/4 cup flour on board or pastry cloth for kneading. 4. Turn out dough and knead until smooth and elastic. Place in greased bowl. Cover well. Set aside to rise until double in bulk, 1 to 1-1/2 hours. 5. Cut risen dough in half for two cofee cakes (braids). Cut each half into 3 pieces. Roll each piece into a roll 16 inches long. Pinch 3 rolls together at one end, braid and pinch other ends together. Place braid on cookie sheet. Make second braid and place on cookie sheet. 6. Let braids rise until double in bulk, about 45 minutes. For topping brush each braid with 1 Tbsp milk and sprinkle with 3 Tbsp sugar. 7. Bake in moderate oven (375) 25 to 30 minutes. Yield: 2 coffee cakes

Title: Carrot-Walnut Bread

Categories: Breads, Vegetables, Nuts
Servings: 4

1 1/2 c Unbleached flour; sifted   1 ts Baking soda
1/2 ts Cinnamon; ground   1/4 ts Nutmeg; ground

1/4 ts Salt 1 c Sugar
3/4 c Cooking oil 2 Eggs; lg
1 1/2 c Carrots; pared, shredded 1/2 c Walnuts; chopped
Sift the flour, baking soda, cinnamon, nutmeg and salt together in a small bowl and set aside. Combine the sugar, oil and eggs in a mixing bowl. Beat, with an electric mixer set on medium speed, for 2 minutes. Add the dry ingredients, stirring just until moistened. Stir in the carrots and walnuts. Pour the batter into a greased 9 X 5 X 3-inch loaf pan and bake, in a preheated 350 degree F. oven for 1 hour or until a cake tester or wooden pick inserted in the center comes out clean. Cool in the pan on a wire rack for 10 minutes, remove from the pan and finish cooling on the wire rack.

Title: Cinnamon-Raisin Bread

Categories: Breads, Fruits, Yeast
Servings: 10
5 1/2 c Unbleached or bread flour 2 pk Active dry yeast; or
2 ts Active dry yeast; bulk 1 c Milk
3/4 c Water 1/4 c Sugar
1/4 c Vegetable oil 2 ts Salt
1 Egg; lg 1 c Raisins
1 c Sugar 1 ts Cinnamon; ground,or to taste
2 ts Butter or margarine; melted
Stir 2 cups of flour and the yeast together in a large mixing bowl. Heat the milk, water, 1/4 cup sugar, oil and salt in a saucepan over very low heat until very warm, (120-130 degrees F.). Ad the liquid mixture to the flour-yeast mixture. Beat, with an electric mixer at medium speed, until smooth, about 3 minutes. Blend in the egg and then stir in the raisins. Gradually stir in enough of the remaining flour to make a moderately soft dough, (It will be slightly sticky and light in weight). Turn the dough out on a lightly floured surface,

adding flour if needed as you knead the dough, and knead until smooth and satiny about 10 minutes. Cover the dough with the bowl and let rest for 20 minutes. Combine the 1 cup of sugar and the cinnamon, then set aside. Punch the dough down and divide in half. Roll out one half, on the floured surface, to a 14 X 7-inch rectangle. Brush with the melted butter and sprinkle with half of the cinnamon-sugar mixture. Beginning at the narrow end, roll up tightly like a jelly roll. Press the edges to seal and fold the ends under. Place in a greased 8 ½ X 4 1/2 X 2 1/2-inch loaf pan. Repeat for the second half. Brush the tops of the loaves with the remaining butter. Cover and let rise in a warm place until doubled, about 45 minutes. Bake in a preheated 375 degree F. oven for 35 to 40 minutes or until the loaves sound hollow when tapped. Remove from the pans immediately and cool on wire racks.

Title: Corn Meal Muffins

Categories: Muffins, Breads, Breakfast
Servings: 4
1 c Unbleached all-purpose flour 4 ts Baking powder
2 tb Granuleated sugar 1 ts Salt
1 c Yellow cornmeal 2 Large eggs
1/4 c Vegetable oil

Grease 12 2 1/2-inch muffin cups. Heat oven to 425 degrees F. Sift flour, baking powder, sugar and salt into medium-sized bowl. Add cornmeal and stir to mix well. In small bowl, beat eggs with fork. Add milk and oil. Add all at once to dry ingredients. Stir mixture only until dry ingredients are mositened. Batter will be lumpy. Drop batter from a tablespoon into the prepared muffin cups, filling each cup 1/2 to 2/3rds full. Bake 15 to 20 minutes, or until golden brown. Remove and serve hot with butter, bacon and eggs.

Title: Cranberry Muffins

Categories: Muffins, Breads, Breakfast
Servings: 4
2 1/4 c Unbleached flour, sifted 1/4 c Sugar
3/4 ts Baking soda 1/4 ts Salt
1 Large egg, slightly beaten 3/4 c Butter/sour milk
1/4 c Vegetable oil 1 c Chopped raw cranberries
1/2 c Sugar
Sift together flour, 1/4 cup sugar, baking soda and salt into bowl. Combine egg, butter/sour milk and oil in small bowl; blend well. Add all at once to dry ingredients, stirring just enough to moisten. Combine cranberries and 1/2 cup sugar; stir into batter. Spoon batter into greased 2 1/2-inch muffin-pan cups, filling 2/3rds full. Bake in 400 degrees F. oven 20 minutes or until golden brow. Serve hot with butter and homemade jelly or jam.

Title: Date Or Raisin Bran Muffins

Categories: Muffins, Breads, Breakfast
Servings: 4
1 c Wheat/oat bran cereal 3/4 c Milk
1 c Unbleached all-purpose flour 2 1/2 ts Baking powder
1/2 ts Salt 1/4 c Granulated sugar
1/2 c Seedless raisins ,,1/2 c Chopped walnuts
1 Large egg 1/4 c Vegetable oil
,,Finely chopped pitted dates may be substituted to get Date Muffins. Mix cereal and milk. Let stand a few minutes until most of the milk is absorbed. Grease 12 2 1/2-inch muffin cups. Heat oven to 400 degrees F. Sift flour, baking powder, salt and sugar into a medium-sized bowl. Stir to mix well. Add dates/raisins and nuts; toss to mix. Add egg and oil to

soaked cereal and beat well with a fork. Pour into flour mixture and stir only until dry ingredients are moistened. Batter will be lumpy. Drop batter into prepared pans, filling each cup half to two-thirds full. Bake about 30 minutes, or until browned. Remove from pan and serve hot with butter and jelly or preserves.

Title: Dillbrot (Dill Bread)
Categories: Breads, Cheese/eggs, Vegetables
Servings: 4
1 pk Yeast; active dry 1 c Cottage cheese; creamed „
2 tb Sugar 1 tb Onion; minced
1 tb Butter; melted 1 Egg; large
1 ts Salt 2 ts Dillseed
2 1/4 c Flour; unbleached or bread
„Creamed Cottage Cheese should be heated to lukewarm.

Dissolve yeast in warm water. Combine all ingredients in a mixing bowl, except add the flour a little at a time (it may take up to 2 1/2 cups of flour). Beat until well mixed and mixture is stiff but not heavy. (Standard bread dough feeling). Cover and let rise in a warm place until doubled. Punch down and put dough in a bread pan, or arrange in a round shape on a greased cookie sheet. Let rise again. Bake for 30 to 45 minutes at 350 degrees F. While warm, bursh loaf with soft butter, sprinkle well with salt. Makes 1 loaf.

Title: Dilly Zucchini Ricotta Muffins
Categories: Muffins, Breads, Dinner
Servings: 4
1 1/2 c Unbleached flour 2 tb Sugar

3 ts Baking powder 1/2 ts Salt
3/4 ts Dill weed 1/4 c Milk
1/2 c Margarine/butter, melted 2 Large eggs
2/3 c Ricotta cheese 1/2 c Shredded zucchini

Heat oven to 400 degrees F. Line with paper baking cups or grease, 12 muffin-pan cups. Lightly spoon flour into measuring cup, level off. In large bowl, combine flour, sugar, baking powder, salt and dill weed, mix well. In medium bowl combine milk, margarine and eggs. Stir in ricotta cheese and zucchini, beat well. Add to dry ingredients, stirring just until moistened (Batter will be stiff). Fill prepared muffin cups 2/3rds full. Bake at 400 degrees F. for 20 to 25 minutes or until golden brown. Immediately remove from pan and serve.

Title: Easy Parker House Rolls

Categories: Breads, Yeast
Servings: 4

1 1/4 c Milk; scalded 3 ts Sugar
2 ts Butter or regular margarine 3/4 ts Salt
2 pk Active dry yeast; or 2 ts Active dry yeast; bulk
1/4 c Lukewarm water; 110 deg. f. 4 1/2 c Unbleached flour
2 ts Butter or margarine; melted

Pour the scalded milk over the sugar, 2 tbls of butter and salt in a mixing bowl. Cool to lukewarm. Sprinkle the yeast over the lukewarm water and stir to dissolve. Add 2 cups of flour, and the yeast mixture to the milk mixture. Beat, with an electric mixer on medium speed, until smooth, about 2 minutes. Gradually add enough of the remaining flour to make a soft dough, then cover and let rest for 15 minutes. Knead the dough a few times on a lightly floured surface until it is no longer sticky and roll out to a 1/2-inch thickness. Cut into rounds, using a floured biscuit cutter. Brush the rounds with the remaining 2 Tbls of melted

butter and crease each roll in the center with the dull edge of a knife. Fold the rolls over on the crease and press the edges together lightly. Place on greased baking sheets and cover. Let rise in a warm place until almost doubled, about 30 minutes. Bake in a preheated 400 degree F. oven for 10 minutes or until golden brown. Remove from the baking sheets and cool on wire racks.
NOTE: These rolls are almost a must at the Holiday dinners coming up shortly.Restaurants and most older cooks make it a tradition to serve them.

Title: Festive Cranberry Loaf

Categories: Breads, Fruits, Nuts
Servings: 4
2 c Unbleached flour; sifted 1 c Sugar
1 1/2 ts Baking powder 1 ts Salt
1/2 ts Baking soda 1/4 c Shortening
1 Egg; lg, beaten 3/4 c Orange juice; fresh
1 ts Orange rind; grated 1 c Raw cranberries; coarse chop
1/4 c Walnuts; chopped 1 ts Unbleached flour

Sift the 2 cups of flour, sugar, baking powder, salt and baking soda into a bowl then, using a pastry blender, cut the shortening in until crumbs form. Combine the egg, orange juice and orange rind and add to the crumb mixture all at once, stirring until just moistened. Combine the coarsely chopped cranberries, walnuts and 1 tb of flour and add the mixture to the batter. Pour into a greased and waxpaper lined loaf pan 8 1/2 X 4 1/2 X 2 1/2-inch loaf pan. Bake in a preheated 350 degree F. oven for 1 hour or until a cake tester or wood pick inserted in the center comes out clean. Cool in the pan for 10 minutes before turning out to cool to room temperature. Wrap the loaf in aluminum foil and let stand over night for better slicing.

Title: Flour Tortillas

Categories: Mexican, Breads
Servings: 12
4 c All purpose flour 1 1/2 ts Salt
1 1/2 ts Baking powder 4 tb Lard or shortening
1 1/2 c Warm water
Combine dry ingredients in a mixing bowl. Cut in shortening. Make a well in the center and add water, a small amount at a time, to form a dough. Knead dough in bowl until smooth and elastic. Cover and wet aside for ten minutes. Form dough into egg-sized balls and flatter between palms. With rolling pin, roll each ball into a 6 inch circle, about 1/8 inch thick. Cook on preheated ungreased skillet over medium high heat, apprx. two min. per side, until tortilla looks slightly speckled. Cover with a clean towel to keep warm and soft until served. The tortillas may be cooled and stored in plastic bags in the freezer for later use.

Title: Golden Raisin Loaves

Categories: Breads, Fruits, Yeast
Servings: 10
2 c Whole wheat flour; stirred 1/4 c Sugar
2 pk Active dry yeast; or 2 ts Active dry yeast; bulk
1 ts Salt 2 ts Cinnamon; ground
3/4 c Water 1/3 c Butter or regular margarine
1/2 c Buttermilk 2 Eggs; lg
1 1/2 c Raisins; golden 2 1/2 c Unbleached flour; sifted
Vegetable oil ------vanilla frosting------
2 c Confectioners' sugar 1/4 ts Vanilla
2 1/2 ts Milk
NOTE: The amount of flour can vary from 2 1/4 to 2 3/4

cups depending on Stir 1 3/4 cups of the whole wheat flour, sugar, undissolved yeast, salt and cinnamon together in a large mixing bowl. Heat the water and butter in a saucepan over low heat to very warm (120-130 degrees F.). Remove from the heat and stir in the buttermilk. Add to the flour-yeast mixture and beat, with an electric mixer on medium speed, until smooth, about 2 minutes. Add the eggs and beat an additional 2 minutes, then stir in the raisins. Gradually add the remaining 1/4 cup of whole wheat flour and enough white flour to make a stiff but light dough. (Heaviness indicates too much flour and the bread will not rise correctly.) Let rest for 5 minutes. Turn the dough out onto a lightly floured surface and knead until smooth, about 5 to 8 minutes. Cover with the mixing bowl and let rest for 30 minutes. Punch the dough down and divide in half. Let rest 10 minutes, then roll each half to a 12 X 7-inch rectangle. Beginning at the 7-inch side, roll up tightly like a jelly roll and seal the edges. Tuck the ends under to form rounded edges, (the loaf should be about 7 X 3-inches in size). Place on a greased baking sheet. Brush with oil and repeat for the second batch of dough. Cover and let rise in a warm place until almost doubled, about 30 minutes. Bake in a preheated 375 degree F. oven for 25 minutes or until the loaves sound hollow when tapped. Remove from the baking sheet and cool on wire racks for 20 minutes. Frost with the vanilla icing if desired.

VANILLA ICING:

Combine the sugar, vanilla, and milk in a bowl and beat until smooth.

Title: Grand Champion Pumpkin Bread
Categories: Breads, Fruits, Vegetables
Servings: 10

3 1/3 c Unbleached flour; sifted 4 ts Pumpkin pie spice
2 ts Baking soda 1 ts Baking powder
1 1/2 ts Salt 2 2/3 c Sugar
2/3 c Cooking oil 4 Eggs; lg
2 c Pumpkin; mashed, canned, 1cn 2/3 c Water
2/3 c Chopped dates

Stir the flour, pumpkin pie spice, baking soda, baking powder, and salt together in a small bowl and set aside. Beat the sugar and oil together in a medium mixing bowl, using an electric mixer set on high, until light and fluffy. Add the eggs, one at a time beating well after each addition, and then beat in the pumpkin. Add the dry ingredients alternately with the water to the sugar mixture, beating well after each addition, using a mixer set on low speed. Stir in the dates and pour the batter into 2 greased 9 X 5 X 3-inch loaf pans. Bake in a preheated 324 degree F. oven for 55 minutes or until a cake tester or wooden pick inserted in the center comes out clean. Cool in the pans on wire racks for 10 minutes, then remove from the pans and continue cooling on the racks.

Title: Instant Potato Lefse
Categories: Breads, Christmas
Servings: 6

1 pk (7 oz) instant potatoes 2 ts Salt
1 tb Butter 1 c Rich milk
1 c Boiling water 1 1/2 c Flour

Place instant potato flakes, salt and butter in mixing bowl. Add boilig water to milk and add to potato mixture. Mix quickly until thick and smooth. Add just enough flour to be able to handle dough. Knead lightly. Form into balls and roll very thin on floured board. Bake on hot electric lefse grill (any griddle will work), turning to brown both sides.

Title: Justin Wilson's Hush Puppies

Categories: Cajun, Breads
Servings: 48

2 c Cornmeal Ground cayenne pepper
1 c Plain flour 2 Eggs, beaten
1 ts Baking powder 1 c Buttermilk
1 ts Salt 1 c Green onion, finely chopped
1/2 ts Soda 2 tb Bacon drippings, hot
1/2 c Parsley, finely chopped 1/2 ts Garlic powder (to taste)

Deep fat for frying Combine all dry ingredients. Add eggs, buttermilk, onions, and oil or bacon drippings. Mix well. Drop in deep hot fat by spoonfuls and brown on all sides. Now, I said above that this makes 48, I've never counted, so I don't know for sure. But it sure does make a bunch. The main reason why I said 48 is because the program, Menu Master, won't let you past that field unless you tell it something. Justin Wilson says, "Hush puppy is an old Southern term that originated after the Civil War. People didn't have enough for themselves to eat let alone feed their dogs, so when the old hounds started barking from hunger, they would throw pieces of fried corn bread to them, yelling, 'Shut up, dog! Hush puppy!"

Title: Kasespatzle (Spaetzle Cheese Noodles)

Categories: German, Breads, Cheese/eggs
Servings: 4

3 tb Butter or margarine 3 Onions;sliced in small rings
3 oz Emmenthaler cheese; grated 1 ts Dry mustard
2 c Spaetzle noodles 2 tb Chives; chopped

Heat butter in frypan, add onions, and brown lightly. Toss cheese with dry mustard. Add cooked noodles to cooked onions and cheese; mix well. Place mixture in an ovenproof casserole. Bake at 300 degrees F. for 20 to 30 minutes or until hot and bubbly. Sprinkle top with chopped chives before serving.

Title: Lefse
Categories: Breads, Christmas
Servings: 6
2 c Milk, scalded 1/2 c Lard
1 tb Salt 4 c Flour
Add lard, salt and 2 cups flour to scalded milk and mix well over low heat. Remove from fire. Sift 2 cups of flour on board, add warm dough and work in flour. Knead well and cool. This dough can be rolled immediately or kept in a cool place for a couple of days. May be stored in a plastic bag. Make a small patty, about hamburger size, with even sealed edges as you would for pastry. Flour board lightly and with a Scandinavian rolling pin roll patty in all directions, keeping the dough round. Roll lightly, stretching dough until it is almost as large as the lefse baker. Use pointed stick to handle dough when it is transferred from the board to the baker. Brown lightly, prick air bubbles, turn and brown other side. It may be necessary to change heat control from high to low. This is a soft bread. Serve with butter, or butter and sugar. (Note: I don't have either a Scandinavian rolling pin or a lefse baker, so I use a regular rolling pin and a griddle. This is like a Swedish tortilla! We usually spread butter and sprinkled sugar over the lefse then rolled them up and DEVOURED them!)

Title: Melt-In-Your-Mouth Rolls
Categories: Breads, Yeast

Servings: 6
2 c Milk 1/4 c Shortening
1/4 c Sugar 2 ts Salt
2 pk Active dry yeast; or 2 ts Active dry yeast; bulk
1/4 c Luke-warm water; (110 deg.f) 7 c Unbleached flour; sifted
2 Eggs; lg

Scald the milk in a saucepan. Pour over the shortening, sugar and salt in a large mixing bowl. Cool to lukewarm. Sprinkle the yeast over the lukewarm water and stir to dissolve. Add the yeast mixture, 3 cups of the flour, and eggs to the milk mixture. Beat, using an electric mixer set on medium speed, for about 2 minutes. Gradually stir in enough of the remaining flour to make a soft dough. Turn the dough out on a lightly floured surface and knead until smooth and satiny, about 8 to 10 minutes. Place the dough in a greased bowl, turning once to grease the top and cover. Let rise in a warm place until double, about 1 hour. Punch the dough down and divide the dough into thirds, then let the dough rest for 10 minutes. Divide each third into 12 pieces and shape each piece into a ball. Place 12 balls, equally spaced, in a greased 9-inch round cake pan. Repeat for the remaining two thirds. Cover and let rise until doubled, 45 to 60 minutes. Bake in a preheated 400 degree F. oven for 12 to 15 minutes or until golden brown. Remove from the pans and cool on wire racks.

Title: Mexicali Spoon Bread Casserole
Categories: Breads, Cheese, Hamburger
Servings: 8
--------meat mixture-------- 1 1/2 lb Lean ground beef
1 c Onion; chopped, 1 lg 1/4 c Green bell pepper; chopped
1 Clove garlic; minced 15 oz Tomato sauce; 1 cn

12 oz Whole kernel corn; 1 cn 1 1/2 ts Salt
Chili powder; to taste 1/8 ts Pepper
1/2 c Ripe olives; sliced ------cornmeal topping------
1 1/2 c Milk 1/2 c Yellow cornmeal
1/2 ts Salt 3/4 c Cheddar cheese; shredded
2 Eggs; lg, beaten

Heat the oven to 375 degrees F. Cook and stir the meat, onion, green pepper and garlic in a large skillet until the onion is tender and the meat is browned. Drain off the excess fat. Stir in the tomato sauce, UNDRAINED corn, 1 1/2 ts salt, the chili powder, pepper and olives. Heat to boiling then reduce the heat and simmer, uncovered, while preparing the cornmeal topping. Mix the milk, cornmeal and 1/2 ts salt in a saucepan. Cook and stir over medium heat just until the mixture boils. Remove from the heat and stir in the cheese and eggs. Turn the hot meat mixture into an ungreased 2 1/2 to 3-quart casserole. Immediately pour the topping onto the meat mixture. Bake, uncovered, until a knife inserted in the topping comes out clean, about 40 minutes. Serve hot.

Title: Mexican Cornbread
Categories: Meats, Breads
Servings: 4
1 lb Ground meat Salt & pepper to taste
1 c Chopped onion 1/2 lb Grated american cheese
3 Jalapeno peppers finely chop 1 c Cornmeal
3 Large eggs 1/2 ts Soda
3 tb Bacon drippings 1 c Sweet milk
1 ts Salt

Make batter by mixing together the cornmeal, eggs, soda, drippings, milk, and salt. Mix well. Brown meat and drain off grease. Grease a 9 x 13-inch baking pan. Add 1/2 batter then sprinkle on the meat, onions, peppers, and last add cheese. Cover with remaining batter. Cook at 350 degrees F. for about 45 minutes. Serve hot.

Title: Molasses Refrigerator Muffins
Categories: Muffins, Breads, Brunch
Servings: 12
4 c Unbleached flour, sifted 2 ts Baking soda
1 ts Salt 1 ts Ground cinnamon
1 ts Ground ginger 1/4 ts Ground cloves
1/4 ts Ground allspice 1/4 ts Ground nutmeg
1 1/3 c Vegetable shortening 1 c Sugar
4 Large eggs, slightly beaten 1 c Molasses
1 c Butter/sour milk 1 c Raisins

Sift together flour, baking soda, salt, cinnamon, ginger, cloves, allspice and nutmeg; set aside. Cream together shortening and sugar in mixing bowl until light anf fluffy, using electric mixer at medium speed. Add eggs beat well. Blend in molasses and butter/sour milk. Add dry ingredients all at once, stirring just enough to moisten. Stir in raisins. Spoon into greased 3-inch muffin-pan cups, filling 1/2 full. Bake in 350 degree oven 20 minutes or until golden brown. Serve hot with butter and jam. NOTE: Batter can be stored in refrigerator in covered container for up to 3 weeks.

Title: Muffins Basic And Variations
Categories: Muffins, Breads, Breakfast
Servings: 4
2 c Unbleached all-purpose flour 1 tb Baking powder
2 tb Granulated sugar 1 ts Salt
1 Large egg 1 c Milk
1/2 c Vegetable oil

Grease 12 2 1/2-inch muffin cups. Heat oven to 400 degrees F. Sift Flour, baking powder, sugar and salt into a medium-sized bowl. Stir to mix well. In a small bowl, beat egg with a fork. Add milk and oil. Add all at once to dry ingredients. Stir mixture only until dry ingredients are moistened. Batter will be lumpy. Drop batter from a tablespoon into prepared muffins pans, filling each cup half to two-thirds full. Bake 15 to 20 minutes, or until golden brown. Remove from pan and serve hot with butter, jam or marmalade.

VARIATIONS: GINGER MUFFINS:
Add 1/2 Cup finely diced candied ginger to flour mixture before adding liquid. BANANA PECAN MUFFINS: Prepare muffin batter but use only 1/2 cup milk. Add 1/2 cup chopped pecans and 1/4 t ground nutmeg to sifted flour. Add 1 cup mashed, peeled banana with the egg, milk and oil.

BLUEBERRY MUFFINS:
Toss 1 cup washed and well-drained fresh or frozen blueberries with sifted flour mixture before adding liquid.

ORANGE MUFFINS:
Cut 2 peeled navel oranges into sections. When batter is in the cups, place an orange section on top of each and sprinkle lightly with granulated sugar.

CHEESE MUFFINS:
Fold 1/2 cup grated sharp yellow cheese into muffin mix with the last few strokes on batter. Serve hot with scrambled eggs and bacon for a special breakfast.

SURPRISE MUFFINS:
Fill muffin cups 1/3rd full of batter. Drop 1/2 t of your favorite jelly in center of batter. Addbatter to fill cup 2/3rds full. Kids just love these as you will.

COCONUT MUFFINS: Add 1 c Shredded coconut with the last few strokes of mixing. For a snack have coconut muffins, butter and milk.

CHIVE MUFFINS:
Fold 1/4 cup chives into the batter during the last few strokes and serve at dinner. Great with a steak and salad.

Title: Oatmeal Muffins
Categories: Breakfast, Breads, Muffins
Servings: 5
1 c Quick-cooking oats 1 c Butter/sour milk
1 c Unbleached flour, sifted 1 ts Baking powder
1/2 ts Baking soda 1 ts Salt
1/3 c Butter or regular margarine
1/2 c Brown sugar, packed
1 Large egg
Combine oats and butter/sour milk in small bowl. Mix well and let stand 1 hour. Sift together flour, baking powder, baking soda and salt; set aside. Cream together butter and brown sugar in mixing bowl, using electric mixer at medium speed. Add egg; beat until light and fluffy. Add dry ingredients alternately with oat mixture to creamed mixture, blending well after each addition. Spoon batter into greased 2 1/2-inch muffin-pan cups, filling 2/3rds full. Bake in 400 degree F. oven 20 minutes or until golden brown. Serve hot with homemade jam or preserves.

Title: Onion-Cheddar Bread
Categories: Breads
Servings: 4
2 1/2 c Unbleached all-purpose flour 1 c Whole wheat flour
1 pk Active dry yeast 1/3 c Warm water (110-115 degrees)
1/2 c Orange juice 1/2 c Water
2 tb Butter or margarine ,,1 Env. onion soup mix
1 tb Sugar 1 ts Salt

5 oz Shredded cheddar cheese Melted butter or margarine
„Butter or margarine should be cut into small pieces.

In medium bowl, combine flours and set aside. In large bowl, dissolve yeast in warm water. Add orange juice, water, butter, onion recipe soup mix, sugar, salt, and 2 cups flour mixture. Mix until smooth. Stir in enough of the remaining flour mixture until soft dough is formed and it pulls away from the sides of the bowl. Turn dough onto lightly floured board, then knead until smooth and elastic, about 10 minutes. Cover and let rise in warm place until doubled, about 1 hour. (Dough is ready if indentation remains when touched) Preheat oven to 375 degrees F. Punch down dough, then turn onto lightly floured board. Press into 10 x 8-inch rectangle; top with 1 cup cheese. roll, starting at 8-inch side, jelly-roll style; pinch ends to seal. Place in 9 x 5 x 3-inch loaf pan, seam side down. Brush with melted butter, then top with remaining cheese. Bake 45 minutes or until bread sound hollow when tapped. Remove to wire rack and cool completely before slicing. Makes 1 loaf.

Title: Parmesan Herb Muffins

Categories: Muffins, Breads, Dinner
Servings: 4
2 c Unbleached flour 1 tb Sugar
1 1/2 ts Baking powder 1/2 ts Baking soda
1/2 ts Sage leaves, crumbled 1/2 c Chopped fresh parsley
1/4 c Grated parmesan cheese 1 1/4 c Butter/sour milk
1/4 c Butter/margarine, melted 1 Large egg

Heat oven to 400 degrees F. Grease bottoms of 12 muffin-pan cups or line with paper baking cups. Lightly spoon flour into measuring cup; level off. In large bowl, combine flour sugar, baking powder, baking soda, sage, parsley and cheese, blend well. Add butter/sour milk, margarine and egg;

stir just until dry ingredients are moistened. Fill prepared muffin cups 2/3rds full. Bake at 400 degrees F. for 15 to 20 minutes or until toothpick inserted in center coumes out clean. Serve hot.

MICROWAVE DIRECTIONS:

Prepare muffin batter as directed above. Using 6 cup microwave-safe muffin pan, line each with 2 paper baking cups to absorb moisture during baking. Fill cups 1/2 full. Sprinkle top of each muffin with cornflake crumbs. Microwave 6 muffins on HIGH for 2 1/2 to 3 minutes or until toothpick inserted in center comes out clean, rotating pan 1/2 turn halfway through baking. Remove muffins from pan and immediatedly discard outer baking cups. Cool 1 minute on wire rack before serving. Repeat with remaining batter.

Title: Pecan Cinnamon Muffins

Categories: Muffins, Breads, Breakfast
Servings: 4
1 1/2 c Unbleached flour, sifted 1/4 c Sugar
1/4 c Brown sugar, packed 2 ts Baking powder
1/2 ts Salt 1/2 ts Ground cinnamon
1 Large egg, slightly beaten 1/2 c Vegetable oil
1/2 c Milk 1/2 c Chopped pecans

Sift together flour, sugar, brown sugar, baking powder, salt and cinnamon into mixing bowl. Combine egg, oil and mil in small bowl; blend well. Add all at once to dry ingredients, stirring just enough to moisten. Stir in pecans. Spoon batter into greased 2 1/2-inch muffin-pan cups, filling each 2/3rds full. Bake in 400 degree F. oven 20 minutes or until golden brown. Serve hot with butter and homemade jelly or jam. Serving Hint: Match the mood of your mealtime by using a variety of pretty napkins to line a muffin basket. For a picnic, choose a red and white checked napkin; for special dinners, use your finest linen napkins; and for Christmas, of course, a bright red napkin.

Title: Pumpkin Bread
Categories: Breads, Fruits, Nuts
Servings: 4
3 1/2 c Unbleached flour; sifted 1 1/2 c Light brown sugar; packed
1 1/2 c Sugar; granulated 2 ts Baking soda
1 1/2 ts Salt 1 ts Cinnamon; ground
1/2 ts Nutmeg; ground 4 Eggs; lg
1 c Salad oil 2/3 c Water
2 c Pumpkin; mashed, canned 1 c Raisins
1 c Walnuts; chopped
Preheat the oven to 375 degrees F, and grease 3 medium (8 1/2 X 4 1/2) loaf
pans, sprinkling a little brown sugar in each. Combine all the dry ingredients in a large bowl and fashion a well in the center. Break in the 4 eggs and add the salad oil, water and pumpkin. Beat thoroughly until well mixed, then add the raisins and nuts. Pour into the prepared pans. Bake 1 hour and 15 minutes or until a cake tester or wooden pick inserted in the center comes out clean. Cool for 5 minutes in the pans before turning onto wire racks to cool. NOTE: This bread can be wrapped in aluminum foil and frozen very satisfactorily.

Title: Pumpkin Muffins
Categories: Dinner, Breakfast, Breads
Servings: 4
1 c Unbleached flour, sifted 2 ts Baking powder

1/4 ts Salt 1/4 ts Ground cinnamon
1/4 c Vegetable shortening 2/3 c Sugar
1 Large egg 1/2 c Canned, mashed pumpkin
2 tb Milk

Sift together flour, baking powder, salt and cinnamon; set aside. Cream together shortening and sugar in mixing bowl until ight and fluffy, using electric mixer at medium speed. Beat in egg. Combine pumpkin and milk in small bowl. Add dry ingredients alternately with pumpkin mixture to creamed mixture, stirring well after each addition. Spoon pagger into paper-lined 2 1/2-inch muffin-pan cups, filling 2/3rds full. Bake in 350 degree F. oven 20 minutes or until golden brown. Serve hot with butter and homemade jam.

Title: Pumpkin Oat Muffins

Categories: Breakfast, Breads, Muffins
Servings: 12

1 c Unbleached flour, sifted 2 ts Baking powder
1 ts Pumpkin pie spice 1/4 ts Baking soda
1/2 ts Salt 3/4 c Canned, mashed, pumpkin
1/2 c Brown sugar, packed 1 Large egg, slightly beaten
1/4 c Milk 1/4 c Vegetable oil
1 c Quick-cooking oats 1/2 c Raisins

Crumb topping Sift together flour, baking powder, pumpkin pie spice, baking soda and salt; set aside. Combint pumpkin, brown sugar, egg, milk, oil, oats and raisins in bowl; blend well. Add dry ingredients all at once, stirring just enough to moisten. Spoon batter into grease 3-inch muffin-pan cups, filling 2/3rds full. Sprinkle with crumb topping. Bake in 400 degree F. oven 18 to 20 minutes or until golden brown. Serve hot with homemade jelly or jam. CRUMB TOPPING: Combine 1/2 c brown sugar (packed), 1 T unbleached flour, 1/4 t pumpkin pie spice and 2 T butter or regular margarine in bowl. Mix until crumbly.

Title: Quick Sticky Buns
Categories: Breads, Yeast
Servings: 24
------------buns------------ 1 1/4 c Milk
1/4 c Butter 3 1/4 c Flour
1/4 c Sugar 1 ts Salt
2 pk Yeast 1 Egg
----------topping----------- 1 c Brown sugar
1 1/2 ts Cinnamon 3/4 c Butter
2 tb Corn syrup 1 c Walnuts

Heat milk and butter to 120 to 130 degrees. Mix together 2 cups flour, sugar, salt, yeast and egg. Add liquid and beat medium four minutes. Stir in rest of flour. Cover and rise until double (30 to 45 minutes). Generously grease 24 muffin cups. Chop nuts. Heat all topping ingredients on low until ingredients are melted and combined. Divide topping between muffin cups. Stir down batter. Drop into muffin cups. Cover and rise until double (20 to 30 minutes). Preheat oven to 375 degrees. Place tins on cookie sheet and bake 12 to 15 minutes until golden brown. Cool three minutes then invert on waxed paper.

Title: Roggenbrot (Rye Bread)
Categories: German, Breads
Servings: 12
2 pk Yeast; active dry 1 1/2 c Milk; lukewarm
2 tb Sugar 1 ts Salt
1/2 c Molasses 2 tb Butter
3 1/4 c Rye flour; unsifted 2 1/2 c Bread flour; unsifted

Dissolve yeast in warm water. In a large bowl combine milk, sugar, and salt. Use a mixer to beat in molasses, butter, yeast mixture and 1 cup of rye flour. Use a wooden spoon to mix in the remaining rye flour. Add white flour by stirring until the dough is stiff enough to knead. Knead 5 to 10 minutes, adding flour as needed. If the dough sticks to your hands or the board add more flour. Cover dough and let rise 1 1 1/2 hours or until double. Punch down dough and divide to form 2 round loaves. Let loaves rise on a greased baking sheet until double, about 1 1/2 hours. Preheat oven to 375 degrees F. Bake for 30 to 35 minutes. Makes 2 round loaves.

Title: Sopaipillas

Categories: Mexican, Breads
Servings: 12
4 c Flour 1 tb Baking powder
2 ts Sugar 1 1/2 ts Salt
1/4 c Shortening or lard 1 1/4 c Water or more if needed
Sift dry ingredients together. Cut in shortening until crumbly. Add water and mix until holds together. Knead 10-15 times until dough forms a smooth ball. Cover and let set for 20 minutes. Divide dough into two parts. Roll dough to 1/8" thickness on lightly floured board. Cut into 3" squares or triangles. Do not allow to dry; cover those waiting to fried. When ready to fry, turn upside down so that surface on bottom while resting is on top when frying. Fry in 3" hot oil until golden brown, turning once. Add only a few at a time to maintain proper temperature. Drain on paper towels.

Title: Sopaipillas 2

Categories: Mexican, Breads
Servings: 12

1 pk Active dry yeast 1/4 c Warm water (110)
1 1/2 c Milk 3 tb Lard or shortening
1 1/2 ts Salt 2 tb Sugar
4 c All purpose flour 1 c Whole wheat flour
1 Oil

In a large mixing bowl, dissolve yeast in warm water. In another bowl combine milk, lard, salt and sugar. Heat to 110 degrees and add to dissolved yeast. Beat in 3 cups of the all purpose flour and all of the whole wheat flour. Add abut 1/2 c all purpose flour and mix until a stiff sticky dough forms. Place dough on a floured board and knead, adding more flour as needed, until dough is smooth and nonsticky. Place doug in a greased bowl turning over to grease top. Cover and let stand at room temp. 1 hour. Punch dough down. The dough may be coverec and chilled as long as overnight. Knead dough on alightly floured board to expel air. Roll dough out, a portion at a time, to slightly less than 1/8" thick. Cut in 2"X 5" rectangles or 3" squares for appetizers. Place on lightly floured pans and lightly cover. If you work quickly you can let cut sopaipillas stay at room temp up to 5 min; otherwise, refrigerate them until all are ready to fry. In a deep wide frying pan or kettle heat 1 1/2 - 2 inches oil to 350 on a deep fat frying thermometer. Fry 2 or 3 at a time. When the bread begins to puff, gently push the bread into the hot oil several times to help it puff more evenly. Turn several times and cook just until pale gold on both sides, 1-2 minutes total. Drain on paper towels. Serve immediately or place in a warm oven until all are fried. Or if made ahead, cool, cover and chill or freeze. To reheat, bake uncovered in a 300 oven, turnig once, just until warm, 5-8 min. Do not overheat or they will become hard. Makes 2 dozen large so paipillas or about 4 dozen small ones.

Title: Souper Baked Sandwich
Categories: Breads, Cheese, Hamburger
Servings: 6
1 1/2 lb Lean ground beef 1/4 c Onion; chopped, 1 sm
1/2 ts Salt 1/2 c Celery; chopped
4 c Herb stuffing cubes; not mix 1 1/2 c Milk
2 Eggs; lg 10 3/4 oz Cream of mushroom soup; 1 cn
1 ts Mustard; dry 1 c Cheddar cheese; shredded,4oz
Heat the oven to 350 degrees F. Cook and stir the meat, onion and celery in a large skillet until the meat is brown. Drain off the excess fat. Stir in the salt. Arrange the stuffing cubes in a greased baking pan, 9 X 9 X 2 or 11 3/4 X 7 1/2 X 1 3/4-inches and top with the meat mixture. Beat the milk, eggs, soup, and mustard together and pour over the meat. Then sprinkle with the cheese and bake uncovered until a knife inserted in the center comes out clean, about 30 to 40 minutes. Cool for 5 minutes and then cut into squares and serve.

Title: Sourdough Banana Bread
Categories: Breads
Servings: 12
1/2 c Shortening 1 c Sugar
1 Large egg 1 c Mashed bananas
1 c Active sourdough starter 2 c Unbleached flour
1 ts Salt 1 ts Baking powder
1/2 ts Baking soda 3/4 c Chopped walnuts
1 ts Vanilla or 1 ts Grated orange peel
Cream together the shortening and sugar, add egg and mix until blended. Stir in bananas and sourdough starter. Add orange peel or vanilla. Stir flour and measure again with salt, baking powder and soda. Add flour mixture and walnuts to

the first mixture, stirring until just blended. Pour into greased 9 x 5-inch loaf pan. Bake in 350 degree oven for 1 hour or until toothpick comes out clean. Cool to cold before slicing.

Title: Sourdough Cornbread
Categories: Breads
Servings: 4
1/2 c Active sourdough starter 2 tb Margarine, melted
1/2 c Cornmeal 1 ts Salt
1 tb Sugar 1/2 c Sour cream or yogurt
2 Large eggs, stirred 1 c Unbleached flour
1/2 ts Cream of tartar 1/2 ts Baking powder
Mix ingredients in the above order, stirring only enough to blend the mixture. Pour into a buttered pan. Bake in a 375 to 400 degree oven for about 15 minutes.

Title: Sourdough Honey Whole Wheat Bread
Categories: Sourdough, Breads
Servings: 4
1 pk Active dry yeast 1 c Warm water
1 ts Salt 2/3 c Sourdough starter
1/2 c Honey 1 1/2 tb Shortening
4 c Whole wheat flour
Dissolve yeast in 1 cup warm water. Mix yeast, starter, honey, salt and shortening with 3 cups flour. Add more flour as needed to make a stiff dough. Knead 150 strokes on a floured surface and place in a greased bowl. Cover and let rise 1 to 1 1/2 hours until doubled in size. Punch down, let double again. Punch down and roll into tight loaf. Grease and place in bread pan. Let double in pan and bake at 400 degrees F. for 35 to 40 minutes or until very dark golden brown, and it sounds hollow when thumped.

Title: Sourdough Pancakes #1

Categories: Breads
Servings: 4

1/2 c Active starter 1/2 c Pancake mix
1 Large egg 1 tb Cooking oil
1/2 c Milk 1/2 ts Soda

Mix all ingredients well. Be careful not to over mix. Small lumps are OK. Lightly grease a hot cast iron griddle. Drop onto griddle with a large spoon while the batter is still rising.

Title: Sourdough Pancakes #2

Categories: Breads
Servings: 4

1 c Active starter 1 Large egg
2 tb Cooking oil 1/4 c Instant or evaporate milk
1 ts Salt 1 ts Baking soda
2 tb Sugar

Mix ingredients together and let the mixture bubble and foam a minute or two, then drop on hot griddle in large spoonfuls.

Title: Sourdough Pancakes #3

Categories: Breads
Servings: 6

2 c Active starter 2 c Unbleached flour
1 ts Baking soda 2 Large eggs, well beaten
1 tb Sugar 1 ts Salt
Bacon fat (2; 3 t)

Mix well and cook on hot griddle. Note: This is good recipe for camping. Instead of fresh eggs, you can use 1 T Powdered eggs.

Title: Sourdough Pizza Shells

Categories: Breads
Servings: 4

1 c Sourdough starter 1 tb Shortening, melted
1 ts Salt 1 c Flour

Mix ingredients, working in the flour until you have a soft dough. Roll out into a flat shape. Dash oil over a dough sheet and place dough on it. Bake about 5 minutes. It doesn't take long, so watch carefully. Have pizza sauce and topping ready and make pizza as usual. Then bake as usual.

Title: Sourdough Pumpernickle

Categories: Breads
Servings: 10

1 1/2 c Active sourdough starter 2 tb Caraway seeds, chopped
2 c Unsifted rye flour 1/2 c Boiling black coffee
1/2 c Molasses 1/4 c Dry skim milk
2 ts Salt 3 tb Melted shortening
1/2 c Whole milk 2 3/4 c Unbleached flour
1 pk Active dry yeast

Pour boiling coffee over chopped caraway seeds. Let the mixture cool and then add it to the rye flour and starter which have previously been mixed well. Let stand for 4 to 8 hours in a warm place, preferabley overnight. Then add the molasses, dry milk, salt, shortening,liquid milk, unbleached flour and yeast. Mix well. Cover the bowl and let rise to double. Then´knead on floured board and shape into two round loaves on baking sheet. Let rise until double again and bake at 350 degrees for 30 minutes or until done.

Title: Spatzle (Spaetzle Noodles)
Categories: German, Breads
Servings: 4

3 c Flour; unbleached 1 ts Salt
1/4 ts Nutmeg 4 Eggs; large, beaten
1/4 c Butter

Sift flour, salt and nutmeg together in a bowl. Pour eggs and 1/4 cup
water into middle of flour mixture, beat with a wooden spoon. Add enough water to make the dough slightly sticky, yet keeping it elastic and stiff. Using a spaetzle machine or a colander with medium holes, press the noodles into a large pot full of boiling salted water. Cook noodles in the water about 5 minutes or until they rise to the surface. Lift noodles out and drain on paper towels. Brown noodles in melted butter over low heat.

Title: Spicy Applesauce Bread
Categories: Breads, Fruits, Nuts
Servings: 6

1 c Raisins 1/2 c Water
1 c Applesauce 1 1/2 c Unbleached flour; sifted
1 ts Baking soda 1/2 ts Cinnamon; ground
1/8 ts Cloves; ground 1/2 c Butter or regular margarine
1 c Sugar 1 Egg; lg
1 ts Vanilla 1/2 c Walnuts; chopped

Combine the raisins and water in a small saucepan. Bring the mixture to a boil then reduce the heat and simmer, covered, for 1 minute. Remove from the heat and stir in the applesauce. Cool to lukewarm. Sift the flour, baking soda, and spices together into a small bowl and set aside. Cream the butter and sugar in a mixing bowl until light and fluffy, using an electric mixer set on medium. Beat in the egg and vanilla. Add the dry ingredients alternately with the applesauce mixture, into the creamed mixture, beating well after each addition. Stir in the walnuts. Turn the mixture into a greased and waxed paper lined 9 X 5 X 3-inch loaf pan. Bake in a preheated 350 degree F. oven for 1 hour or until a cake tester or wooden pick comes out clean when inserted in the center of the loaf. Cool in the pan for 10 minutes before turning out on a wire rack to finish cooling.

Title: Spicy Apricot Oat Muffins

Categories: Muffins, Breads, Breakfast
Servings: 6
2 c Unbleached flour, sifted 1/2 c Sugar
3 ts Baking powder 1 ts Salt
2 ts Pumpkin pie spice 1/2 c Quick-cooking oats
1 c Chopped dried apricots 1/2 c Chopped walnuts
2 Large eggs, slightly beaten 1 1/3 c Milk
1/4 c Vegetable oil

Sift together flour, sugar, baking powder, salt and pumpkin pie spice into large mixing bowl. Stir in oats, apricots, and walnuts. Combine eggs, milk and oil in small bowl; blend well. Add all at once to dry ingredients, stirrin just enough to moisten. Spoon batter into greased 3-inch muffin-pan cups, fill 2/3rds full. Bake in 350 degree F. oven 30 minutes or until golden brown. Serve hot with butter and homemade jam or jelly.

Title: Toronto Bran Muffins

Categories: Breads, Quick

Servings: 12
1 1/4 c Hot milk 2 tb Oil
3 Eggs
Combine cereal with hot milk in a 1-1/2 quart mixing bowl and let it ´stand about 10 minutes---or until the cereal has absorbed all of the milk. With the electric mixer on high speed, beat in the oil and eggs till completely blended. Remove the beaters. Switch to a sturdy spoon and dump in the cake mix, stirring only to moisten all of it thoroughly--- but don't over mix or over beat or the muffin texture will be heavy and tough. The batter will be a bit lumpy. Cover the bowl and let the batter stand 15 minutes while you preheat the oven to 400 F, and grease 12 muffin tin wells in Crisco, evenly. Divide batter equally between the 12 wells. If you are using cupcake tin wells, you will have 15 muffins. Bake at 400 for 20 to 25 minutes, or till golden brown. Wipe tops of each while still warm in softened butter or margarine.

Title: True Garlic Bread
Categories: Breads, Garlic
Servings: 6
Garlic puree(2 roasted head) 1/4 lb Unsalted butter, softened
2 tb (2 pk) dry yeast 1/2 c Warm water (115-120 degrees)
2 1/2 c Warm water 2 tb Kosher salt
3 1/4 c Whole wheat flour 3 1/4 c Unbleached all purpose flour Cornmeal Cream together the garlic puree and butter. (This may be done days in advance and refrigerated. Bring to room temperature before using). Combine the yeast with 1/2 cup warm water in large bowl. Stir with a fork or small whisk. Add an additional 2 1/2 cups water. Add salt. Stir in the flour, 1 c at a time, beginning with the whole wheat. Use

a whisk until the dough becomes stiff, then switch to a wooden spoon. Turn the dough onto a well floured work surface. Knead rhythmically for 10 to 15 minutes, until the dough is smooth, springy, non sticky, and elastic. Add more flour as you knead if necessary. The dough is ready if you can poke to fingers into it and the resulting indentations spring back. Cover the dough with a cloth and let rest while you wash, dry and generously butter the bowl. Knead the dough a few more turns, then form it into a ball and place it in the bowl. Turn it to coat with butter. Cover the bowl and put it in a warm, draft-free place until the dough has doubled in bulk, about 1 1/2 hours. It has risen sufficiently when you can gently poke a finger into the dough and the hole reamins. (Don't poke too enthusiastically or the dough will collapse.) When doubled, flour your fist and punch the dough down. Knead it a few times and then let it rest. Sprinkle 1 large or 2 small baking sheets with a liberal amount of cornmeal. Divide the dough into 3 equal parts. While you work with 1 piece, keep the other 2 covered. Flour your work surface. With a rolling pin, roll each piece of dough into a rectangle approximately 14-inches long X 7-inches wide. Spread it with softened garlic butter. Roll the long edge toward the opposite long edge, as if you were rolling up a rug. Pinch ends closed. Place loves on the baking sheets. With a sharp knife or razor blade, slash the loves lightly at 2-inch intervals. Cover with a cloth and place in a warm draft-free place to rise until doubled, about 1/2 hour. Meanwhile preheat oven to 400 degrees F. Bake for 35 to 40 minutes with a pan of boiling water on the oven floor. Spray loaves with water several times during the baking process. (This helps the bread form a thick crusty shell.) To test for doneness, rap the loaf with your knuckles. The loaf should sound hollow. Cool on wire racks, but the loaves are delicious eaten warm right out of the oven.

Title: Walnut Brown Bread
Categories: Breads, Fruits, Nuts
Servings: 10
3 c Raisins 3 c Water
1/4 c Shortening 5 1/2 c Unbleached flour; sifted
2 c Sugar 4 ts Baking soda
2 ts Salt 2 Eggs; lg, slightly beaten
1 c Walnuts; chopped
Combine the raisins and water in a 3-quart saucepan and bring to a boil. Boil, uncovered, for 5 minutes, then remove from the heat and add the shortening. Cool to lukewarm. Sift the flour, sugar, baking soda and salt together into a mixing bowl and add the eggs, walnuts and raisin mixture. Stir until just moistened. Spoon the batter into 6 greased (1-lb) vegetable cans. Bake in a preheated 350 degree F. oven for 1 hour or until a cake tester or wooden pick inserted in the center of each loaf comes out clean. Cover with aluminum foil for the last 15 minutes of baking to prevent over browning. Cool in the cans for 10 minutes before turning out onto wire racks to cool to room temperature.

Title: Weizen Keimbreat (Molasses Brown Bread)
Categories: Breads
Servings: 4
2 1/2 c Whole-wheat flour 1 1/2 c Wheat germ
1/3 c Brown sugar 1/2 ts Salt
1 c Raisins; mixed dark & light 2 ts Baking soda
1 7/8 c Buttermilk 1/3 c Molasses
Preheat oven to 325 degrees F. Grease a 9 X 5 X 3-inch pan. Combine flour, wheat germ, brown sugar, salt and raisins in a mixing bowl. Mix well. In a second mixing bowl, mix

baking soda, buttermilk and molasses, using a wooden spoon. This mixture will start to bubble. Immediately mix it into the dry ingredients. Spoon the batter into the greased pan. Bake at once. The bread is done when a toothpick comes out clean, about 1 hour. Turn out of the pan and cool on a wire rack. Makes 1 loaf.

Title: Citrus Dumplings
Categories: Citrus, Breads
Servings: 2
1/2 ts Finely Shredded Orange Peel 1/2 c Orange Juice
2 ts Cornstarch 1/4 ts Ground Cinnamon
11 oz Mandarin Orange Sect., Drain 1/2 c Bisquick
2 tb Sugar 2 tb Milk
1 ts Sugar Dash Ground Cinnamon

In a 1-quart casserole stir together orange juice, cornstarch and 1/4 t ground cinnamon. Micro-cook, uncovered, on 100% power for 1 1/2 to 2 minutes or till thickened and bubbly, stirring every 30 seconds. Stir in drained mandarin orange sections and finely shredded orange peel. Micro-cook, uncovered, on 100% power for 1 to 1 1/2 minutes or till mixture is heated through. Meanwhile for dumplings, stir together Bisquick and 2 T sugar. Add milk, stirring just till moistened. Drop mixture into four mound atop the hot orange mixture. Micro-cook, uncovered, at 50% power for 6 to 7 minutes or till dumplings are just set. Stir together the 1 t sugar and dash of ground cinnamon. Sprinkle sugar mixture atop dumplings.

Title: AARONSON CORN MUFFINS
Categories: Breads, Aaronson, Nw
Servings: 1
1 1/3 c Flour 1 c Sour cream

2/3 c Cornmeal 3 X-lg eggs
1/2 c Sugar 5 tb Butter; melted
3 ts Baking powder 12 oz Can Green Gian Mexicorn;optl
1/2 ts Baking soda 1/2 c Bacon; coarsely chopped
pn Salt Cupcake papers

I like to add the Mexicorn and bacon to this recipe. It certainly does enhance the flavor, but if you want plain corn muffins, you can certainly omit these 2 ingredients. Preheat oven to 400~. You'll need either one or two 12 unit muffin tins, lined with cupcake papers. Whisk the dry ingredients together, throughly, in a bowl and set aside. Whisk the sour cream, eggs and melted butter together until well-blended. Make a well in the dry ingredients, pour in cream/butter/egg mixture and if you're adding the corn and bacon, add them now. Using a spatula, fold the ingredients together, just until combined--DON'T OVERMIX. Spoon the mixture into the lined muffin tins, filling them evenly, about 3/4 full. Bake for 20-25 minutes, testing until a wooden pick comes out clean.

Title: BREAD PUDDING.

Categories: Desserts, Chocolate, Breads, Puddings
Servings: 6

Bread; to fill dish 2/3 full 2 c Milk
2/3 c Sugar 2 Eggs
2 tb Cocoa 1 ts Vanilla

Into a greased casserole dish break up enough bread to fill it 2/3 full. Over this pour 2/3 cup sugar, 2 Heaping Tbsp cocoa that have been mixed together. Toss all together lightly (to coat the bread). To 2 cups of milk add 2 well beaten eggs and 1 tsp vanilla. Pour this over the bread and it should just cover the pieces. Bake at 350 for about 45 minutes. Serve with milk ...or with a lump of butter melting into the nice warm pudding. Or with Cool Whip, etc.

Title: Altdeutxche Brotchen (Old German Muffins)

Categories: German, Breads, Desserts, Fruits
Servings: 4

3/4 c Butter Or Margarine 1/2 c Sugar
2 Eggs; Large 1 tb Rum
1 ts Vanilla Extract 3 tb Milk
1/2 ts Cinnamon 2 ts Baking Powder
2 1/4 c Flour; Unbleached 1/4 c Almonds; Ground
1 tb Orange Rind; Grated 1/4 c Raisins; If Desired

Cream butter and sugar. Beat in eggs, rum, vanilla, and milk. Mix
cinnamon, baking powder, and flour. Add flour mixture to butter mixture.
Gently mix in almonds, orange rind, and raisins. Pour batter into greased
muffin tins, filling half full. Bake at 375 degrees F. for 25 to 30 mminutes, or until browned. Makes 18 muffins.

Title: WHOLE WHEAT SOURDOUGH

Categories: Breadmaker, Breads
Servings: 8

-JUDY GARNETT PJXG05A 2 ts Wheat germ
2 ts Yeast 1/2 ts Ginger
2 c Whole wheat bread flour 2 tb Olive oil
1 1/3 c Unbleached bread flour 1 tb Honey
2 tb Buttermilk powder 1/2 c Whole wheat s/d starter (you
2 tb Vital wheat gluten 1 c Water ; (i use bottled h20)
2 tb Lecithin 1/2 Margarine, room temp.
2 ts Salt ; lite

I used the whole wheat starter and experimented with your whole wheat bread recipe in the DAK today. It turned out great. Basically, I just halved your recipe and added a few things. My DAK is a 3 cup flour model, is yours? If I'm using whole wheat or rye flour, I can add more flour because it doesn't rise as much. Also, whenever I use whole wheat, etc. I add vital wheat gluten and lecithin to aid elasticity and to help it rise.

Title: GARDEN HERB BREAD

Categories: Breads, Breadmaker, Brunch, Holiday
Servings: 8

---------------**REGULAR LOAF**-------------------------------
2 c White Bread Flour 1 ts Thyme
1 tb Dry Milk 1/2 ts Basil
1 tb Sugar 1 tb Butter
1 ts Salt 3/4 c Water
1 ts Chives 1 ts FAST RISE Yeast OR
1 ts Marjoram 2 ts ACTIVE DRY Yeast

--------------**LARGE LOAF (12 SERVINGS**-------------
3 c White Bread Flour 1/2 tb Thyme
2 tb Dry Milk 1 ts Basil
2 tb Sugar 2 tb Butter
1 1/2 ts Salt 1 1/4 c Water
1/2 tb Chives 2 ts FAST RISE Yeast OR
1/2 tb Margoram 3 ts DRY ACTIVE Yeast

NOTE: I rewrote the recipe to follow order of my machine. It works
wonderfully in my Panasonic.
This bread tastes like stuffing! It is WONDERFUL!!!! Here are some hints
from the book: 1. Use dried herbs that are flaked and not ground. If using
ground, reduce the amt. by half. If using fresh herbs, double the recipe.

2. This recipe can be made with the regular, rapid, or delayed time bake
cycles.

Title: WALNUT BREAD - PAN-1
Categories: Breadmaker, Breads
Servings: 1
 Don Fifield 1 tb Butter
2 1/4 c Bread flour 1/4 c Walnuts (1 oz); chopped
1 tb Sugar 15/16 c Water (7 1/2 fl.oz)
1 tb Dry milk 1 ts Dry yeast
1 ts Salt
Timer OR Bake (Rapid) mode may be used. Place all ingredients (except liquids and yeast) inside the bread pan. Add liquid ingredients. Close cover and place dry yeast into the yeast holder. Press start.

Title: YOGURT BREAD - PAN-1
Categories: Breadmaker, Breads
Servings: 1
 Don Fifield 1 tb Butter
2 1/4 c Bread flour 2 tb Sesame seeds
1 tb Sugar 1/2 c Yogurt (4 1/2 oz)
1 tb Dry milk 1/2 c Water
1 ts Salt 1 ts Dry yeast
Bake (Rapid) mode may be used. Place all ingredients (except liquids and yeast) inside the bread pan. Add liquid ingredients. Close cover and place dry yeast into the yeast holder. Press start.

Title: ZUCCHINI BREAD - PAN-1

Categories: Breadmaker, Breads
Servings: 1
 Don Fifield 1 ts Cinnamon
2 1/4 c Bread flour 1/2 ts Ground cloves
1 tb Dry milk 3 tb Zucchini; grated
1 ts Salt 3/4 c Water
1 tb Butter 1 ts Dry yeast
1/4 c Walnuts (1 oz); chopped

Bake (Rapid) mode may be used. Place all ingredients (except liquids and yeast) inside the bread pan. Add liquid ingredients. Close cover and place dry yeast into the yeast holder. Press start.

Title: DINNER ROLLS - PAN-1

Categories: Breadmaker, Breads, Rolls
Servings: 1
 Don Fifield TOPPINGS:
2 1/4 c Bread flour 1 Egg
3 tb Sugar -(for brushing on top)
2 tb Dry milk 3/4 tb Poppy seeds; (optional
1 ts Salt -for sprinkling on top)
2 1/2 tb Butter 3/4 tb Sesame seeds; (optional
5/8 c Water (5 fl.oz) -for sprinkling on top)
1 ts Dry yeast

1. Place first 5 ingredients inside the bread pan. Add liquid ingredients.Close cover and place dry yeast into the yeast holder. SELECT: BASIC DOUGH MODE. Press start. (Breadmaker completes the basic dough mode (2
hours and 25 minutes later) 2. Divide the dough into 12

equal portions.Roll each portions into a ball. Cover with a plastic wrap and rest for 20 minutes. 3.

Title: BRIOCHE - PAN-1
Categories: Breadmaker, Breads
Servings: 1

Don Fifield 3 lg Eggs
2 1/4 c Bread flour 1/4 c Water
1 1/2 tb Sugar 2 ts Dry yeast
1 tb Dry milk 1 Egg; beaten for brushing
1 ts Salt -on top
6 tb Butter

1. Place first 5 ingredients inside the bread pan. Add eggs and water.

Close cover and place dry yeast into the yeast holder. SELECT: BASIC DOUGH MODE. Press start. (Breadmaker completes the basic dough mode 2 hours and 25 minutes later) 2. Place dough in greased bowl. Cover. Rest the dough in fridge for 30 minutes. 3. Divide dough into 8 equal portions. Roll each portion into a ball. Cover with a plastic wrap and rest for 20 minutes. 4.Using edge of the hand, pinch off about 1/4th of the dough without detaching it. Roll the dough on the bench so that both parts are round. 5.Place the dough in the tin large-end first. With fingertips, press the small ball around its circumference into the large one. 6. Place tins on baking pan. (could use muffin tins???) Spray water on top. Proof at 90 deg. for 30 to 50 minutes or until the larger ball rises above the tin. 7. Brush with beaten egg. 8. Bake in 350 deg. oven for 10 to 15 minutes or until golden brown.

Title: CROISSANTS - PAN-1

Categories: Breadmaker, Breads
Servings: 1

Don Fifield 2 ts Dry yeast
2 1/4 c Bread flour FOR LATER USE:
1 1/2 tb Sugar 5 oz Butter;
2 tb Dry milk -chiled for folding in the
1 ts Salt -dough
1 tb Butter 1 Egg; beaten for brushing
2/3 c Water -on top

1. Place first 5 ingredients inside the bread pan. Add water. Close cover and place dry yeast into the yeast holder. SELECT: BASIC DOUGH MODE. Press start. (Bread maker completes the basic dough mode 2 hours and 25 minutes later) 2. Place dough in greased bowl. Cover. Rest the dough in fridge for 30 minutes. 3. Roll 5 oz of chilled butter between two sheets of waxed paper into a 8 x 7 inch rectangle. Place back in the refrigerator. Chill at least 1 hour. 4. Roll out the dough on a lightly floured surface into a 10 x 10 1/2 inches rectangle. 5. Place the rolled out butter over two-thirds of the dough. Fold the third without butter over the center third. 6. Fold the remaining third on top. Seal edges. Rest the dough in the refrigerator for 20 to 30 minutes. 7. Place the dough at right angles to the previous position in #5. Roll out into 10 x 10 1/2 inches. Fold into thirds. Wrap and place into refrigerator for 20 to 30 minutes. Fold and roll twice more. Wrap and chill after each rolling. After the final folding, chill several hours or overnight. 8. Cut dough crosswise into thirds. Cut each third in thirds. cut each third diagonally to form two triangles. 9. Roll up each triangle loosely, starting from the side oposite the point. Curve ends. 10. Place seam side down on a greased baking pan. 11. Spray water on top. Proof
at 90. deg. for 30 to 50 minutes or until nearly doubled. 12. Brush croissants with beaten egg. 13. Bake in 375 deg. oven for 10 to 15 minutes or until golden brown.

Title: FRENCH BREAD (BAGUETTE) - PAN-1

Categories: Breadmaker, Breads
Servings: 1

 Don Fifield 3/4 c Water
2 1/4 c Bread flour 1 ts Dry yeast
1 ts Salt FOR TOPPING:
1 1/2 ts Sugar 2 tb Poppy seeds; optional
1 1/2 ts Buttar

1. Place first 4 ingredients inside the bread pan. Add water. Close cover
and place dry yeast into the yeast holder. SELECT: BASIC DOUGH MODE. Press start. (Breadmaker completes the basic dough mode 2 hours and 25 minutes later) 2. Divide dough into 2 equal portions. Roll each portions into a ball. 3. Place the dough in a greased bowl. Cover. Rest for about 20 minutes. (Place in the refrigerator during the summer time.) 4. Roll each ball into a rectangle, using a rolling pin. 5. Starting at one short edge, roll the dough up tightly into a thin log, pinching the edges to seal. Taper and round ends. 6. Place on a greased baking pan. Spray water on top.Proof at 90 deg. for 60 minutes or until nearly doubled. 7. Brush with water. With a sharp knife, make 3 or 4 diagonal cuts about 1/4 inch deep across top of the logs. 8. Sprinkle with poppy seeds if desired. 9. Bake in 375 deg. oven for 25 to 30 minutes or until golden brown. (If your oven allows for steaming, bake with steam for first 10 minutes.)

Title: DANISH ROLLS - PAN-1

Categories: Breadmaker, Breads, Rolls
Servings: 1
 Don Fifield 2 ts Dry yeast
1 3/4 c Bread flour (8 1/5 oz) FILLING:
1/2 c All purpose flour (2 1/3 oz) 1/3 c Raisins (3 oz)
4 tb Sugar 1/4 c Sliced almonds (2/3 oz)
3 tb Dry milk OR
1 ts Salt 1/2 c Mixed nuts; chopped
1/3 c Butter (2 1/10 oz) 1 tb Cinnamon
1/2 c Water 2 tb Sugar
1 sm Egg 1 Egg; beaten for top
1. Place first 6 ingredients inside the bread pan. Add water. Close cover and place dry yeast into the yeast holder. SELECT: BASIC DOUGH MODE. Press start. (Breadmaker completes the basic dough mode 2 hours and 25 minutes later) 2. Place the dough in a greased bowl. Cover. Rest for about 30 minutes in the refrigerator. 3. Roll out the dough on a lightly floured surface into a 10 x 16 inch rectangle. 4. Spread the filling over the dough. 5. Starting at one short edge, roll the dough up tightly into a log. 6. Brush with beaten egg over the sealed end. 7. Cut the log into 10 equal portions. 8. Place on a greased baking pan. Spray water on top. Proof at 90 deg. for 20 to 30 minutes. 9. Brush rolls with beaten egg. 10. Bake in 375 deg. oven for 10 to 15 minutes or until golden brown.

Title: DOUGHNUTS - PAN-1

Categories: Breadmaker, Breads
Servings: 1
 Don Fifield 1 ts Dry yeast
1 1/2 c Bread flour (7 oz) TOPPINGS:
3/4 c All purpose flour (3 1/2 oz) 3 oz Semi sweet chocolate;

3 tb Sugar -melted
2 tb Dry milk 1/2 c Blanched almonds; chopped
1 ts Salt 1/2 c Powdered sugar
2 1/2 tb Butter 1/2 c Whipped cream
3/4 c Water 1/2 c Cinnamon sugar (2 3/4 oz)

1. Place first 6 ingredients inside the bread pan. Add water. Close cover
and place dry yeast into the yeast holder. SELECT: BASIC DOUGH MODE. Press start.
(Breadmaker completes the basic dough mode 2 hours and 25 minutes later) 2. Divide the dough into 12 equal portions. Roll each portion into a ball. 3. Place on a lightly floured surface. Cover with a plastic wrap and rest for 20 minutes.)
4. Shape each ball as desired, in a ring, twisted, or in an oval shape. Place on a greased baking pan. 5. Proof at 90 deg. For 30 minutes or until nearly doubled. 6. Deep fry the doughnuts in 360 deg. Oil until golden brown. Let cool. 7. Garnish with your choice of toppings. 8, If desired, cut a hole on one end of doughnut and fill with jelly or your favorite filling.

Title: LIGHT WHOLE WHEAT BREAD - PAN-1

Categories: Breadmaker, Breads
Servings: 1

 Don Fifield 1 tb Butter
1 1/8 c Whole wheat flour (5 1/4 oz) 1 tb Molasses
1 1/8 c Bread flour (5 1/4 oz) 15/16 c Water (7 1/2 fl.oz)
1 tb Dry milk 1 ts Dry yeast
1 ts Salt

Timer OR Bake (Rapid) mode may be used. Place all ingredients (except liquids and yeast) inside the bread pan. Add liquid ingredients. Close cover and place dry yeast into the yeast holder. SELECT: WHOLE WHEAT BAKE

MODE. Press start. 5:00 will show.

Title: MILLET BREAD - PAN-1

Categories: Breadmaker, Breads
Servings: 1
 Don Fifield 1 tb Butter
1 1/8 c Whole wheat flour (5 1/4 oz) 3 tb Toasted bran
1 1/8 c Bread flour (5 1/4 oz) 1 tb Molasses
1/4 c Millet flour 1 c Water
1 tb Dry milk 1 ts Dry yeast
1 ts Salt
Timer OR Bake (Rapid) mode may be used. Place all ingredients (except liquids and yeast) inside the bread pan. Add liquid ingredients. Close cover and place dry yeast into the yeast holder. SELECT: WHOLE WHEAT BAKE MODE. Press start. 5:00 will show.

Title: MULTIGRAIN BREAD II - PAN-1

Categories: Breadmaker, Breads
Servings: 1
 Don Fifield 1 ts Flax seeds
1 1/8 c Whole wheat flour (5 1/4 oz) 1 ts Cornmeal
1 c Bread flour (4 7/10 oz) 1 tb Dry milk
2 tb Triticale flour „1 ts Salt
2 tb Soy flour 1 tb Butter
1 tb Oats 1 tb Molasses
2 tb Toasted bran 1 c Water
1 tb Cracked wheat cereal 1 ts Dry yeast
1 ts Millet flour
„If triticale flour is unavailable, use 1 tb all purpose flour and 1 tb rye flour. Place all ingredients (except liquids and

yeast) inside the bread pan. Add liquid ingredients. Close cover and place dry yeast into the yeast holder. SELECT: WHOLE WHEAT BAKE MODE. Press start. 5:00 will show.

Title: WHOLE WHEAT APPLE-RAISIN BREAD - PAN-1

Categories: Breadmaker, Breads
Servings: 1

 Don Fifield 1/4 c Apple sauce (2 oz)
1 1/8 c Whole wheat flour (5 1/4 oz) 1/4 c Raisins (1 1/2 oz)
1 1/8 c Bread flour (5 1/4 oz) 1/2 ts Cinnamon
1 tb Dry milk 2/3 c Water
1 ts Salt 1 ts Dry yeast
1 tb Butter

Bake (Rapid) mode may be used. Place all ingredients (except liquids and
yeast) inside the bread pan. Add liquid ingredients. Close cover and place
dry yeast into the yeast holder. SELECT: WHOLE WHEAT BAKE MODE. Press
start. 5:00 will show.

Title: WHOLE WHEAT DATE-NUT BREAD - PAN-1

Categories: Breadmaker, Breads
Servings: 1

 Don Fifield 1/3 c Dates; (1 1/2 oz); chopped
2 1/4 c Whole wheat flour 1/4 c Pecans (1 oz); chopped
1 tb Dry milk 15/16 c Water (7 1/2 fl.oz)
1 ts Salt 1 ts Dry yeast

1 tb Butter
Timer OR Bake (Rapid) mode may be used. Place all ingredients (except liquids and yeast) inside the bread pan. Add liquid ingredients. Close cover and place dry yeast into the yeast holder. SELECT: WHOLE WHEAT BAKE MODE. Press start. 5:00 will show.

Title: LOGGERS BREAD DIANA'S VERSION
Categories: Breads, Breadmaker
Servings: 1
1 c Whole wheat flour 2 ts Brown sugar
1/2 c Oat flour 1 ts Honey
1 1/2 c Bread flour 1 ts Molasses
3 tb Applesauce 3/4 ts Salt
1 ts Margarine 1 c Water
3 tb Powdered buttermilk 1 tb Yeast
add all to bm make on dough cycle for rolls.

Title: BANANA NUT BREAD
Categories: Breadmaker, Breads, Fruits
Servings: 6
2 1/3 c Bread Flour 1/4 c Nuts;chopped
2 tb Brown sugar 1/2 c Banana's;mashed2 small ones
1 tb Dry milk 3/4 c Water
1 ts Salt 1 ts Cinnamon; or nutmeg
1 tb Butter 1 ts Yeast
Just add as your B/M requires. I baked it on Bake Light in my Pan-1Lb'er. It came out nice and high and Light, but I thought it could have more banana 's. I used 1/2 cup but would go to 2 small Banana's.Was also good toasted. Good Luck

Title: WHOLE WHEAT HONEY-WALNUT BREAD - PAN-1

Categories: Breadmaker, Breads
Servings: 1

 Don Fifield 1/4 c Walnuts (1 oz); chopped
2 1/4 c Whole wheat flour 2 ts Honey
1 tb Dry milk 15/16 c Water (7 1/2 fl.oz)
1 ts Salt 1 ts Dry yeast
1 tb Butter

Timer OR Bake (Rapid) mode may be used. Place all ingredients (except liquids and yeast) inside the bread pan. Add liquid ingredients. Close cover and place dry yeast into the yeast holder. SELECT: WHOLE WHEAT BAKE MODE. Press start. 5:00 will show.

Title: WHOLE WHEAT ORANGE ANISE BREAD - PAN-1

Categories: Breadmaker, Breads
Servings: 1

 Don Fifield 2 tb Orange zest
2 1/4 c Whole wheat flour 1 1/2 ts Anise
1 tb Dry milk 1/2 c Orange juice
1 ts Salt 1/2 c Water
1 tb Butter 1 ts Dry yeast

Bake (Rapid) mode may be used. Place all ingredients (except liquids and yeast) inside the bread pan. Add liquid ingredients. Close cover and place dry yeast into the yeast holder. SELECT: WHOLE WHEAT BAKE MODE. Press start. 5:00 will show.

Title: WHOLE WHEAT PEANUT SESAME - PAN-1

Categories: Breadmaker, Breads
Servings: 1
 Don Fifield 1/4 c Peanut butter (2 oz)
2 1/4 c Whole wheat flour 2 tb Sesame seeds
1 tb Dry milk 1 c Water
1 ts Salt 1 ts Dry yeast
1 tb Butter
Timer OR Bake (Rapid) mode may be used. Place all ingredients (except liquids and yeast) inside the bread pan. Add liquid ingredients. Close cover and place dry yeast into the yeast holder. SELECT: WHOLE WHEAT BAKE MODE. Press start. 5:00 will show.

Title: WHOLE WHEAT YOGURT BREAD - PAN-1

Categories: Breadmaker, Breads
Servings: 1
 Don Fifield 1 tb Sugar
2 1/4 c Whole wheat flour 2 tb Sesame seeds
1 tb Dry milk 1/2 c Yogurt (4 1/2 oz)
1 ts Salt 1/2 c Water
1 tb Butter 1 ts Dry yeast
Bake (Rapid) mode may be used. Place all ingredients (except liquids and yeast) inside the bread pan. Add liquid ingredients. Close cover and place dry yeast into the yeast holder. SELECT: WHOLE WHEAT BAKE MODE. Press start. 5:00 will show.

Title: PIZZA - PAN-1

Categories: Breadmaker, Breads
Servings: 1
 Don Fifield 1 ts Dry yeast
2 1/4 c Bread flour TOPPINGS:
1 ts Salt 2/3 c Pizza sauce (10 oz)
1 1/2 ts Vegetable oil 2 c Mozzarella cheese (8 oz)
3/4 c Water Garnishes of your choice

1. Place first 3 ingredients inside the bread pan. Add water. Close cover and place dry yeast into the yeast holder. SELECT: BASIC DOUGH MODE. Press start. (Breadmaker completes the basic dough mode 2 hours and 25 minutes later) 2. Divide the dough into 4 equal portions. Roll each portion into a ball. 3. Place on a lightly floured surface. Cover with a plastic wrap and rest for 20 minutes. 4. Roll out each ball into a flat circle. 5. Place on a greased baking pan. Prick the surface with a fork. 6. Brush with 2 tablespoons pizza sauce. Sprinkle mozzarella cheese on top. Garnish with ingredients of your choice. 7. Bake in 500 deg. oven for 12 to 15 minutes or until ingredients are cooked and the dough is crisp and slightly brown.

Title: WHOLE WHEAT BAGELS - PAN-1

Categories: Breadmaker, Breads
Servings: 1
 Don Fifield 2/3 c Water
1 1/8 c Whole wheat flour (5 1/4 oz) 1 1/2 ts Dry yeast
1 1/8 c Bread flour (5 1/4 oz) TOPPINGS:
1 ts Salt 3/4 tb Poppy seed (optional)
1 tb Butter 3/4 tb Sesame seeds (optional)
2 tb Molasses

1. Place first 4 ingredients inside the bread pan. Add molasses and water. Close cover and place dry yeast into the

yeast holder. SELECT: WHOLE WHEAT DOUGH MODE. Press start. (Breadmaker completes the basic dough mode 3 hours and 15 minutes later) 2. Rest in a greased covered bowl in refrigerator for 20 minutes. 3. Divide the dough into 6 equal portions. Roll each portion on a lightly floured surface into a log, approximately 3/4 inch thick and 8 inches long, using the palm of your hand. 4. Seal the ends together tightly to make a ring with a 1 1/2 to 2 inch hole in the center. 5.Place on a greased baking pan. Spray water on top. Proof at 90 deg. for 30 minutes .
6. Bring 1 gallon water with 1 tb sugar to a boil. 7. Reduce to a simmer. Cook 4 or 5 bagels at a time for 7 minutes, turning once. Drain well. 8. Place on a greased baking pan. 9. Sprinkle tops with poppy seeds or sesame seeds, if desired. 10. Bake in 45 deg. oven for 25 to 30 minutes until golden brown, turning them over after half the baking time.

Title: WHOLE WHEAT SOFT PRETZELS - PAN-1
Categories: Breadmaker, Breads
Servings: 1
 Don Fifield 5/8 c Water (5 fl.oz)
1 1/8 c Whole wheat flour (5 1/4 oz) 1 ts Dry yeast
1 1/8 c Bread flour (5 1/4 oz) TOPPINGS:
1 tb Dry milk 1 Egg; beaten
1/2 ts Salt 3/4 tb Black sesame seeds(optional)
1 tb Shortening 1/4 c Coarse salt (optional)
2 tb Molasses
1. Place first 5 ingredients inside the bread pan. Add molasses and water.
Close cover and place dry yeast into the yeast holder. SELECT: WHOLE WHEAT DOUGH MODE. Press start. (Breadmaker completes the basic dough mode 3 hours and 15 minutes later) 2. Divide the dough into 8 equal

portions. Roll each portion on a lightly floured surface into a ball. Cover with a plastic wrap and rest for 20 minutes. 3. Using the palm of the hand, roll each unit on a lightly floured surface into a rope of about 10 inches long. 4. Twist once where the dough overlaps. 5. Lift ends across to opposite edges. Tuck ends under. 6. Place on a greased baking pan. Spray water on top. Proof at 90 deg. for 30 to 50 minutes. 7. Brush with beaten egg. Add any desired toppings. 8. Bake in 375 deg. oven for 15 to 22 minutes.

Title: WHOLE WHEAT PRUNE BREAD - PAN-1
Categories: Breadmaker, Breads
Servings: 1
 Don Fifield 1/4 c Prunes (1 oz); chopped
2 1/4 c Whole wheat flour 1 tb Molasses
1 tb Dry milk 1 c Water
1 ts Salt 1 ts Dry yeast
1 tb Butter
Bake (Rapid) mode may be used. Place all ingredients (except liquids and yeast) inside the bread pan. Add liquid ingredients. Close cover and placedry yeast into the yeast holder.
 SELECT: WHOLE WHEAT BAKE MODE.
Pressstart. 5:00 will show.

Title: DANISH PASTRIES - PAN-1
Categories: Breadmaker, Breads
Servings: 1
 Don Fifield 1/2 c Water
1 3/4 c Bread flour (8 1/5 oz) 2 ts Dry yeast
3/4 c Cake Flour (3 1/2 oz) 1/2 c Butter or marg.; for folding

2 1/2 tb Dry milk -in the dough
3/4 ts Salt 1 Egg; beaten
3 1/2 tb Butter (1.4 oz) -for brushing on top
Fillings: 1/2 - 3/4 c apricot jam or marmalade 1/4 - 1/3 c canned fruit
filling or preserves 1/2 - 3/4 c nut streusel 1/2 - 3/4 c cheese filling

1. Place first 5 ingredients inside the bread pan. Add water. Close cover and place dry yeast into the yeast holder. SELECT: BASIC DOUGH MODE. Press start. (Breadmaker completes the basic dough mode 2 hours and 25 minutes later) 2. Place dough in greased bowl. Cover. Rest the dough in fridge for 30 minutes. 3. Roll 5 oz of chilled butter between two sheets of waxed paper into a 8 x 7 inch rectangle. Place back in the refrigerator. Chill at least 1 hour. 4. Roll out the dough on a lightly floured surface into a 10 x 10 1/2 inches rectangle. 5. Place the rolled out butter over two-thirds of the dough. Fold the third without butter over the center third. 6. Fold the remaining third on top. Seal edges. Rest the dough in the refrigerator for 20 to 30 minutes. 7. Place the dough at right angles to the previous position in #5. Roll out into 10 x 10 1/2 inches. Fold into thirds. Wrap and place into refrigerator for 20 to 30 minutes. Fold and roll three times more. Wrap and chill after each rolling. After the final folding, chill several hours or overnight. 8. Roll out the dough into 10 x 10 1/2 inches. Cut into 6 squares. Roll each out into about 7 inch square. 9. Place the filling of your choice in the center of each square. Brush the four corners lightly with water to help them seal when pressed together. 10. Fold opposite corners over the center. Press down firmly to seal together. Then fold the other two corners over the center and press all four corners tightly together. 11. Place on greased baking pan. Spray water on top. 12. Proof, brush with beaten egg and bake in 357 deg. oven for 10 to 15 minutes or until golden brown.

Title: HARVEST ROUND BREAD (BREADMAKER)
Categories: Breads, Breadmaker
Servings: 1

-RENEE SCOTT (DNTM47A) 1 ts Salt
1 c Whole wheat flour 1/2 c Carrots
1 tb Honey 3/4 c Milk
5/8 c Oatmeal 1/4 c Raisins
1 tb Molasses 1/4 c -water
1 pk Yeast 1/4 c Nuts
1 c White flour 3/16 c Margarine

NOTE: This recipe was resized; follow the directions for your B/M. Because I am still so new at this „P BB I wrote my note in the wrong place so here goes again! My bread making is improving, thanks to „P and B M Magic! I love the book. On a trip to New England I bought bread in a town square, it was wonderful! Later I wrote the baker for the recipe and she kindly sent it. I've only tried it once (I'm new to bread making). But now I'd like to try it in my BM. (the directions follow for assembling ingredients, etc. but since I want to make it in my BM, I'm not including them. Divide dough in two. Divide each half into 3 and make 3 ropes. Braid them and make into a circle. Attach both ends,repeat with other half. The bread was delicious and I would appreciate any help someone can give me. San Diego

Title: GAYE'S SOURDOUGH TIPS
Categories: Breads, Breadmaker, Sourdough
Servings: 1

You will find that your sourdough breads will have more

"tang" and will rise higher in the BM if you follow this procedure: „Remove a cup)or more) of your starter from the fridge and bring to room temp. „Feed with 1 cup flour and 1 cup (or slightly less) water „Let the starter do its thing. It will become bubbly and foamy. Watch for its 'peak'. This usually occurs 8 to 10 hours after feeding. It is best to keep the starter warm (75 to 85 degrees). If it cold out, leave it in the oven with the light turned on!„Make your bread during the peak...while the starter is VERY active.„Dump the unused starter back into the mother pot. Following this method,you can even make sourdough in the b/m without yeast. Really!„Variation: Separate your starter into two batches. Create a "beer" starter with one batch. You will feed this pot with flat beer and flour instead of water and flour. A very unique and delicious taste!

„To create your own sourdough recipe:
Substitute 7/8 cup start for 1 cup liquid
Reduce flour by 1/4 to 1/2 cup

Title: SWEDISH LIMPA BREAD

Categories: Breads, Breadmaker, Holiday
Servings: 1
-Dottie Cross TMPJ72B 1 tb Butter
2 1/4 c Bread flour 1 tb Orange peel; chopped
1/4 c (1 oz.) rye flour 1 1/2 ts Caraway seeds
2 tb Brown sugar 1/2 ts Fennel seed
1 tb Dry milk 15/16 c (7-1/2 fl. oz.) water
1 ts Salt 1 ts Dry yeast
Combine ingredients in order according to your own bread machine instructions. Hope you enjoy! It's delicious bread!
Makes (1) 1 pound loaf

Title: COTTAGE DILL BREAD FOR BREAD MACHINE

Categories: Breads, Breadmaker
Servings: 8
-Electric Bread

--------------------------------**REGULAR LOAF**-------------------------------

1/2 c Water 1 1/4 c Cottage cheese
2 c White bread flour 1/2 tb Dry onion
1 tb Dry milk 1/2 tb Dill seed
1 tb Sugar 1/2 tb Dill weed
1 ts Salt 1 ts Fast rise yeast; ,,,,OR,,,,
1 tb Butter 2 ts -Active dry yeast

--------------------------------**LARGE LOAF**-------------------------------

3/4 c Water 3/4 c Cottage cheese
3 c White bread flour 1 tb Dry onion
1 1/2 tb Dry milk 1 tb Dill seed
2 tb Sugar 1 tb Dill weed
1 1/2 ts Salt 2 ts Fast rise yeast; ,,,,OR,,,,
1 1/2 tb Butter 3 ts -Active dry yeast

--- servings are based on 8 for regular loaf and 12 for large loaf. Hints: Use small curd, lowfat cottage cheese. This recipe can be made with the regular or rapid bake cycles. Be sure to follow loading instructions for your particular bread machine.

Title: ZOJI'S HEARTY OATMEAL BREAD

Categories: Breadmaker, Breads
Servings: 1
-S DUNLAP USN (RET) XRVR35A 2 2/3 c Bread flour

1 1/4 c Water 1/2 c "quick" oatmeal
1 1/2 tb Powdered milk 3 tb Vital gluten;
2 tb Brown sugar -(optional, but good)
3 tb Butter; (margerine) 1 pk Yeast
1 1/2 ts Salt

Bake on the "regular" cycle, and you'll get a truly fine and tasty "white" loaf that won't last very long. This is my contribution to your 1993....how about a few of your "bulletproof" favorites in return? Have the very finest of New Years....

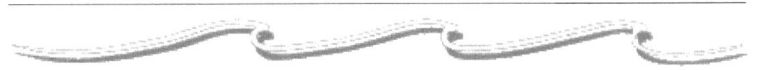

Title: CREAM CHEESE BREAD
Categories: Breadmaker, Breads, Dairy
Servings: 1
-PEGGY SEEVERS (PDMT15A) 3 tb Sugar
1/3 c Milk 1 ts Salt
1 c Cream cheese; (I cube mine) 3 c Bread flour
1/4 c Margarine; or butter 2 1/2 ts Yeast
1 Egg

Here is the recipe for Cream Cheese bread
cook this on the light crust setting and if you want to add choc chips,raisins or other dried fruits, use the setting for adding these at the beep.

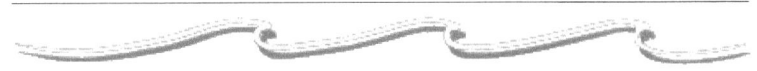

Title: DEDE'S BUTTERMILK BREAD
Categories: Breads, Breadmaker
Servings: 1
1 1/8 c Buttermilk or 1 1/2 ts Salt
4 tb Dry buttermilk powder and 1 tb Butter or margarine

1 1/8 c Water 3 tb Honey
(for Welbilt/Dak machines 1/4 ts Baking soda,, Add 2 T more buttermilk) 1 1/2 ts Red Star active dry yeast 3 c Bread flour ,,Prodigy "research" has shown that if using powdered buttermilk we should omit the baking soda. Place all ingredients in bread pan, select Light Crust setting, and pres Start. From Bread Machine

Title: LISA'S CORNY BREAD
Categories: Breads, Breadmaker
Servings: 10
3 c Flour 1 1/2 ts Dry Yeast
1 tb Sugar 7/8 c Milk; warmed
1 ts Salt 1/4 c Water; plus enough for dough
1/2 c Yellow Cornmeal 1 1/2 tb Butter
Add all ingred. into Bread machine in order per your manufacturer. NOTE:
Very nice texture and flavor. A definite DO AGAIN!

Title: ANADAMA BREAD - PAN-1
Categories: Breadmaker, Breads
Servings: 1
 Don Fifield 1 tb Molasses
2 1/4 c Bread Flour 1 tb Olive oil
1 tb Dry milk 15/16 c Water (7 1/2 fl.oz)
1 ts Salt 1 ts Dry yeast
1/4 c Cornmeal (1/2 oz)
Timer OR Bake (Rapid) mode may be used. Place all ingredients (except liquids and yeast) inside the bread pan. Add liquid ingredients. Close cover and place dry yeast into the yeast holder. Press start.

Title: BASIC WHITE BREAD - PAN-1

Categories: Breadmaker, Breads
Servings: 1

 Don Fifield 1 tb Butter (2/5 oz)
2 1/4 c Bread flour (10 1/2 oz) 2 tb Sugar (3/5 oz)
1 tb Dry milk (1/5 oz) 7/8 c Water (7 fl.oz)
1 ts Salt (1/5 oz) 1 ts Dry yeast (1/10 oz)
Timer OR Bake (Rapid) mode may be used. Place all ingredients (except liquids and yeast) inside the bread pan. Add liquid ingredients. Close cover and place dry yeast into the yeast holder. Press start.

Title: DOUBLE BRAN BREAD - PAN-1

Categories: Breadmaker, Breads
Servings: 1

 Don Fifield 1 tb Butter
2 1/4 c Bread Flour 1/3 c Bran flakes (1 oz)
1 tb Brown sugar 1/4 c Toasted bran (3/4 oz)
1 tb Dry milk 1 c Water
1 ts Salt 1 ts Dry yeast
Timer OR Bake (Rapid) mode may be used. Place all ingredients (except liquids and yeast) inside the bread pan. Add liquid ingredients. Close cover and place dry yeast into the yeast holder. Press start.

Title: CARROT-SPICE BREAD - PAN-1

Categories: Breadmaker, Breads
Servings: 1

Don Fifield 1/4 c Carrots (1 oz); grated
2 1/4 c Bread Flour 2 ts Allspice
1 tb Dry milk 1 tb Honey
1 ts Salt 3/4 c Water
1 tb Butter 1 ts Dry yeast

Bake (Rapid) mode may be used. Place all ingredients (except liquids and yeast) inside the bread pan. Add liquid ingredients. Close cover and place dry yeast into the yeast holder. Press start.

Title: CRACKED WHEAT-SUNFLOWER BREAD - PAN-1

Categories: Breadmaker, Breads
Servings: 1
Don Fifield 1/4 c Unsalted sunflower seeds
2 1/4 c Bread Flour -(1 oz)
1 tb Dry milk 1 tb Honey
1 ts Salt 1 c Water
1 tb Butter 1 ts Dry yeast
1/4 c Cracked wheat cereal (1 oz)

Bake (Rapid) mode may be used. Place all ingredients (except liquids and yeast) inside the bread pan. Add liquid ingredients. Close cover and place dry yeast into the yeast holder. Press start.

Title: HERB BREAD - PAN-1

Categories: Breadmaker, Breads
Servings: 1
Don Fifield 2 tb Parsley
2 1/4 c Bread Flour 1 tb Caraway seeds
2 tb Sugar 1 tb Dill
1 tb Dry milk 15/16 c Water (7 1/2 fl.oz)

1 ts Salt 1 ts Dry yeast
1 tb Butter
Timer OR Bake (Rapid) mode may be used. Place all ingredients (except liquids and yeast) inside the bread pan. Add liquid ingredients. Close cover and place dry yeast into the yeast holder. Press start.

Title: MILK BREAD - PAN-1
Categories: Breadmaker, Breads
Servings: 1
 Don Fifield 1 tb Butter
2 1/4 c Bread Flour 15/16 c Milk (7 1/2 fl.oz)
2 tb Sugar 1 ts Dry yeast
1 ts Salt
Bake (Rapid) mode may be used. Place all ingredients (except liquids and yeast) inside the bread pan. Add liquid ingredients. Close cover and place dry yeast into the yeast holder. Press start.

Title: MULTGRAIN BREAD - PAN-1
Categories: Breadmaker, Breads
Servings: 1
 Don Fifield 1 tb Butter
2 1/4 c Bread Flour 1 ts Cornmeal
2 tb Whole wheat flour 1 tb Cracked wheat cereal
2 tb Soy flour 2 tb Bran flakes
2 tb Triticale flour ,,1 ts Flax seeds
1 ts Millet flour 1 tb Honey
1 tb Dry milk 1 c Water
1 ts Salt 1 ts Dry yeast
,,IF TRITICALE FLOUR IS UNAVAILABLE, USE: 1 tb ALL-PURPOSE FLOUR AND 1 tb RYE FLOUR.

Place all ingredients (except liquids and yeast) inside the bread pan. Add liquid ingredients. Close cover and place dry yeast into the yeast holder. Press start.

Title: **OATMEAL-APPLESAUCE BREAD - PAN-1**
Categories: Breadmaker, Breads
Servings: 1
 Don Fifield 1/4 c Oatmeal (4/5 oz)
2 1/4 c Bread flour 1/4 c Applesauce (2 1/10 oz)
1 tb Sugar 1/2 ts Cinnamon
1 tb Dry milk 5/8 c Water (5 fl.oz)
1 ts Salt 1 ts Dry yeast
1 tb Butter
Bake (Rapid) mode may be used. Place all ingredients (except liquids and
yeast) inside the bread pan. Add liquid ingredients. Close cover and place
dry yeast into the yeast holder. Press start.

Title: **ORANGE BREAD - PAN-1**
Categories: Breadmaker, Breads
Servings: 1
 Don Fifield 1 tb Butter
2 1/4 c Bread flour 1 tb Orange zest; chopped
1 ts Sugar 7/16 c Orange juice (3 1/2 fl.oz)
1 tb Dry milk 1/2 c Water
1 ts Salt 1 ts Dry yeast
Bake (Rapid) mode may be used. Place all ingredients (except liquids and yeast) inside the bread pan. Add liquid ingredients. Close cover and place dry yeast into the yeast holder. Press start.

Title: EGG BREAD - PAN-1
Categories: Breadmaker, Breads
Servings: 1

 Don Fifield 1 tb Butter
2 1/4 c Bread Flour 1 sm Egg
1 tb Sugar 3/4 c Milk; or enough to make
1 ts Sugar -16/16 c with the whole egg
1 tb Dry milk 1 ts Dry yeast
1 ts Salt

Bake (Rapid) mode may be used. Place all ingredients (except liquids and yeast) inside the bread pan. Add liquid ingredients. Close cover and place dry yeast into the yeast holder. Press start.

Title: FRUIT NUT BRAN BREAD - PAN-1
Categories: Breadmaker, Breads
Servings: 1

 Don Fifield 1/4 c Bran flakes (4/5 oz)
2 1/4 c Bread Flour 3 tb Toasted bran
2 tb Brown sugar 1/4 c Sliced almonds (4/5 oz)
1 tb Dry milk 1/4 c Dried fruit bits (1 2/5 oz)
1 ts Salt 1 c Water
1 tb Butter 1 ts Dry yeast

Place all ingredients (except liquids and yeast) inside the bread pan. Add liquid ingredients. Close cover and place dry yeast into the yeast holder. Select BAKE (LIGHT) mode. Press start.

Title: CHEESE & PEPPERONI BREAD - PAN-1

Categories: Breadmaker, Breads
Servings: 1
 Don Fifield 2 ts Parmesan cheese, grated
2 1/4 c Bread flour 1/2 ts Garlic powder
1 tb Sugar 1/2 ts Onion powder
1 tb Dry milk 1/4 ts Oregano
1 ts Salt 1 ts Olive oil
1/4 c Pepperoni (1 oz); chopped 3/4 c Water
1/4 c Provolone cheese (1 1/5 oz); 1 ts Dry yeast
-chopped

Place all ingredients (except liquids and yeast) inside the bread pan. Add liquid ingredients. Close cover and place dry yeast into the yeast holder. Press start.

Title: POPPY SEED-LEMON BREAD - PAN-1

Categories: Breadmaker, Breads
Servings: 1
 Don Fifield 1 tb Butter
2 1/4 c Bread flour 2 tb Poppy seeds
1 tb Sugar 1 tb Lemon peel
1 tb Dry milk 15/16 c Water (7 1/2 fl.oz)
1 ts Salt 1 ts Dry yeast

Bake (Rapid) mode may be used. Place all ingredients (except liquids and yeast) inside the bread pan. Add liquid ingredients. Close cover and place dry yeast into the yeast holder. Press start.

Title: PUMPERNICKEL BREAD - PAN-1

Categories: Breadmaker, Breads
Servings: 1
 Don Fifield 1 tb Butter
2 1/4 c Bread flour 3 tb Cornmeal

1/4 c Rye flour (1 oz) 2 tb Cocoa
1/4 c Whole wheat flour(1 1/3 oz) 2 tb Molasses
1 tb Dry milk 15/16 c Water (7 1/2 fl.oz)
1 ts Salt 1 ts Dry yeast
Place all ingredients (except liquids and yeast) inside the bread pan. Add liquid ingredients. Close cover and place dry yeast into the yeast holder. Press start.

Title: PUMNPKIN BREAD - PAN-1
Categories: Breadmaker, Breads
Servings: 1
 Don Fifield 1 tb Butter
2 1/4 c Bread flour 1/4 c Pumpkin; cooked and mashed
1 tb Sugar -(1 4/5 oz)
1 tb Dry milk 3/4 c Water
1 ts Salt 1 ts Dry yeast
Bake (Rapid) mode may be used. Place all ingredients (except liquids and yeast) inside the bread pan. Add liquid ingredients. Close cover and place dry yeast into the yeast holder. Press start.

Title: RAISIN BREAD - PAN-1
Categories: Breadmaker, Breads
Servings: 1
 Don Fifield 1 tb Butter
2 1/4 c Bread flour 1/4 c Raisins (1 1/2 oz)
1 tb Sugar 1/2 tb Cinnamon (optional)
1 tb Dry milk 7/8 c Water
1 ts Salt 1 ts Dry yeast
Place all ingredients (except liquids and yeast) inside the bread pan. Add liquid ingredients. Close cover and place dry yeast into the yeast holder.Select BAKE (LIGHT) mode.

Press start.

Title: RYE BREAD - PAN-1
Categories: Breadmaker, Breads
Servings: 1

 Don Fifield 1 ts Salt
2 1/4 c Bread flour 1 tb Butter
1/4 c Rye flour (1 oz) 1 c Water
2 tb Sugar 1 ts Dry yeast
1 tb Dry milk

Timer may be used. Place all ingredients (except liquids and yeast) inside the bread pan. Add liquid ingredients. Close cover and place dry yeast into the yeast holder. Press start.

Title: SPICY CHEESE LOAF - PAN-1
Categories: Breadmaker, Breads
Servings: 1

 Don Fifield 1 ts Dry mustard
2 1/4 c Bread flour 1/4 ts Black pepper
2 tb Sugar 1/2 c Cheddar cheese; shredded
1 tb Dry milk 1 tb Worcestershire sauce
1 ts Salt 7/8 c Water
1 tb Butter 1 ts Dry yeast

Bake (Rapid) mode may be used. Place all ingredients (except liquids and yeast) inside the bread pan. Add liquid ingredients. Close cover and place dry yeast into the yeast holder. Press start.

Title: NO-FAT BAGELS FOR BREADMACHINE
Categories: Breadmaker, Breads, Low-cal, Jewish

Servings: 6

-Judy Garnett pjxg05a 3 c Flour
1 pk Yeast 1 Egg white
3/4 c -Warm water; 110 deg 1 1/2 -water

Place yeast and flour to bread pan of machine. Add egg white and warm water. Program for Manual, White Bread and press start. Allow bread to knead two times and then remove from pan. Shaping Bagels: Divide dough into 12 portions. Roll each piece into a smooth ball. Punch a hole in center of dough and shape like a bagel. Cover and let rise 20 minutes. In a large pot, bring 1 gal of water to a boil. Add 3 bagels at a time and simmer for 5 minutes turning once. Drain. Beat egg white and water together lightly. Brush bagles with egg white and water glaze. For variety sprinkle with onion or garlic bits or sesame or poppy seeds/ Bake in preheated 375 deg oven 30 mins. or until brown. Makes 6. No Salt No Sugar No Fat .

Title: BAGELS (BREADMAKER)

Categories: Breads, Breadmaker, Jewish
Servings: 12

---------------------**SMALL** ---------------------------------

2/3 c Water 2/3 c Whole wheat flour
1 tb Honey 1 1/3 c Bread flour
1 ts Salt 1 ts Yeast

---------------------**MEDIUM** ---------------------------------

1 c Water 1 c Whole wheat flour
1 1/2 tb Honey 2 c Bread flour
1 1/2 ts Salt 1 1/2 ts Yeast

------------------**LARGE** ---------------------------------

1 1/3 c Water 1 1/3 c Whole wheat flour
2 tb Honey 2 2/3 c Bread flour
2 ts Salt 2 1/2 ts Yeast

Set for dough cycle. Let the machine knead the dough once, and then let the dough rise for only 20 minutes in the machine. Even if your cycle runs longer, simply remove dough after 20 minutes and turn off the machine. Divide the dough into the appropriate number of pieces. Each piece should be rolled into a rope and made into a circle, pressing the ends together. You may find it necessary to wet one end slightly to help seal the ends together. Place these on a well greased baking sheet, cover and let rise only 15 to 20 minutes. Meanwhile, bring to a slight boil in a "non aluminum pan", (Donna German uses a cast iron frying pan) about 2 inches of water. Carefully lower about 3 or 4 bagels at a time into the water, cooking for about 30 seconds on each side. Remove bagels, drain on a towel, sprinkle with poppy seeds, sesame seeds or dried onion bits if desired and place on the greased baking sheet. Bake in a preheated 550 degree oven for 8 minutes.

Title: APPLE OATMEAL BREAD WITH RAIS

Categories: Breadmaker, Breads

Servings: 1

1/2 c Old fashioned rolled oats 1 1/2 tb Nonfat dry milk powder

5/8 c Water 1 1/2 tb Applesauce,,

1/2 c Unsweetened applesauce 1/3 c Raisins

2 3/4 c Bread flour 1 ts Ground cinnamon

1 1/2 ts Salt 1 1/2 ts Yeast,,

2 tb Brown sugar

Place in bread pan. Select light crust setting. ,,Welbilt/Dak 1 1/2 pound machines take 2 teaspoons. Recipe calls for 1 1/2 T butter...I use applesauce. Hold back some water to begin with. Did not use raisin setting. Flavor outstanding. Very moist, but not soggy. 1 1/2 lb. loaf - Bread Machine Magic

Title: OLD-FASHIONED WHEAT BREAD
Categories: Breadmaker, Breads
Servings: 1

-----------**ONE POUND LOAF**-----------------------------
3/4 c Water 1/3 c Whole Wheat Flour
1 1/2 tb Canola Oil 2 tb Powdered Milk
1 1/2 tb Maple Syrup 1 ts Fine Sea Salt
1 2/3 c Unbleached All-Purpose Flour 1 1/2 ts Active Dry Yeast

Put all the ingredients in the inner pan in the order listed, or in the reverse order if the manual for your machine specifies dry ingredients first andliquids last. Select Basic Wheat cycle, **LIGHT SETTING**
(or thequivalent setting for your machine. Push Start.

Title: POTATO KUGEL BREAD
Categories: Breadmaker, Breads
Servings: 6

------------**MAKES A MEDIUM LOAF**------------------
3/4 c Mashed Potatoes „1 tb Sugar
3/4 c Potato Water 3 c Bread Flour
2 1/4 tb Vegetable Oil 1 1/2 ts Yeast
3/4 ts Salt 2 ts Wheat Germ

„Mashed Potatoes = Use boiled or instant, but add minced onion, parmesan cheese and horseradish. The dough is very liquid and the bread will not rise very high but it makes a chewy bread similar in texture to a knish or a potato kugel.

Title: Quick Sourdough Bread
Categories: Breadmaker, Breads
Servings: 12
2 1/4 c Bread Flour 1/2 c Dairy sour cream

1 tb Wheat Germ 1 tb Vinegar
1 1/2 ts Sugar 1/2 Egg white
1 ts Salt 1/2 tb Water
1/4 ts Ginger 1 ts Poppy seed
1/2 c Water 2 ts Yeast
Load as directed for your bread machine.

Title: Wonder Bread--Golden Egg Bread
Categories: Breadmaker, Breads
Servings: 12
2 1/2 ts Yeast 2 Eggs
3 c Bread flour 6 tb Vegetable oil
1 1/2 ts Salt 3/4 c Water
4 tb Sugar
Load according to your machine's directions. Bake on light.

Title: Lemon Poppy Seed Bread
Categories: Breadmaker, Breads
Servings: 12
3/4 c Water 2 tb Honey
3 c Bread flour 1/2 c Almonds, toasted & sliced
1 1/2 tb Dry milk 1 tb Lemon peel
1 ts Salt 3 tb Poppy seeds
1 1/2 tb Butter 2 ts Lemon extract
3/4 c Lemon Yogurt 2 ts Yeast
You can also use sour cream instead of the yogurt for a bit of a different
taste. Load as directed for your bread machine.

Title: Walnut-Onion Herb Bread

Categories: Breads, Breadmaker
Servings: 8

1 1/4 tb Active dry yeast 1/4 c Chopped fresh dill
2 tb Sugar Or
1 c Warm water (105-115) 1 1/2 tb Dried dill
1 c Warm milk (105-115) 4 1/2 c Flour
1 Egg 1/3 c Minced white onion
2 ts Salt 2/3 c Coarsely chopped walnuts
2 tb Walnut oil or unsalted buttr

„This recipe is for making bread in a casserole dish with no kneading. To make it in a bread machine cut liquid and flour in half. In a small bowl, sprinkle the yeast and a pinch of sugar over the warm water. Stir to dissolve and let stand until foamy, about 10 minutes. In a large bowl, combine the mild, remaining sugar, egg, salt, oil or butter, dill and 1 ½ cups flour. Beat with a wisk or heavy duty mixer until smooth. Add the yeast mixture and remaining flour 1/2 cup at a time, beating vigorously about 2 minutes. Batter will be sticky. Cover with plastic wrap and let rise in a warm area until doubled in bulk, about 1 hour. Sprinkle the onion and walnuts over the top of the batter and stir down, beating vigorously to evenly distribute. Turn into a well greased 3-quart casserole or souffle dish, 9-inch springform pan, or 9-inch kugel of tube mold. Cover loosley with plastic wrap and let rise in a warm area until doubled in bulk, about 30 minutes. Preheat the oven to 375 degrees. Bake in the center of the oven until the top is crusty brown, hollow when tapped and a cake tester inserted into the center comes out clean, about 45-50 minutes. Run a sharp knife around the sides of the pan and turn out of the pan onto a rack to cool right side up. Variation: add 4 ounces mozzarella cheese, cut into cubes. „For Bread machine, dump in all ingredinets and push start.

Title: SAUCY APPLE BREAD
Categories: Breadmaker, Breads, Apples
Servings: 1
------------------**1 POUND LOAF-**----------------------------
-Marie Frainier ,,DGCP02C,,2 1/2 tb Honey
1/2 c Apple cider 1/3 ts Vanilla extract
1 1/3 c White bread flour 2 1/2 tb Unchopped walnuts
3/4 c Plus (see Below) 2 1/2 tb Beaten egg
1 tb Wheat flour 1/3 c Unsweetened applesauce
1 ts Salt 1/3 c Unpeeled granny smith apples
2 1/2 tb Plain yogurt 1 1/4 ts Yeast (active dry)
,,,,,,core and dice unpeeled apple.

Title: APPLE OAT BREAD
Categories: Breadmaker, Breads, Apples
Servings: 1
------------**1 POUND LOAF-**-------------------------------
-Marie Frainier ,,DGCP02C,,1 tb Concentrated apple juice
1/2 c Water 2 ts Lemon juice
1 1/3 c White bread flour 1 tb Honey
2/3 c Wheat flour 2 tb Yogurt
2 ts Dry milk 2 ts Molasses
1 ts Salt 1/4 c Oats
2 ts Butter 2 ts Yeast (active dry)
1/2 c Canned/chopped apples

Title: WHOLE WHEAT SUNFLOWER BREAD
Categories: Breadmaker, Breads, Bmm
Servings: 1

1 pound loaf 1 ts Salt
1/3 c Old fash rolled oats 1 tb Applesauce
5/8 c Buttermilk 1 tb Brown sugar
1 Egg Grated rind 1 orange
1 c Whole wheat flour 1/4 c Sunflower seeds
1 c Bread flour 1/4 ts Baking soda
2 ts Wheat gream 3 ts Yeast
Crust light. Bake.

Title: BASIC WHITE BREAD
Categories: Breadmaker, Breads, Pam vkbb14a, Bmm
Servings: 1
--1 1/2 pound loaf 1 1/2 ts Salt
1/2 c Water 1 1/2 tb Butter/marg/applesauce
5/8 c Milk 3 tb Sugar
3 c Bread flour 1 1/2 ts Yeast

Title: EGG BREAD
Categories: Breadmaker, Pam vkbb14a, Breads, Bmm
Servings: 1
1 1/2 pound loaf 1 1/2 ts Salt
3/4 c Milk 3 tb Applesauce
2 Eggs 1/4 c Sugar
3 c Bread flour 1 1/2 ts Yeast
Crust light.

Title: BASIC WHOLE WHEAT
Categories: Breadmaker, Pam vkbb14a, Breads, Bmm
Servings: 1

1 pound loaf 1 c Bread flour
1/4 c Water 1 ts Salt
3/8 c Milk 1 tb Applesauce (oil)
1 Egg 1 tb Honey
1 c Whole wheat flour 2 ts Yeast
Crust light Bake.

Title: SAN DIEGO SUNSHINE
Categories: Breadmaker, Pam vkbb14a, Breads, Bmm
Servings: 1
1 pound loaf 1 1/2 tb Applesauce (butter)
3/4 c Water 1 tb Brown sugar
1 1/3 c Bread flour 1 tb Honey
2/3 c Whole wheat flour Grated rind of 1 orange
1 ts Salt 1 1/2 ts Yeast
Crust: light. Bake.

Title: Luscious Luau Bread
Categories: Breadmaker, Breads
Servings: 1
3/4 c Water,,,,2 tb Shredded carrots
1 tb Dry milk,,,,1/4 c Flaked, shredded coconut
1 tb Butter (cut up) 1/2 c Crushed pineapple
2 1/3 c Bread flour 1/3 c Chopped macadamia nuts
1/2 ts Salt 2 ts Yeast
1 1/2 tb Brown sugar ,,,,,,1/2 t cinnamon if desired
Drain the pineapple well. Juice may be substituted for up to 2/3 of the
water. ,,,,May use regular milk for water and powdered milk.
Put all ingredients into pan. Select light crust, sweet bread.

Title: LINDA'S EASY POTATO BREAD

Categories: Breadmaker, Pam vkbb14a, Breads, Bmm
Servings: 1

1 1/2 pound loaf 1 1/2 ts Salt
1/4 c Instant potato flakes 1 1/2 tb Applesauce (butter)
3/4 c Milk 1 1/2 tb Sugar
3/8 c Water 2 ts Yeast
3 c Bread flour
crust light.

Title: MIDNIGHT-SUN BREAD

Categories: Breadmaker, Pam vkbb14a, Breads, Bmm
Servings: 1

1 1/2 pound loaf 2 tb Honey
1 1/8 c Buttermilk Grated rind 1 small orange
3 c Bread flour 1 1/2 ts Caraway seeds
1 1/2 ts Salt 1/2 c Raisins
2 tb Applesauce (butter) 2 ts Yeast
Bake Light

Title: ENGLISH TOASTING BREAD

Categories: Breadmaker, Pam vkbb14a, Breads, Bmm
Servings: 1

1 1/2 pound loaf 2 ts Sugar
3/4 c Milk 1/4 ts Baking soda
3/8 c Water 2 ts Yeast
3 c Bread flour Cornmeal
1 ts Salt

This si a special bread, coated with cornmeal, so it needs to be baked in a loaf pan in the oven. Heavenly with orange marmalade. Put all in b/m except cornmeal. Dough setting. When machine beeps, remove bread pan & turn out dough onto floured counter top. Grease an 8 1/2x 4 1/2 x 2 1/2-inch loaf pan; sprinkle all sides with cornmeal. Place dough into prepared loaf pan. With your hands, carefully press it evenly into pan. Sprinkle the top with cornmeal. Cover and let rise in a warm oven for 20 to 30 min or until dough almost reaches top of pan. To warm oven slightly, turn oven on Warm setting for 2 minutes then turn off) Preheat oven to 400F & bake 25 min. Cool.

Title: TANGY BUTTERMILK CHEESE BREAD
Categories: Breadmaker, Pam vkbb14a, Breads, Bmm
Servings: 1
1/2 pound loaf 1 1/2 tb Sugar
1 1/8 c Buttermilk 3/4 c Grated extra-sharp cheese
3 c Bread flour 1 1/2 ts Yeast
1 1/2 ts Salt
Use extra sharp cheese. Bake light.

Title: BMM HERB BREAD
Categories: Breadmaker, Pam vkbb14a, Breads, Bmm
Servings: 1
1 1/2 pound loaf 1 1/2 tb Sugar
3 tb Applesauce (butter) 1/2 ts Dried dill
1/2 c Chopped onion 1/2 ts Dried basil
1 c Milk 1/2 ts Dried rosemary
3 c Bread flour 1 1/2 ts Yeast
1 1/2 ts Salt

Place all ingred. including onion mix in pan. select light crust & press´start.

Title: ANITA'S ITALIAN HERB BREAD
Categories: Breadmaker, Pam vkbb14a, Breads, Bmm
Servings: 1
1 1/2 pound loaf 1 tb Sugar
1 1/8 c Buttermilk 1/2 c Parmesan cheese
3 c Bread flour 1/4 ts Dried basil
1 1/2 ts Salt 1/4 ts Dried oregano
1 1/2 tb Applesauce (oil) 1 1/2 ts Yeast
Crust light. Bake.

Title: HEAVENLY WHOLE WHEAT BREAD
Categories: Breadmaker, Pam vkbb14a, Breads, Bmm
Servings: 1
1 pound loaf 3 tb Applesauce (butter)
3/4 c Water 1 tb Sugar
1 1/3 c Whole wheat flour 3 tb Instant Potato flakes
2/3 c Bread flour 1 1/2 ts Yeast
1 ts Salt
Good!! Crust: light. Bake.

Title: DEBBIE'S HONEY WHOLE WHEAT BREAD
Categories: Breadmaker, Pam vkbb14a, Breads, Bmm
Servings: 1
1 pound loaf 2 ts Applesauce
3/4 c Milk 3 tb Honey
2 c Whole wheat flour 2 ts Yeast
1/2 ts Salt

Crust light. Bake.

Title: **MADELEINE'S NEIGHBORLY BREAD**
Categories: Breadmaker, Pam vkbb14a, Breads, Bmm
Servings: 1
1 pound loaf 1/4 c Plain mashed potato,,
3/8 c Milk 1 ts Salt
1/4 c Potato water 1 tb Applesauce (butter)
1 1/3 c Whole wheat flour 1 tb Honey
2/3 c Bread flour 2 ts Yeast
Crust light.

Title: **APPLE-BUTTER WHEAT BREAD**
Categories: Breadmaker, Pam vkbb14a, Breads, Bmm
Servings: 1
1 pound loaf 1 ts Salt
5/8 c Water 1 tb Applesauce (butter)
1 c Allpurpose flour 3 tb Apple butter
1 c Whole wheat flour 1 1/2 ts Yeast
Crust light. Bake.

Title: **DAILY BREAD**
Categories: Breadmaker, Pam vkbb14a, Breads, Bmm
Servings: 1
1 pound loaf 1 ts Salt
3 tb Millers bran 1 tb Applesauce
1/4 c Milk 3 tb Honey
3/8 c Water 1/4 c Sunflower seeds
1 Egg 2 ts Yeast

2 c Whole wheat flour
Crust: light. Bake.

Title: SHREDDED-WHEAT BREAD
Categories: Breadmaker, Pam vkbb14a, Breads, Bmm
Servings: 1
1 pound loaf 1 tb Applesauce
1 Large shredded-wheat biscuit 1 1/2 tb Brown sugar
7/8 c Water 1 1/2 tb Honey
2 c Whole wheat flour 2 ts Yeast
1 ts Salt
Crust light. Bake.

Title: MOM'S BREAD ROLLS FOR THE BM
Categories: Breads, Breadmaker
Servings: 24
,,JAN CARGILL ,,,,VHPK03A 1/2 tb Salt
2/3 c Milk 1 tb Shortening
2/3 c Water 1 pk Yeast or 1 env. dry yeast
1 1/3 tb Sugar 3 c Flour
Dissolve yeast in a 1/4 cup of lukewarm water. Combine milk,water,sugar ,salt and shortening. Stir until dissolved and lukewarm. Add yeast (dissolved in water). Sift flower (about 6 cups) only enough so you can knead it-(so it wont stick to fingers) for 10 Min.. Place in greased bowl and let rise (warm room) 1 1/2 hrs. (or until doubled in bulk) Punch down with knife and let rise again 1/2 hr. .Cut up in small pieces and roll around in hands and place in tin . (To form a small ball). Let rise for 11/4 hrs. (Put dough on floured board to work with). Bake in oven for 30 to 40 min at 350 degrees. Recipe from Island Pond, Vermont The ingredient amounts

have been adjusted for the BREAD MACHINE. You will need to follow your bread machine directions for making the bread. The above directions are for BY HAND bread making only.

Title: Herman Starter

Categories: Breads, Breadmaker
Servings: 1
2 tb Or 2 envelopes active dry 1 c Sugar
Yeast 2 c All purpose white flour
1/4 c Warm water 2 c Milk (see note)

DAY,1: Sprinkle yeast over warm water. Add 1 tablespoon of the sugar and let stand a few minutes until yeast is active and swelling. Combine remaining sugar,flour and milk in a 4 t0 6 quart glass,plastic or pottery bowl or container.(Do not use metal bowls or utensils as these may retard starter growth). With a wooden spoon, stir in active yeast mixture. Cover loosely with a towel so Herman can breathe. Let stand in a warm draft free place overnight. DAYS,2, 3,and 4: Stir daily with a wooden spoon. Keep covered. Keep cool. DAY,5: Stir in 1/2 cup sugar,1 cup milk and 1 cup flour. Let stand 24 hours. DAYS,6, 7, 8, and 9: Stir daily with a wooden spoon. DAY,10: Repeat DAY 5, stirring in 1/2 cup sugar,1 cup milk and 1 cupflour. THIS gives you enough starter to use freely in recipes and/or give away. Herman may be replenished as needed but can go no more than 5 days at room temperature between feedings. After feeding, wait 24 hours before using the renewed starter. DAILY stirring helps keep yeast mold from forming.Most directions specify that Herman not be refrigerated since cooler temperatures slow the growth and "souring" of the starter. It is, however, a safer course for busy cooks with fast growing starters. Herman also is freezer-friendly and may be kept on ice between baking impulses if you get bored.

NOTE: If desired, substitute buttermilk for milk in starter for more flavor and less fat. If more starter is needed, additions may be doubled when 2 or more cups of starter are used.....

Title: BREAD FAT SUBSTITUTE - APPLESAUCE
Categories: Tips, Breads, Apples, Breadmaker
Servings: 1

Try substituting unsweetened applesauce for the fats called for in your bread recipes. This even works with chocolate cake! Many can't tell any difference in taste and the pectin in the applesauce keeps the bread moist longer. I buy the small Motts individual containers so I don't have a large jar going bad in the fridge. I've read that you can use up to one tablespoon of applesauce per cup of flour. If you do make this substitution hold out about 1/8 to 1/4 cup of the liquid in the recipe and add it back in a tsp. at a time during the kneading cycle.

Title: Hawaiin sweet bread
Categories: Breads, Breadmaker
Servings: 1

3 ts Dry yeast 1/4 ts Lemon extract
5 tb Sugar 1/4 ts Vanilla extract
3 c Bread flour 2 Eggs
3/4 ts Salt 4 tb Butter
2 tb Dry milk 1 c Warm water
2 tb Instant potato flakes

Title: OAT-WHEAT BAGEL BREAD

Categories: Breadmaker, Breads
Servings: 1
1 1/2 ts Yeast - 1 1 1/2 ts Cinnamon 1
1 1/2 ts Gluten - 1 1 ts Salt - 1 1/2
1 1/2 c Oat flour 1 3 tb Honey - 2
1 1/2 c Whole wheat flour - 1 1 c Water - 5 1/2 oz
1437 cal - 1030 - Amounts are for 1 1/2 pound loaves - amounts to the right
are for 1 pound loaves.

Title: ANOTHER SOURDOUGH STARTER

Categories: Breads, Sourdough, Starter
Servings: 1
Make a starter of 1 bottle stale beer with equal parts of flour. Let set as usuall until you have a sourdough starter (about 3 days) then mix
1 cup starter with
2 cup warm water,
4 T sugar and
2-1/2 cups flour. Beat till
smooth. Set in gas oven (turn off) and let sit 28 hours. Beat in 3 eggs,
1T salt,
1 Cup sour cream,
1/3 cup bacon grease and enough flour to make a
soft dough. (about 7-8 cups) knead till smooth. Let rise till doubled punch down and let rise again. Form into 2 loves. Let rise. Bake 375 about 30 minutes. IT has taken anywhere from 3 hours to 12 hours to rise so hang in there. This was the sourest sourdough I'd ever eaten but it was to die for.

Title: BASIC SOURDOUGH STARTER (WITH POTATO)
Categories: Breads, Sourdough, Starter
Servings: 1
1/2 tb Active dry yeast
Lg baking potato peeled,cube 1 ts Sugar
1 c White flour

Cook potato in water to cover until tender. Pour off liquid to measure 1 c, saving potato for other use. Let potato water cook to lukewarm. In a glass or ceramic bowl that has been scalded, place flour, yeast and sugar; add lukewarm potato water and stir in well. Cover with plastic wrap and pierce with fork to release gases. Place in a warm, draft-free location at an even 85F for 2 days; stir several times daily. (do not let sourdough starter rise above 95F because higher temp are favorable to less desireable microorganisms) Refrigerate until ready to use. Replenish with one c flour and 3/4 c water and let stand overnight or 12 hrs in a warm location before refrigerating again. When replenishing, add lukewarm water with flour. Starter should be at room temp when using in recipes, always after having stood 12 hrs from addition of replenishing flour and water. At least 1 c should remain to refrigerate.

Title: WHOLE-WHEAT SOURDOUGH STARTER
Categories: Breads, Sourdough, Starter
Servings: 1
1 ts Active dry yeast
1 1/2 c Whole wheat flour 1 1/2 x Lukewarm water

In a glass or ceramic bowl or jar that has been scalded, combine flour and yeast, add water and blend well. Cover with plastic wrap and pierce with fork to release gases. Place in a warm, draft-free location at an even 85F for 18-24 hrs; stir several times daily. Refrigerate until ready to use. If you have several starters, keep whole wheat separate from others to preserve its own distinctive flavor. Whole wheat starter does not have as much rising action as that made with white flour; you may have to plan longer rising times. To replenish, always use whole wheat flour.

Title: YOGHURT SOURDOUGH STARTER
Categories: Breads, Sourdough, Starter
Servings: 1
NFXS18B 2 tb Natural plain yoghurt
1 c Low fat milk 1 c White flour
Heat milk to 100F on thermometer. Remove from heat and stir in yoghurt. Pour into scalded glass jar or bowl, cover with plastic and place in a warm location for 18 hrs. Consistency will be like thin yoghurt. Stir in flour until well blended, cover again with plastic and pierce with fork to release gases. Place in a warm draft-free location at an even 85F for 2 days; stir several times each day. It should have a strong sourdough smell and show bubbles. Refrigerate until ready to use. When replenishing starter, add lukewarm milk instead of water.

Title: BASIC SOURDOUGH STARTER
Categories: Breads, Sourdough, Starter
Servings: 1
NFXS18B 3/4 c Milk
1 ts Active dry yeast 1 c Flour ,,
1/4 c Warm water
Dissolve yeast in warm water in 3-qt glass bowl. Stir in milk.

Stir in flour gradually. Beat until smooht. Cover with towel; let stand in warm, draft-free place until starter begins to ferment, about 24 hrs. (bubbles will appear on surface of starter) If starter has not begun fermentation after 24 hr, discard and begin again. If fermentation has begun, stir well; cover tightly with plastic wrap and return to warm, draft-free place. Let stand until foamy, 2-3 days. When starter has become foamy, stir well; pour into 1-qt crock or glass jar with tighlty fitting cover. Store in frig. Starter is ready to use when a clear liquid has risen to top. Stir before using. Use 1 c starter in recipe; reserve remaining starter. Add 3/4 c milk and 3/4 c flour to reserved starter. Store covered at room temp until bubbles appear, about 12 hrs, refrigerate. Use starter regularly, every week to 10 days. If the volume of the breads you bake begins to decrease, dissolve 1 t yeast in 1/4 c warm water. Stir in 1/2 c milk, 3/4 c flour and the remaining starter.

,,DO NOT USE SELF RISING FLOUR,,NOTE:
Start bread at night to bake in the morning - or vice versa. Before adding the milk and flour to remaining starter, bake your bread and judge the volume

Title: SOURDOUGH RYE STARTER
Categories: Breads, Sourdough, Starter
Servings: 1
1 1/2 c Lukewarm water
2 c Rye flour Onion slice optional
1 tb Yeast
In a glass or ceramic bowl, or jar that has been scalded, combine flour and yeast, add water and blend well. Add onion slice, cover with platic wrap and pierce plastic with fork to release gases. Place in a warm, draft-free place, at an even 85F for 3 days.; stir several times daily. Remove onion

slice and refrigerate until ready to use. Onion imparts a strong flavor and this starter can only be used with compatible rye recipes; rye starter without onion can be used in any rye sourdough recipe. To replenish, always use rye flour. If starter does not seem bubbly after replenishing and standing 12 hrs, sprinkle 1 t yeast over and stir in well. Like whole wheat starter, you may have to plan longer rising times for dough made with this one.

Title: ALASKA SOUREST DOUGH
Categories: Starter, Sourdough, Breads
Servings: 2

1 pk Yeast 1 tb Vinegar
2 1/4 c Warm water 1 ts Salt
2 tb Sugar
2 c Bread flour

1Disolve yeast in 1/4 cup warm water. Add sugar vinegar,salt,all purpose flour. Add remaining water until a creamy batter is formed. Place in a glass bowl,cover and let sit until it starts to ferment. About 3 days. It will take on a powerful boozy smell. Stir again until creamy and measure out what is called for in the recipe. Replenish starter with equal amounts of flour and water. Store in the fridge and bring to room temp before using. It says to allow to ferment for one week between uses but I don't.I do let it sit out overnight after I feed it. This starter took about 1 1/2 months to become really sour.

Title: CARAWAY RYE
Categories: Breads, Breadmaker, Jewish
Servings: 1

1 c Flour; better for bread flo 1 tb Caraway seeds
1 c Flour; all purpose 1 tb Butter
1/2 c Rye flour 1 c Warm water
3/4 ts Salt 1 1/4 ts Yeast
Add in the order required for your BM It is on the sweet side. Re- ally our
favorite.

Title: Pizza

Categories: Breadmaker, Breads
Servings: 1
2 1/4 c Bread flour TOPPINGS:
1 ts Salt 2/3 c Pizza sauce (10 oz)
1 1/2 ts Vegetable oil 2 c Mozzarella cheese (8 oz)
3/4 c Water Garnishes of your choice
1 ts Dry yeast
1. Place first 3 ingredients inside the bread pan. Add water. Close cover and place dry yeast into the yeast holder.
SELECT: BASIC DOUGH MODE.
Press start. (Breadmaker completes the basic dough mode 2 hours and 25 minutes later) 2. Divide the dough into 4 equal portions. Roll each portion into a ball. 3. Place on a lightly floured surface. Cover with a plastic wrap and rest for 20 minutes. 4. Roll out each ball into a flat circle. 5. Place on a greased baking pan. Prick the surface with a fork. 6. Brush with 2 tablespoons pizza sauce. Sprinkle mozzarella cheese on top. Garnish with ingredients of your choice. 7. Bake in 500 deg. oven for 12 to 15 minutes or until ingredients are cooked and the dough is crisp and slightly brown.

Title: SOURDOUGH STARTER AND BREAD

Categories: Sourdough, Starter, Breads, Breadmaker
Servings: 1

2 c Skim milk
2 c Bread flour
1 Pk Yeast

Place milk in a glass container and allow to stand at room temperature for 24 hours. Stir in flour and yeast. Leave uncovered in a warm place for 2-5 days, depending on how long it takes it to bubble and sour. If it starts to dry out, stir in enough tepid water to bring it back to the original consistency. Once it has a good sour aroma and is full of bubbles, it is ready to use. Try to maintain about 1 and 1/2 cups of starter. Each time part of the starter is used, replenish with a mixture of equal parts milk and flour. Leave at room temperature several hours or overnight, or until it begins to fill with bubbles. Then cover and store in refrigerator. Starter is best if used at least once a week. If starter isn't, used for 2 or 3 weeks, spoon out and discard about half and replenish as described. Given attention, a starter becomes more flavorful with age. Starter can be frozen if it is not to be used for several weeks. This will slow down yeast action and should be left at room temperature for 24 hours after thawing.

Sourdough Bread:

2/3 cup skim milk
1 cup sourdough starter
3 cups bread flour 2 Tbs.sugar
2 tsp. lite salt
1 & 1/2 tsp. yeast
2 Tbs. liquid Butter Buds Combine above

thoroughly (using half of the flour) and let stand uncovered to ferment overnight in a warm place. Next morning, after the mixture has risen and fallen, stir down any crust that may have formed. Add the rest of the flour. When thoroughly mixed, turn out onto a board covered with a little flour so it

won't stick. Shape dough into 2 loaves, put into bread pans, brush lightly with liquid Butter Buds, and let rise covered until almost doubled in size. Bake in a pre-heated 400F. oven 45-50 minutes. Note: This recipe works GREAT in a bread machine. Simply put all of the ingredients in the machine, adding the dry ingredients first. Yields: 2 loaves (24 slices)
Per slice
Fat: 0.21g Calories: 96
Cholesterol:0.42 mg Carbohydrate:19.7g
Protein:2.89g Sodium:10.3mg

Title: Three Cheese Bread

Categories: Breads, Breadmaker
Servings: 16
3/4 c Water 1/2 c Shredded Swiss Cheese
3 c Bread Flour 1/3 c Creamed Cottage Cheese
2 tb Sugar 3 tb Grated Parmesan Cheese
1 1/2 ts Salt 2 ts Regular Active Yeast
2 tb Margarine or Oil
Place ingredients in bread pan in the order recommended by the
manufacturer. Don't use the delayed timer cycle since the cheese may
spoil. Bake on light crust.
NOTE: Due the differing moisture content of cheese, you may need to watch
the dough ball to determine if it is too moist or too dry.

Title: Blueberry Muffins

Categories: Muffins, Breads, Fruit
Servings: 12

1 c Sugar 3/4 ts Nutmeg
1/4 c Margarine 1/2 ts Vanilla extract
1 c Milk 1/4 ts Salt
1 lg Egg 1 c Blueberries, fresh or
1 1/3 c Flour -unsweetened frozen, thawed
2 ts Baking powder -and drained
3/4 ts Cinnamon

Preheat oven to 375. Prepare muffin tins with paper liners. In medium bowl, cream sugar and margarine on low speed of electric mixer until smooth. Add milk, egg, 2/3 cup of flour, baking powder, cinnamon, nutmeg, vanilla and salt. Mix just until thoroughly blended. Gently mix in remaining 2/3 cup of flour (batter should be lumpy).Fold in blueberries. Fill tin liners 3/4 full. Bake until golden, 20 to 30 minutes.

Title: Hamburger Pizza

Categories: Cheese, Ground beef, Breads
Servings: 8

--------------------**CRUST**----------------------------------
2 1/2 c Bisquick Baking Mix 2/3 c Water; Hot
1 pk Active Dry Yeast
----------------**MEAT MIXTURE**-------------------------------
1 lb Lean Ground Beef 2 ts Oregano Leaves
1/2 c Onion; Chopped 1/4 ts Pepper
15 oz Tomato Sauce
------------------**TOPPING**----------------------------------
1/2 c Green Pepper; Chopped (opt) 1 c Parmesan Cheese; Grated
2 c Mozzarella Cheese; Shredded

Heat the oven to 425~. Mix the baking mix and yeast and

stir in the hot water. Turn the dough onto a well-floured surface and knead until smooth, about 20 times. Let the dough rest a few minutes. While the dough is resting, cook and stir the meat and onion in a large skillet until the onion is tender and the meat is brown. Drain off the excess fat. Stir in the tomato sauce, oregano leaves, and pepper and set aside. Divide the dough in half. Roll each half on an ungreased baking sheet into a rectangle, 13x9" or on a pizza pan 12" in diameter. Pinch the edges to make a slight rim. Spread the meat mixture almost to the edges. Top with the green pepper and cheeses. Bake until the crust is brown and the filling is hot and bubbly, 15 to 20 minutes. Cut into squares or wedges and serve.
NOTE: If desired, you can use shredded Cheddar Cheese for the Mozzarella in the above recipe.

Title: Spiced Apple Muffins

Categories: Breads, Fruits, Muffins, Apples
Servings: 12
1/3 c Shortening 1/2 ts Cinnamon
1/2 c Sugar 1/4 c Milk
1 Egg 1 c Apple sauce
1 1/2 c Sifted flour 1/3 c Melted butter
2 ts Baking powder 1/2 ts Sugar
1/2 ts Salt 1 ts Cinnamon
1/2 ts Nutmeg

Cream together shrotening and sugar. Add egg. Sift dry ingredients, add dry ingredients alternately with milk to creamed mixture. stir in apple sauce. Fill greased muffin cups 3/4 full and Bake at 400 F 20-25 minutes. Cool for 10 minutes, then dip each muffin top into melted butter, followed by mixture of sugar and cimmamon. Serve warm or cold.

Title: Apple Butter Bread
Categories: Breads, Fruits, Apples
Servings: 1

1 1/2 c Flour 1 Egg
2 tb Flour 4 tb Melted butter
2 tb Baking powder 1/2 c Apple butter
1/2 c Brown sugar 1/4 c Milk
1 ts Cinnamon 1/4 c Apple cider
1/2 ts Nutmeg 1/2 c White raisins,soaked in
1/2 ts Salt 2 tb Orange juice

Preheat oven to 350 F. In large bowl, mix flour, baking powder, sugar, spices and salt. Make a well in center and add egg, butter, apple butter, milk and cider. Mix quickly. Add drained raisins. Pour into greased loaf pan. Bake for 45 minutes.

Title: Apple Banana Bread
Categories: Breads, Fruits, Apples
Servings: 8

1/2 c Butter, softened 2 c Flour
1/2 c Brown Sugar 1 ts Baking Powder
1/2 c Granulated Sugar 1 ts Baking Soda
2 Eggs 1/2 ts Cinnamon
3 tb Sour Cream 2 Apples, cored and chopped
1 Banana, mashed 1/2 c Chopped Walnuts
1 ts Vanilla

Preheat oven to 350 deg F.

Cream butter and sugars, and beat in eggs. Stir in sour cream, banana and vanilla. In separate bowl, combine flour, baking powder, soda and cinnamon. Gradually add to butter mixture. Gently stir in apples and nuts. Spoon into greased bread pan and bake 1 hour.

Title: Apple Pancakes II
Categories: Breads, Apples
Servings: 1
1 c Flour 1/2 c Milk
1/4 ts Salt 1 Egg; beaten
1 1/2 ts Baking powder 1/2 ts Vanilla
1 tb Butter; melted 1 1/4 c Applesauce
Sift flour, salt and baking powder. Combine butter, milk and egg. Stir into flour. Add vanilla and applesauce. Beat well. Spoon batter onto a hot, well greased griddle, allowing enough batter to make 4 " cakes. When edges are lightly browned, turn and cook on second side. Serve hot with maple syrup or apple jelly and lots of butter.

Title: 7-Up Apple Dumplings
Categories: Breads, Apples
Servings: 10
2 c Sugar 10 Large apples
1 ts Cinnamon 1 Can biscuits
1/2 ts Nutmeg 1 ts Nutmeg
1 Stick butter 1 ts Cinnamon
20 oz 7-up
1/2 stick butter
In saucepan combine first group of sugar, cinnamon, nutmeg, butter and the 7- up. Heat until melted, set aside. Peel and core apples, separate dough from 1 can biscuits. Separate and roll out each biscuit individually and place 1 apple in each. Combine second group of sugar, cinnamon and nutmeg. Sprinkle 1 tsp. of this mixture in center of each apple along with 2 T. butter. Fold biscuit around apple and

pinch dough. Put dumplings in 9 x 13" pan. Pour sauce over each dumpling. Bake at 375 degrees for 45 minutes.

Title: Apple Rolls
Categories: Breads, Rolls, Apples
Servings: 2
2 c Flour 1/4 c Shortening
4 ts Baking powder 2 tb Melted butter or butter
3/4 c Milk -substitute
4 c Pared, sliced apples 1 ts Cinnamon
1/4 c Brown sugar 1 c Brown sugar
1/2 ts Salt

Sift flour, measure, and sift with baking powder and salt. Cut in shortening with 2 spatulas. Add milk, Mix quickly and lightly. Turn onto lightly floured board. Roll in oblong sheet 1/4 inch thick. Brush with melted butter. Cover with apples. Sprinkle with 1cup sugar and the cinnamon which have been mixed. Roll like a jelly roll. Cut in slices 1 ½ inches thick. Sprinkle 1/4cup brown sugar over bottom of well-oiled pan. Place rolls, cut down, in pan. Bake in hot oven (425 F) about 40 minutes. 8 servings. 1941

Title: Apple Pancake Puff
Categories: Breads, Apples, Low-cal
Servings: 4
1 tb +1 t rc margarine 1 ts Cinnamon
3 Small mac. apples;cored & 2 Large eggs
Cut into 1/4" thick slices 1/2 c Skim milk
2 tb Dark raisins 1/4 c + 2 Tb. flour
3 tb Granulatd sugar 1 ts Vanilla extract
2 tb Orange juice

In heavy med. ovenproof skillet, melt 2 tsp of the

margarine. Add apples, raisins, 1 T sugar, and orange juice and cinnamon. cook, stirring freq. 6-8 minutes, until apples are just tender. Remove apples to bowl. Preheat oven to 425d. In small bowl, w/ electric mixer, beat eggs until foamy. Gradually add milk, flour, the remaining 2 TB. sugar and the vanilla; beat 2 minutes longer, until batter is smooth. Add remaining 2 tsp. margarine to same skillet. Place in oven to melt, abt 1 minute. Pour batter into skillet;bake 10 minutes. Remove from oven and spoon apple mixture into center of pancake. Return to oven and bake 12-15 min. longer until puffed and golden. Cut into quarters. Each serving: 1/2 Fa, 1/2 P, 1/2 B, 1 FR, 60 cal.

Title: Apple Bread #2
Categories: Breads, Apples
Servings: 2
1/2 c Butter 1 tb Butter (melted)
2 c Peeled, diced,apples 2 tb Buttermilk
1 c Sugar 1/4 c Packed brown sugar
1/2 c Chopped walnuts 2 c All purpose flour
2 Eggs 1/4 ts Cinnamon
1/2 c Raisins 1 ts Vanilla
1 ts Baking soda

Cream butter, slowly adding sugar, beat until light and fluffy. Add eggs, one at a time, beating well after each addition. Dissolve baking soda in buttermilk, add to batter, mixing well. Stir in flour. Add vanilla and stir well. Stir in apples, walnuts and raisins. Spoon into 2 greased and floured loaf pans. Drizzle melted butter over loaves. Combine brown sugar and cinnamon, sprinkle over loaves. Bake at 350 for about 40 to 45 min.Cool in pan for 5 minutes and then cool completely on rack.

Title: Apple Bread

Categories: Breads, Apples
Servings: 12
4 c Apples, sliced 2 lg Eggs
1 c Butter 2 ts Cinnamon
2 c Sugar 1/2 c Hazelnuts, chopped
2 c Flour, pastry
Core and peel apples before slicing. Melt butter. Preheat oven to 350. Mix all ingredients together in large work bowl. Pour batter into greased 9"x5" bread pan. Bake one hour.

Title: Ange's Apple Bread
Categories: Breads, Apples
Servings: 2
2 c Sugar 1 ts Baking soda
1 c Oil 1 ts Cinnamon
3 Eggs 2 ts Vanilla extract
3 c All purpose flour 2 c Chopped peeled apples
1 ts Salt 1 c Nuts
Grease 2 loaf pans. In a large bowl beat together the sugar, oil and eggs. In a separate bowl sift together the flour, slt, baking soda, and cinnamon. Add the dry ingredients to the sugar mixture. Add the vanilla, apples, and nuts. Pour the batter into the prepared pans. Bake in a 325F over for 1 hour.

Title: Walnut Apple Bread
Categories: Breads, Apples
Servings: 1

1 1/2 c All-purpose flour, sifted 1 1/2 c Wheat cereal flakes, crushed
2 ts Baking powder 1 c Walnuts, coarsely chopped
1/2 ts Baking soda 1/4 c Apple, chopped
1/2 ts Salt 1 Egg, slightly beaten
1 ts Cinnamon 1/4 c Brown sugar, firmly packed
1/4 ts Nutmeg 2 ts Vegetable oil
1/8 ts Allspice 1 1/2 c Buttermilk, lowfat

Grease or spray 9x5x3 in. loaf pan. Preheat oven to 350F. Mix and sift flour, baking powder, baking soda, salt and spices into bowl. Stir in cereal, walnuts and apple. Combine egg, brown sugar, buttermilk and oil; add to dry mixture. Stir just enough to moisten dry ingredients. Do not beat. Spoon into pan. Bake at 350F one hour or until toothpick inserted into center comes out clean. Makes 1 loaf.

Title: Sourdough Apple Sorcery

Categories: Breads, Sourdough, Apples
Servings: 4
3/4 c White flour 1/2 ts Ground cinnamon
3/4 c Whole wheat flour Egg
2/3 c Lightly toasted wheat germ 1/2 c Brown sugar
1/2 ts Salt 1/2 c Safflower oil
1/2 ts Baking soda 1 c Sourdough starter, room temp
1 ts Baking powder 1 c Unsweetened thick applesauce

Combine flours, wheat germ, salt, baking soda, baking powder and cinnamon and blend well. In lg bowl, beat egg lightly and blend in sugar and oil. Mix in starter and applesauce and mix well. Add mixture and stir just until dry ingredients are moistened. Spoon into 4 prepared ,,,,#4 loaf pans and bake in oven preheated to 350 for 50 mins or until bread tests done. Cool on wire rack 10 mins, turn out, turn right side up, remove waxed paper and cool. ,,,,To keep quick breads from sticking to pan, line pan with strip of waxed paper; oil pan, place paper in pan invert paper so that batter is on oiled surface.

Title: Apple Breakfast Bread
Categories: Breads, Apples
Servings: 2
2 c Flour 3 Apples
1 ts Salt 4 ts Baking powder
2 tb Brown sugar 4 tb Shortening
3/4 c Milk 2 c Chopped raisins
1 ts Cinnamon 1 Egg, well beaten
2 tb Melted butter or butter 2 tb Brown sugar
-substitute Sift flour, measure, and sift with baking powder, salt, and sugar. Cut in shortening and add raisins. Add sufficient milk to which egg has been added to make a stiff dough. Mix thoroughly. Pour into well-oiled shallow pan. Brush dough with melted butter. Pare, quarter, and core apples and cut in thin slices. Arrange in rows in the dough, allowing edges to overlap. Brush apples with more melted butter and sprinkle with cinnamon and brown sugar which have been mixed together. Bake in moderate oven (400 F) 20 minutes or until apples are tender. 9 servings. (1941)

Title: Sourdough Apple Pancakes
Categories: Sourdough, Breads, Apples
Servings: 4
2 c Starter 1 tb Sugar
1 Egg; beaten White flour; kneaded
1/2 c Applesauce 1/2 ts Baking soda
2 tb Butter; melted

add egg, applesauce, melted butter, sugar and salt to the starter and mix briefly. Add flour to attain desired consistency mix until lump free. Just before baking dissolve baking soda in a tablespoon of water and gently blend with the batter pour 2 to 3 inch rounds on a hot (400) griddle. Cook 2 to 4 minutes and turn for an additional 2 minutes.

Title: STRAWBERRY-ORANGE MUFFINS

Categories: Muffins, Fruits, Breads, Nw
Servings: 16
2 1/4 c All-purpose flour 1 Egg
2 ts Baking powder 1 tb Finely grated orange zest
1 ts Baking soda 1 c Fresh strawberries; thinly
1/2 ts Salt -sliced 1/8"; pat dry
3/4 c Sugar -between paper towels to
1/2 c Milk -keep juices from coloring
1/2 c Sour cream -the batter
1/3 c Vegetable oil 1/3 c Strawberry jam

Preheat an oven to 400~. Butter standard muffin tins. In a large bowl stir and toss together the flour, baking powder, baking soda and salt. Set aside. In a medium bowl whisk together the sugar, milk, sour cream, oil, egg and orange zest until mixed; stir in the strawberries. Add to the combined dry ingredients and stir just until blended. Place a spoonful of batter in each prepared muffin cup. Top each with a scant teaspoon of strawberry jam. Spoon the remaining batter over the jam, filling each cup about two-thirds full. Bake until a toothpick inserted in the center of the muffin comes out clean, 15-18 minutes. Cool in the tins for 5 minutes, then remove. Makes about 16 standard muffins.

Title: Boboli Topping 23

Categories: Breads, Boboli, Cheese/eggs, Pizza
Servings: 1

Here are some of the pizza combinations. All have mozzarella cheese in addition to the other ingredients.

HAWAIIAN--pineapple, bacon or canadian bacon, homemade tomato sauce.

GRILLED TERIYAKI CHICKEN--
with grilled chicken marinated in an orange teriyaki sauce, red onions, scallions and sweet peppers.

GOAT CHEESE--bacon, red onions, 3 color peppers, freshtomatoes and mild goat cheese.

SHRIMP PESTO
--with shrimp, fresh tomatoes, Mediterrean olives, sund-dried tomatoes, and homemade pesto sauce.

SOUTHWESTERN BURRITO
--with grilled chicken breast marinated in lime and herbs, homemade black beans, fire-roasted mild chilies, sweet white onions and cheddar cheese. Serve with green tomatillo salsa and sour cream.

FIVE CHEESE AND TOMATO--Fresh sliced tomatoes, basil leaves, buffalo mozzarella, fontina, smoked gouda, and romano cheeses.

Title: BOBOLI CRUST

Categories: Pizza, Crust, Italian, Breads, Nw
Servings: 2

2 1/2 c BREAD flour 2 sm Cloves garlic; thinly sliced
1/2 ts -Salt 2 tb Rosemary,,
3/4 ts Active dry yeast 3 tb Bertolli Light olive oil
1 c -Warm water

Preheat oven to 400 degrees. Combine flour, salt, yeast and

water in bowl. Blend well, turn out onto floured surface. Knead well, about 15 minutes. Place in lightly greased bowl, not buttered, cover with a damp cloth and let rise for 1-1/2 hours (until doubled in bulk). Turn dough out, punch down and knead for 5 minutes or so. Return to bowl and let rise until doubled in bulk. Punch down and turn out on lightly floured board. Roll and press out to about 1/2 inch thickness. This recipe makes about 1-12 inches-so you can judge whether to double or reduce the recipe. Rub surface of baking (cookie) sheet with oil and transfer the dough round to the sheet. Make several indentations with the point of a knife in the dough and insert garlic slices and rosemary into indentations. Rub olive oil (pour) onto surface and gently smooth over the surface. Salt and pepper surface LIGHTLY. Bake 10-12 minutes or until just golden. Remove from oven and TAKE OUT THE GARLIC SLIVERS! You can now top the crust, freeze it, eat it the way it is, smille at it (YOU DID IT!) Remember, when you top it the crust is all read 2/3 baked and will require only enough time so that the cheeses, etc. are bubbly.

Title: Swedish Oven Pancakes

Categories: Breads, Breakfast, Brunch, Main dish
Servings: 6
3 c Milk 4 tb Butter, melted
4 Eggs 1 ts Salt
2 c Flour 2 tb Sugar

Beat eggs well. Add milk, melted butter, salt and flour. Bake in a greased 9 X 13 pan in 425F oven for 25-30 minutes. Cut into squares and serve immediately with butter and syrup. Variations: Omit butter. Saute 3 strips bacon, cut up, until crisp. Put drippings and bacon in bottom of pan and pour batter over. Bake 375F for 30 minutes. Serve with berry and

cream topping: 1/2 pint cream, whipped and 1 jar preserves (ie: raspberry, strawberry, apricot etc.)
Serve with sour cream mixed with brown sugar.

Title: Lemon Bread
Categories: Breads, Breadmaker
Servings: 1
------------**FOR 1-1/2 LB. LOAF**--------------------------
1 pk Yeast 3/4 c Milk; scalded
3 c Bread flour 1 Egg + 1 yolk; room temp.
1/4 c Sugar 1/4 ts Lemon extract
1/2 ts Salt 2 ts Dried or freshly grated
1/4 c Butter; room temperature -lemon peel
Place all ingredients into breadmaker pan in the order above, select white bread and push start.

Title: Pumpernickel Bread
Categories: Breads, Breadmaker
Servings: 1
-------------**FOR 1-1/2 LB. LOAF**----------------------------
1 1/2 pk Yeast 1 1/2 ts Salt
2 c Rye flour 1 tb Unsweetened cocoa
1/2 c Unprocessed whole-bran 3 tb Molasses
-cereal 1 tb Vegetable oil
1 3/4 c Bread flour 1 1/4 c Warm water
2 ts Caraway seed
Add all ingredients in the order listed, select white bread and push start.

Title: Drew's Famous Onion Dill Bread

Categories: Breads, Breadmaker
Servings: 1

------------**FOR 1-1/2 LB. LOAF-**--------------------------
1 pk Yeast 1 1/2 ts Salt
3 1/3 c Flour 1 Egg; unbeaten, room temp
1/4 ts Baking soda
---------**MIX TOGETHER, WARM AND ADD-**-------------
1/4 c Water 3 tb Minced dried onion
3/4 c Cottage cheese 2 tb Whole dill seed
3/4 c Sour cream 1 1/2 tb Butter
3 tb Sugar

Place dry ingredients and egg into inner pan. Warm next set of ingredients, add, select white bread, and push start. Lightly brush the top with a little melted butter at baking time if you wish.

Title: Diet Rite Bread
Categories: Breads, Breadmaker
Servings: 1
-----------**FOR 1-1/2 LB. LOAF--**--------------------------
1 pk Yeast 1 1/4 c Diet rite soda, or Club soda
3 c Bread flour -at room temperature

Place all ingredients into pan, select white bread, and push start.

Title: Potato Loaf Bread
Categories: Breads, Breadmaker, Brunch
Servings: 1
----------------**FOR 1-1/2 LB. LOAF**----------------------------
1 pk Yeast 2 1/2 ts Sweet butter
3 c Bread flour 2 tb Instant mashed potato flakes

1 tb Sugar 1 c Hot milk
1 1/2 ts Salt
Place the first 5 ingredients into the pan. Sprinlke the potato flakes over
the hot milk and stir. Let cool slightly. Add milk, select white bread, and
push start.

Title: Real Chocolate Bread
Categories: Breads, Breadmaker
Servings: 1
----------------**FOR 1-1/2 LB. LOAF**----------------------------
1 pk Yeast 1 Egg; unbeaten
3 c Bread flour 1/4 c Soft butter, or margerine
1/2 c Sugar 1/2 ts Vanilla
1/4 c Unsweetened cocoa 1 c Warm milk
Add all ingredients in the order given, select whiter bread, and push start.

Title: Beer Cheese Bread
Categories: Breads, Breadmaker, Brunch
Servings: 1
------------**FOR 1-1/2 LB. LOAF**----------------------------
1 pk Yeast 10 oz Beer; at room temperature
3 c Bread flour 4 oz Processed American cheese
1 tb Sugar -(2 slices)
1 1/2 ts Salt 4 oz Jack cheese; or any other
1 tb Butter -(cut in 1/4" cubes)
Warm beer and American cheese over low heat on top of stove or in microwave. Cheese doesn't need to melt completely. Stir. Add all ingredients listed, select white bread

and push start.

Title: Bloody Mary Bread
Categories: Breads, Breadmaker, Brunch
Servings: 1
------------**FOR 1-1/2 LB. LOAF-**---------------------------
1 pk Yeast 6 oz Can of spicy V-8 juice; at
3 c Bread flour -room temperature
1 ts Salt 1 tb Vodka
1 tb Sugar 1 tb Water
1 tb Soft butter 1 Egg
Place all ingredients into pan, select white bread and push start.
Serve with a stalk of celery.

Title: California Dip Bread
Categories: Breads, Breadmaker, Brunch
Servings: 1
----------**FOR 1-1/2 LB. LOAF**----------------------------
1 pk Yeast 1/4 ts Baking soda
3 1/3 c Flour 1 Egg; room temperature
---------**MIX TOGETHER, WARM AND ADD**-----------
3/4 c Cottage cheese 1 1/2 tb Butter
3/4 c Sour cream 1/4 c Water
3 tb Sugar 1 pk Lipton's onion soup mix
Place the first 4 ingredients into the pan. Slightly warm the next 6 ingredients and pour into pan. Select white bread and push start.
NOTE: Vary the amount of soup mix to suit your taste.

Title: Buttermilk Cheese Bread
Categories: Breads, Breadmaker, Brunch
Servings: 1

-------------**FOR 1-1/2 LB. LOAF**---------------------------

1 pk Yeast 1 tb Sugar
3 c Bread flour 1 c Buttermilk; room temperature
1 ts Baking powder 1/4 c Warm water
1 ts Salt 1 c Grated sharp cheddar cheese

Pour in all ingredients in the order listed. Select white bread and push start.

Title: Anadama Bread
Categories: Breads, Breadmaker
Servings: 1

------------**FOR 1-1/2 LB. LOAF**---------------------------

1 pk Yeast 1/3 c Molasses
3 1/2 c Bread flour 1 ts Salt
1/3 c Yellow cornmeal 2 ts Butter
1 1/2 c Boiling water

Place cornmeal into a bowl. Carefully pour boiling water into cornmeal, stirring to make sure it is smooth. Let stand for about 30 minutes. Stir in molasses, salt and butter. Place yeast into the B/M pan, bread flour, then cornmeal mixture. Select white bread and push start. NOTE: An early American recipe. This has become a favorite in many homes.

Title: Applesauce Bread
Categories: Breads, Breadmaker, Brunch

Servings: 1

------------**FOR 1-1/2 LB. LOAF**----------------------------

1 pk Yeast 1/2 ts Cinnamon
2 1/4 c Bread flour 1 pn Nutmeg
3/4 c Wheat flour 2/3 c Warm applesauce
1/2 ts Salt 1/2 c Warm applejuice
4 tb White sugar 1/2 c Grated fresh apple

Put all ingredients into the pan, select white bread, and push start.

Title: Banana Wheat Bread

Categories: Breads, Breadmaker, Breakfast
Servings: 1

------------**FOR 1-1/2 LB. LOAF**----------------------------

1 pk Yeast 1/4 c Honey
1 1/2 c Bread flour 1/4 c Warm water
1 1/2 c Wheat flour 1 Egg
1/2 ts Salt 1/4 c Oil
2 Medium ripe bananas; sliced 1/2 ts Vanilla
-right into pan 1 ts Poppy seeds;(optional) Add ingredients into the pan in the order listed, select white bread, and push start.

Title: Blueberry Bread

Categories: Breads, Breadmaker, Breakfast
Servings: 1

------------**FOR 1-1/2 LB. LOAF**----------------------------

1 pk Yeast 1 cn Blueberries (16-1/2 oz);well
3 c Bread flour -drained, reserve liquid
1/2 ts Salt 1/4 c Retained juice
2 tb Sugar 1/4 c Water; approximately

1 tb Butter or margerine
Add all dry ingredients into pan. Put well drained berries into a 2-cup measuring cup, add 1/4 cup juice and enough water to equal 1-1/3 cups (we found it to be 1/4 cup water) Select white bread and push start.

Title: Cheddar Cheese Bread
Categories: Breads, Breadmaker, Brunch
Servings: 1
---------------**FOR 1-1/2 LB. LOAF**----------------------------
1 pk Yeast 2 tb Sugar
3 c Bread flour 1 1/4 c Warm water
1/4 c Nonfat dry milk 1 1/2 c Grated sharp cheddar; (6 oz)
1 tb Soft butter -at room temperature
1 ts Salt
Put all ingredients into the pan, select white bread, and push start.

Title: Chocolate Chip Bread
Categories: Breads, Breadmaker, Brunch
Servings: 1
-----------**FOR 1-1/2 LB. LOAF**----------------------------
1 pk Yeast 4 tb Soft butter
3 c Bread flour 1 Egg
2 tb Brown sugar 1 c Warm milk
2 tb White sugar 1/4 c Water
1 ts Salt 1 c Chocolate chips
1 ts Cinnamon
Put the first 10 ingredients into the pan, select white bread and push start. When the Auto Bakery "beeps" 5 minutes from the end of the second mixing, add the chocolate chips.

NOTE: The chips tend to get a little well done, so turn the darkness control a bit toward light. This bread has a cake-like texture.

Title: Easy Wheat And Honey Bread
Categories: Breads, Breadmaker, Breakfast, Brunch
Servings: 1
-----------FOR 1-1/2 LB. LOAF-----------------------------
1 pk Yeast 2 tb Honey
3/4 c Whole wheat flour 2 tb Butter; at room temperature
2 1/2 c Bread flour 1 Egg; at room temperature
1 ts Salt 1 c Plus 1 Tbsp. warm water
Put all ingredients in pan, select white bread and push start.

Title: Eileen's Corn-chillies-cheese Bread
Categories: Breads, Breadmaker, Brunch
Servings: 1
-----------FOR 1-1/2 LB. LOAF-----------------------------
1 pk Yeast 1/2 c Cheddar cheese, shredded
3 c Bread flour 1 Egg
3/4 c Yellow cornmeal 1 tb Soft butter
1/2 c Whole kernel canned corn; 1/2 ts Salt
-drained 2 ts Sugar
1 tb Canned Ortega chillies; 1 1/4 c Warm water
-chopped Put all ingredients into pan, select white bread, and push start.

Title: French Bread # 1
Categories: Breads, Breadmaker
Servings: 1

----------FOR 1-1/2 LB. LOAF----------------------
1 pk Yeast 2 tb Butter (sweet gives the most
3 c Bread flour -(authentic taste)
2 tb Sugar 1 c Less 1 Tbsp. hot water
1 ts Salt 2 Stiffly beaten egg whites
Whip the whites until stiff and set aside.
Place the first 6 ingredients in the pan, select "French" bread and push start. Once all ingredients are moist, dump in the egg whites.
NOTE: If you choose, lightly brush the top with a mixture of 1 Tbsp. Water, dash salt and 1/4 tsp. cornstarch after the 2nd mixing is over, and sprinkle with sesame or poppy seeds.

Title: French Bread # 2
Categories: Breads, Breadmaker
Servings: 1
--------------FOR 1-1/2 LB. LOAF----------------------
1 pk Yeast 1 ts Sugar
2 c Bread flour 1 ts Soft butter
1 ts Salt 1 c Plus 1 Tbsp. warm water
Put all ingredients in inner pot, select "French" bread and push start.

Title: Golden Egg Bread
Categories: Breads, Breadmaker
Servings: 1
-----------FOR 1-1/2 LB. LOAF----------------------
1 pk Yeast 6 tb Vegetable or corn oil
3 c Bread flour 1 1/2 ts Salt
4 tb Sugar 3/4 c Warm water
2 Eggs; room temperature

Combine all ingredients in the pan in the order listed, select white bread and push start.
Great for sandwiches. It rises tall and cuts beautifully.

Title: Golden Raisin Bread
Categories: Breads, Breadmaker
Servings: 1
----------**FOR 1-1/2 LB. LOAF-**---------------------------
1 pk Yeast 2 tb Soft butter
2 c Bread flour 3/4 c Golden raisins
1 c Whole wheat flour 1/4 ts Ground ginger
1/4 c Wheat germ 1/2 ts Cinnamon
1/4 c Brown sugar 1 1/2 c Warm water
1 ts Salt
Put all the ingredients in the pan in the order listed, select white bread and push start.
NOTE: A sweet, different version of raisin bread

Title: Granola Bread
Categories: Breads, Breadmaker
Servings: 1
---------**FOR 1-1/2 LB. LOAF**----------------------------
1 pk Yeast 1 1/2 ts Sugar
3/4 c Whole wheat flour 3/4 c Warm water
2 c Bread flour 1/2 c Buttermilk
1 c Granola; grind finely in 2 tb Sweet butter; warm
-blender 2 tb Honey
3/4 ts Salt 1 Egg
Add all ingredients, select white bread and push start.

Title: Hawaiian Coconut Bread

Categories: Breads, Breadmaker
Servings: 1

------------**FOR 1-1/2 LB. LOAF**---------------------------

1 pk Yeast 3/4 c Coconut; shredded
3 c Bread flour 3/4 c Macadamia nuts (whole is
2 ts Salt -fine or use almonds)
1 tb Sugar 1/2 c Crushed pineapple; well
1/4 c Nonfat dry milk powder -drained
1 Egg 1/2 c Pineapple juice from above
1/4 c Soft butter 1/4 c Warm water

Drain the pineapple, reserve liquid. Add all ingredients in the order listed above, pineapple and juice "last". Select white bread and push start.

Title: Henzi's Seed Bread

Categories: Breads, Breadmaker
Servings: 1

--------**FOR 1-1/2 LB. LOAF**----------------------------

1 pk Yeast 1 ts Salt
1 tb Sugar 1/3 c Golden raisins
1 1/2 c Bread flour 1/3 c Chopped pecans or walnuts
1 1/2 c Wheat flour 1/3 c Sunflower seeds
2/3 c Rye flour 1/3 c Poppy seeds
1/2 c Cornmeal 2 tb Caraway seeds
1/2 c Unprocessed bran

------------**LIQUID INGREDIENTS**--------------

1 c Warm water 4 tb Honey
1/3 c Warm milk 1 Egg
1 tb Oil

Add all dry ingredients. Then pour in the liquids, measure

the oil before the honey and watch the honey slip right off the spoon. Select white bread and push start. This loaf may sag a bit in the center, but does not affect the texture or taste.

Title: Maple Oatmeal Bread

Categories: Breads, Breadmaker
Servings: 1
----------**FOR 1-1/2 LB. LOAF**----------------------------
1 pk Yeast
1/3 c Maple syrup
1 c Quick cooking (Quaker) oats
 1 tb Cooking oil
3 c Bread flour
1 1/4 c Plus
1 Tbsp. very warm water
1 ts Salt

Put all the ingredients into the pan, select white bread and push start.

Title: Mint And Yogurt Bread

Categories: Breads, Breadmaker
Servings: 1
------------**FOR 1-1/2 LB. LOAF**----------------------------
1 pk Yeast -fresh lemon
3 c Bread flour 2 ts Honey
1 c Plain yogurt; room temp. 1 ts Melted butter
3 tb Fresh mint; chopped 1/4 c Plus 1 Tbsp. warm water
Grated yellow rind of 1

Add all of the above ingredients, select white bread and push start.

Title: Mom's Basic White Bread
Categories: Breads, Breadmaker
Servings: 1
-----------**FOR 1-1/2 LB. LOAF**----------------------------
1 pk Yeast
2 tb Nonfat dry milk powder
3 c Flour
1 tb Butter
1 tb Sugar
1 1/4 c Warm water (110 degrees)
1 ts Salt

Pour the yeast to one side of the inner pan. Add the rest of theingredients in the order given. Select white bread, and push start.

Title: Old Fashioned Graham Flour Bread
Categories: Breads, Breadmaker
Servings: 1
---------**FOR 1-1/2 LB. LOAF**----------------------------
1 pk Yeast
1 ts Salt
2 c Bread flour
1 tb Honey
2 c Graham flour
1 tb Soft butter
1/4 c Nonfat dry milk powder
1 1/2 c Warm water

Combine all ingredients in pan, select white bread and push start.

Title: Orange Bread

Categories: Breads, Breadmaker
Servings: 1

----------**FOR 1-1/2 LB. LOAF**----------------------------

1 pk Yeast
1 Egg; room temperature
3 c Bread flour
2 tb Grated orange rind
1/4 c Sugar
1 c Orange juice
1 ts Salt
1/4 c Hot water
1 tb Soft butter

Add all the ingredients to the pan, select white bread and push start.

Title: Peanut Butter Bread

Categories: Breads, Breadmaker
Servings: 1

-----------**FOR 1-1/2 LB. LOAF**----------------------------

1 pk Yeast
1/2 c Chunky peanut butter
3 c Bread flour
1 1/4 c Very warm water
1/4 c Brown sugar; packed

Add all the ingredients in the order listed, select white bread and pushstart.

Title: Pecan-red Onion Bread

Categories: Breads, Breadmaker
Servings: 1
-----------**FOR 1-1/2 LB. LOAF**----------------------------
1 pk Yeast
1 c Plus
1 Tbsp. warm milk
3 c Bread flour
1/4 c Soft butter
1 1/2 ts Sugar
1/2 c Chopped fresh red onion
1 1/2 ts Salt
3/4 c Chopped pecans or walnuts

Combine all ingredients in the order given. Select white bread and push start. Get ready for an unusual treat.

Title: Pepper Spice Bread
Categories: Breads, Breadmaker
Servings: 1
----------**FOR 1-1/2 LB. LOAF**----------------------------
1 pk Yeast
2 tb Corn syrup
3 c Brotmehl
1/4 c Pekannüsse (oder anderen Nüssen)
1/2 ts Salz
1/2 ts frisch gemahlener schwarzer Pfeffer
1/4 c Zucker
1 ts ganze Anissamen
1/4 c fettarmer Milch-Pulver
1/4 ts Zimt
1/4 c weiche Butter
1/4 ts Piment
1 Ei 3/4 c sehr warmes Wasser
2 Tb Honig

Alle Zutaten in der angegebenen Reihenfolge setzen Sie, wählen Sie Weißbrot und push starten.
Hinweis: Dieses Rezept produziert einen leichten braunen Laib mit einem einzigartigen, würzigen Geschmack.

Titel: Prune Brot
Kategorien: Brot, Brotbackmaschine
Portionen: 1

-----------**FOR 1-1/2 LB. LOAF**----------------------------

1 Pk Hefe
1 Tb weiche butter
3 c Brotmehl
1 c Pflaumen Pitted; Schneiden Sie in
3 Tb brauner Zucker - Viertel
1 ts Salz
1 1/4 C warmem Wasser

Durchschneiden Sie die Pflaumen mit einer Schere. Geben Sie alle Zutaten in die Pfanne geben, wählen Sie Weißbrot und anschieben. Hinweis: Pflaumen aktivieren Sie diese in einem dunklen, feuchten, süßes Brot. Geschmack ist ähnlich eine Pflaume Dänisch. Die Maschine zerkleinert und breitet sich die Pflaumen im gesamten.

Titel: Roggenbrot
Kategorien: Brot, Brotbackmaschine
Portionen: 1

-----------**FOR 1-1/2 LB. LOAF**----------------------------

1 Pk Hefe 1 Tb Honig
2 c Roggen Mehl 1TB Margarine
2 c Brot Mehl 1 ts Boden Piment (optional)
2 Tb Nonfat trocken Milchpulver 1 Tb Kümmel (optional)
1 Tb Zucker 1 1/2 c warmem Wasser

1 ts Salz

Fügen Sie alle oben genannte Zutaten, wählen Sie weißes Brot und Push Start. Hinweis: Kümmel und Piment, können hinzugefügt werden, um eine ungewöhnliche würzige Roggen zu machen, oder für eine gute Populationsroggen weglassen

.Titel: Roggenbrot mit Bier und Orange

Kategorien: Brot, Brotbackmaschine
Portionen: 1

------------**FOR 1-1/2 LB. LOAF**--------------------------

---BROT ZUTATEN---

1 Pk Hefe 1 c Bier; erwärmt
1 c mittlere Roggen Mehl
2 Tb Melasse
2 1/2 c Mehl
2 ts geriebenen orange Schale
2 Tb Weizenkeime
2 Tb Butter; erweicht
1 ts Salz
1/4 c warmen Wasser

---**MIX FÜR GESCHLAGENE BUTTER**---

1 Stick süße butter - Likör Ihrer Wahl
1 Tb Honig
1/4 ts Mandelextrakt
2 Tb Amaretto oder jeder süß

Fügen Sie alle "Brot Zutaten" in Pfanne geben, wählen Sie Weißbrot und anschieben.

Hinweis: Das Bier verleiht diesem herzhaften Roggen einen ausgezeichneten Geschmack. Dieses Brot servieren mit gesüßter Schlagsahne Butter.

Titel: Gesalzene Erdnuss Brot
Kategorien: Brot, Brotbackmaschine
Portionen: 1
----------**FOR 1-1/2 LB. ROAST**--------------------------
1 Pk Hefe
1/2 ts Salz
1 c Vollkorn Mehl
 2 Tb Butter
2 c Brot Mehl
1 Ei; Raumtemperatur
1/3 c fettfreie Trockenmilch
 3/4 c gehackte gesalzene Erdnüsse
3 Tb Zucker
1 c heißes Wasser
Zutaten Sie alle, einschließlich die Erdnüsse direkt aus dem Glas, wählen Sie Weißbrot und anschieben. Trockenen gerösteten Nüssen können verwendet werden.

Titel: Spaghetti Brot
Kategorien: Brot, Brotbackmaschine
Portionen: 1
--------------**FOR 1-1/2 LB. BREAD**--------------------------
1 Pk Hefe 1/3 c geriebenen Parmesan-Käse
3 c Brot Mehl 1 ts getrocknete italienische Gewürzmischung
1 Tb Zucker 1 Tb Olivenöl
1 ts Knoblauch Salz 1 1/2 c warmen Wasser
Alle Zutaten hinzufügen, wählen Sie Weißbrot und push-Start. Servieren mit
Spaghetti.

Titel: Squaw Brot
Kategorien: Brot, Brotbackmaschine
Portionen: 1

------------FOR 1-1/2 LB. LOAF----------------------------

1 Pk Hefe
1 c Roggen Mehl
1 Tb brauner Zucker
1/4 c Instant fettfreie Trockenmilch
2 c Brot Mehl - Pulver
1 c Vollkorn Mehl
1 1/2 ts Salz

---**VERFLÜSSIGEN SIE IN BLENDER**---

1 1/4 c warmen Wasser 2 Tb Rosinen
2 3/4 Tb Öl 2 Tb brauner Zucker
2 Tb Honig

Kombinieren Sie Wasser, Öl, Honig, Rosinen und brauner Zucker zu und mischen Sie bis Flüssigkeit. Trockene Zutaten in der angegebenen Reihenfolge, Gießen Sie in flüssigen, wählen Sie weiß Brot und Push starten.

Titel: Sonnenblumen Brot
Kategorien: Brot, Brotbackmaschine
Portionen: 1

----------**FOR 1-1/2 LB. BREAD**---------------------------

1 Pk Hefe
1 Tb Zucker
1/2 c unverarbeitete Kleie Flocken
3TB Melasse
3 c Brot Mehl
2 Tb weiche butter
1/4 c Sonnenblumenkerne
1 1/4 c warme Milch

1 ts Salz
Fügen Sie alle Zutaten in der angegebenen Reihenfolge, wählen Sie weißes Brot und Push Start.
Hinweis: Ideal zum Servieren mit Suppe oder Salat für ein leichtes Mittagessen.

Titel: Süße Rosinen-Nuss-Brot
Kategorien: Brot, Brotbackmaschine
Portionen: 1
-----------**FOR 1-1/2 LB. LOAF-**----------------------------
1 pk Yeast 4 tb Melted butter; cooled
3 tb Sugar 1/4 c Honey
3 c Bread flour 1 1/2 ts Salt
3/4 c Warm milk 1/3 c Raisins
1/4 c Warm water 1/3 c Golden raisins
2 Eggs; room temperature 3/4 c Nuts „
„Pistachios or peanuts
Simply dump in all ingredients in the order listed, select white bread and
push start.

Title: Third Bread
Categories: Breads, Breadmaker
Servings: 1
----------**FOR 1-1/2 LB. LOAF**----------------------------
1 pk Yeast 1 1/2 ts Salt
3/4 c Rye flour 1/2 c Honey
3 c Bread flour 1 1/2 c Very warm water
3/4 c Yellow cornmeal
Put ingredients into pan in the order listed, select white bread and pushstart.

NOTE: Using two flours and a meal, this is called third bread and was found in many old cookbooks. It is a light, honey colored bread. It will sink a bit in the middle, but has a chewy crust and a sweet, very satisfying flavor.

Title: Wheat-wheat-wheat Bread

Categories: Breads, Breadmaker
Servings: 1
--------**FOR 1-1/2 LB. LOAF**----------------------------
1 pk Yeast
3 tb Honey
1/8 ts Ginger
1 cn Evaporated milk (12 oz.)
2 1/2 c Bread flour
2 tb Salad oil
1 1/4 c Whole wheat flour
1/2 c Cracked wheat
1/2 c Wheat germ
1/2 c Boiling water
1 ts Salt

Put dry ingredients in first. Cover the 1/2 cup cracked wheat with boiling water, stir, and let cool. Then add cooled cracked wheat, select white bread and push start.
NOTE: Cracked wheat is available in health food stores.

Title: Whole-wheat Bread

Categories: Breads, Breadmaker
Servings: 1
---------**FOR 1-1/2 LB. LOAF**----------------------------
1 pk Yeast
1 ts Salt

2 1/2 c Whole wheat flour
2 tb Soft butter
1 c Bread flour
3 tb Nonfat dry milk
1 tb Sugar
1 1/2 c Warm water

Add all ingredients in the order listed, select white bread and push start.

NOTE: A nutritious real whole wheat bread good for sandwichwes and "great" for toast.

Title: Honey Bacon Bread

Categories: Breadmaker, Breads
Servings: 16
3 tb Soft butter
2 ts Yeast 1 1/4 ts Salt
5 ts Gluten 1/2 c Soft bacon bits,,
3 1/2 c Wheat flour 1 1/4 c Very warm water + more if ne
1/2 c Honey

,,(don't use the crunchy kind) it looks too dry add a little more) . I don't deserve any credit for this wonderful bread. Turned out great. It is heavy (2 1/2 lbs.) I also used the crunchy bacon bits but I soaked them in warm water for about 30 minutes. Only had to add 2 Tbsp of water to the 1-1/4 cup.

Title: French Onion-Cheese Bread

Categories: Breadmaker, Breads
Servings: 1
123 - 1 ts Salt
1 tb Dried minced onion

1 pk Yeast 1/2 c Kraft French Onion
1/4 ts Ginger Spreadery Cheese
1/4 ts Sugar Snack +1 Tablespoon
3 c Better for Bread flour 1 Egg;(or 1/4 c Egg Beaters)
1/2 c Wheat flour 1 tb Vegetable oil
2 tb Gluten 10 1/2 oz Cond.French Onion soup; heat

Add all ingredients into the pan in the order listed. MB Select white bread and push "Start." Wonderful for sandwiches or any-meal accompaniments, this bread can also provide a spectacular presentation from first- course French onion soup for a haute cuisine dinner. Spread 1 full-round slice per person with butter (or Kaplan's Better Than Butter) and dust with grated Parmesan cheese. Cut circles out of the centers with a coffee can, place outer rings and circles on a cookie sheet and slide under an oven broiler to brown. To serve: put one cutout in the bottom of each soup bowl, ladle in hot soup, then place the crusty outer rings atop the bowls.

Title: Chicken & Stuffing Bread

Categories: Breadmaker, Breads
Servings: 1
- 16 1/4 oz. package
1 pk Yeast Stove Top instant
1/4 ts Ginger Stuffing mix)
1/4 ts Sugar 1 tb Onion;dried/minced
2 1/4 c Better for Bread flour 1 ts Salt
1/2 c Wheat flour 1/2 ts Poultry seasoning
2 tb Gluten 1/3 c Celery;1/4" pieces/fresh
1 1/4 c Chicken Flavor M/w 1/4 c
Mushrooms;can/slices/drain Stuffing Mix (or 1/2 1 Egg

Add all ingredients into the pan in the order listed. MB Select white bread and push "Start."

Title: Buttered Popcorn Bread
Categories: Breads, Breadmaker
Servings: 1
- 5 c Popcorn;popped/buttered/
Dak Gazette II Salted and crushed
1 pk Yeast Crushed by hand or
1/4 ts Ginger In a food processor
1/4 ts Sugar Until reduced to
2 1/2 c Better for Bread flour 2 1/2 cups
2 ts Gluten 1 tb Popcorn oil;or veg. oil
1 tb Butter Buds 1 1/2 c Very warm water
Salt
Add all the ingredients into the pan in the order listed;

Title: Portly Cheese Bread
Categories: Breads, Breadmaker
Servings: 1
1/8 ts Baking soda Dak Gazette II
1 c Port-wine cheese food;
1 pk Yeast (Kraft Spreadery) or
3 1/4 c Better for Bread flour Cold-pack port-wine
2 tb Gluten Cheese spread
2 tb Parmesan cheese
1 Egg
1 tb Sugar
3 tb Port wine
1 ts Salt
1 c Very warm water
Add all the ingredients in the order listed; select white bread and push "Start." A wine-and-cheese-tasting party all by itself, this bread is also a wondrous snack when spread with additional port-wine cheese.

Title: Pretzels And Beer Bread

Categories: Breads, Breadmaker
Servings: 1
- 1 ts Salt
Dak Gazette II 1/8 ts Baking soda
1 Ingredient 1 1/3 c Pretzel sticks;thin/broken
1 pk Yeast In half
1/4 ts Ginger 1 Egg white
1/4 ts Sugar 1 tb Vegetable oil
3 c Better for Bread flour 12 oz Light beer plus ->
2 tb Gluten 1/4 c Water; heated

Add all ingredients into the pan in the order listed. Select white bread and push "Start" Containing no cholesterol and negligible sugar; this exciting bread is perfect for party snacks or sandwiches.

Title: Raspberry Marshmallow Bread

Categories: Breads, Breadmaker
Servings: 1
- 2 tb Canola oil
Dak Gazette II 2/3 c Water; + ->
1 pk Yeast 1/2 c Raspberry liquid; heated
2 3/4 c Better for Bread flour
10 oz Red raspberries;frozen in
2 tb Gluten Heavy syrup.
1 ts Salt Defrost; drain and
1/8 ts Baking soda Reserve liquid and
1/2 c Miniature marshmallows Berries.
1/4 c Egg Beaters

Place the first 9 ingredients into the pan in the order listed; set darkness control at 11 o'clock. Select white bread and push "Start." Add the reserved, well-drained raspberries (2/3cup) when the breadmaker "beeps," 88 minutes into the cycle. (33 minutes with Dak Turbo II) Shared by Barb Day Delightful with fruit salad, or for a cholesterol-free fiber-flled breakfast treat, spread toasted slices with Kaplan's Better than Butter.

Title: Grandma Ida's Challah
Categories: Breads, Jewish
Servings: 2
6 c FLOUR (approx) 1/2 c SUGAR
1 pk YEAST, DRY 1 ts SALT; HEAPING
1 EGG; WELL-BEATEN 1 1/3 c WATER; LUKEWARM
1/2 c OIL RAISINS, OPTIONAL
Mix dry ingredients (yeast, flour, sugar, and salt) in large bowl, using 4 cups of the flour. Make a well in the center. Into the well, put the eggs, oil, and water. Stir to dampen flour. Add enough flour so that dough becomes smooth and cleans sides of bowl if you are using a dough hook. Else knead on floured board. Place dough in oiled and let rise until double in bulk. Divide dough in half and each half into 3 or 4 pieces. For each loaf, roll out the pieces into ropes and braid from the middle to the ends. Place loaves on a greased cookie sheet or in greased loaf pans. Brush the top of each loaf with egg glaze if desired. Allow to rise again until double. Bake 30 - 45 min 350. ~
FOR BUNS: USE 2/3+ CUPS SUGAR
AND 2 EGGS. ~ ,,,,TO DECREASE RISING TIME: ,,,,PLACE DOUGH IN BOWL - DO NOT GREASE! ,,,,PLACE 1 CUP OF WATER IN CORNER OF MICROWAVE OVEN. ,,,,COVER DOUGH

LOOSELY WITH SARAN OR DAMP LINT-FREE TOWEL. ,,,,NUKE FOR 3 MINUTES 20% POWER. (MAX OF 112 DEGREES!!!) ,,,,LET REST FOR 3 MINUTES. ,,,,NUKE FOR ANOTHER 3 MINUTES 20% POWER. ,,,,LET REST FOR 6 MINUTES. ,,,,AFTER PUNCHING DOWN AND BRAIDING, CAN LET RISE NORMALLY IN PANS OR REPEAT NUKING PROCESS IF USING MICROWAVE SAFE PANS. ~ TO MAKE ROUND LOAVES: PAT DOUGH INTO A 9 X 13 RECTANGLE. PAT RAISINS INTO THE DOUGH, THEN ROLL UP TIGHT FROM THE LONG SIDE TO 32". MAKE A PINWHEEL OF IT, TUCKING THE OUTSIDE END UNDER THE LAST TURN.

Title: Caraway Puffins
Categories: Muffins, Breads
Servings: 1
3 tb Butter 1 ts Grated Lemon Peel
1/2 c Creamed Cottage Cheese 3/4 ts Caraway Seed
1/3 c Sugar 1 1/2 c Biscuit Mix
1 Egg 1/2 c Milk
Cream butter, cottage cheese and sugar. Add grated Lemon peel, caraway seed and egg. Beat with mixer til smooth. Stir in biscuit mix and milk alternately. Do not beat. Spoon batter into greased muffin pans, filling 2/3 full. Bake at 400 for 20 min. or til lightly browned.

Title: Honey Wheat Bread - in a Bag
Categories: Breads
Servings: 40
4 c All purpose flour 1/4 c Honey
3 1/4 c Whole wheat flour 1/4 c Non-fat dry milk powder

2 pk Active dry yeast 2 tb Vegetable oil
2 1/2 c Warm water 1 tb Salt
DIRECTIONS: 1. Combine 1 C all purpose flour, 2 pkg yeast, 1 C warm water and 1 T honey in a 2 gal heavy duty freeze plastic bag (Ziploc Jumbo) 2. Squeeze upper part of bag to force out air. Close top of bag tightly between thumb and index finger. Rest bag on table, mix by working bag with fingers about 20 seconds or until all ingredients are completely blended. Let bag rest about 15 minutes. 3. Add remaining ingredients, except flour. 4. Mix by working bag with fingers. Add Whole wheat flour; mix thoroughly. Then gradually add remaining all purpose flour until a stiff dough is formed, about 2-1/2 C or until dough pulls away from bag. 5. Turn dough out onto floured surface. Divide dough in half. Knead each half 5 minutes or until dough is smooth and elastic. Add more flour, if necessary. Cover with plastic bag. Let rest 10 minutes. 6. Flatten dough into a 12 x 7 inch rectangle. At narrow end fold corners to center to form a point. Beginning with point roll dough tightly towards you. Pinch the edges to seal. Press dough at each end to seal and fold ends under. 7. Place seam down in a greased 8-1/2 x 4-1/2 x 2-1/4 loaf pan. Repeat with second loaf. 8. Cover loosely with plastic bag and let rise in warm place 45-60 minute or until doubled. Uncover. Bake on lower rack in 400 F oven 30-35 minutes or until deep golden brown. Remove from pan immediately. Cool on rack. Makes 2 (1-3/4 lb) loaves.

VARIATIONS: MOUNTAIN TOP BREAD:
Brush tops with melted butter or margarine. Sprinkle with all purpose flour. Repeat with second loaf. Let rise 45-60 minutes. Before baking, carefully make a shallow cut with sharp knife down center of each loaf. Bake as directed.

COUNTRY CRUST BREAD: After greasing loaf pans, coat bottoms and sides of pans with whole wheat germ, wheat bran or whole wheat flour. Shape loaves; place seam side down in prepared pans. Brush tops of loaves with vegetable oil. Sprinkle tops of loaves with 1/4 C wheat germ or whole wheat flour. Let rise and bake as directed. ICED **HONEY RAISIN BREAD:** For two loaves, in small bowl, mix together 1 C raisins, 1/2 C packed brown sugar and 2 tsp cinnamon. Flatten each dough piece into 12 x 7 inch rectangle and brush each piece with softened butter or margarine. Sprinkle raisin mixture on dough. Press raisins in lightly. Shape into loaves, let rise and bake as directed. When cool, frost loaves with Easy Icing. Beat until smooth 1 C powdered sugar and about 1 T hot water.

Title: PARTY BUNDT BREAD:

Shape loaves as directed except do not seal ends. Pinch loaves together to form a ring. Place ring seam side up in greased 12 C bundt pan. Let rise until dough reaches top of bundt pan, about 45-60 min. Bake in 375 F oven 40-45 min. Invert immediately and cool on rack. When cool, drizzle with Honey-Nut Glaze. Stirring constantly, bring to boil 1/4 C coarsely chopped nuts,
1/4 C packed brown sugar,
1/4 C honey and 2 T butter or margarine.

SOFT AND SALTY PRETZELS. Divide dough into 24 equal pieces. Roll each piece into 18 inch rope. Twist ropes into pretzel shape and place on greased baking sheets. Brush pretzels with vegetable oil and sprinkle with coarse salt. Cover; let rise until doubled, about 1/2 hour. Bake in 425 oven 15 to 20min or until golden brown. Cool on rack and store in container with loose fitting cover.

SUBSTITUTIONS: Molasses, brown sugar or granulated sugar may be used in place of honey. 1 C lukewarm milk and 1-1/2 C warm water may be used in place of nonfat dry milk and water. Softened butter or margarine may be used in place of vegetable oil. All purpose flour may be used in place of whole wheat flour. Two 9x5x3 inch loaf pans may be used.

Title: Cheese Cornbread
Categories: Breads
Servings: 18
3 c Stone ground yellow 5 Eggs
-cornmeal 3/4 c Safflower or corn oil
3 c Unbleached flour 3 1/2 c Buttermilk
2 1/2 tb Baking powder 2 c Cheddar cheese
2 tb Sugar -sharp, shredded
1 1/2 ts Salt

In a mixing bowl, combine cornmeal, flour, baking powder, sugar and salt; mix well. Separately beat eggs with oil and buttermilk. Add with cheese to cornmeal mixture, stirring enough only to mix all ingredients well. Spoon into two 8 x 12" greased baking pan. Bake in a preheated 425 degree oven for 20 to 25 minutes or until cornbread is brown around the edge and firm to the touch. Cut into squares and serve hot.

Title: Patio Skillet Bread
Categories: Breads
Servings: 10
1 1/2 c Flour 3 Eggs, slighty beaten
1 1/2 c Cornmeal 2 c Milk
2 tb Sugar 1/3 c Shortening, melted
4 ts Baking powder 1 1/2 c Celery, chopped
2 1/2 ts Salt 1/4 c Pimiento, chopped
2 ts Poultry seasoning 1/4 c Onion, minced

Mix flour, cornmeal, sugar, baking powder, salt and poultry seasoning. Beat eggs and mix with milk and shortening. Add to first mixture. Stir until just mixed. Stir in celery, pimiento and onion. Pour mixture into greased 10 inch skillet or baking pan. Bake at 400F, 35-45 minutes or until well browned and done. Serve hot with butter. This bread goes well with meat and potatoes cooked outdoors on grill.

Title: Walnut Apricot Bread
Categories: Breads
Servings: 12
3 ts Baking powder 2/3 c Walnut meats
3/4 ts Salt 1 c Milk
3 c Flour 1 Egg; well-beaten
1/2 c Brown sugar; firm packed 4 tb Butter
1 c Dried apricots; cut-up

Sift the baking powder, salt, and flour together; sift once more. Add the sugar and mix again; then add the apricots and the nuts. Combine the milk, egg, and butter, and beat lightly; add this to the flour mixture and blend well. Bake in a buttered loaf pan in a 350 oven for one hour.

Title: Buttermilk Oat Bread
Categories: Breads, Bm, Oatmeal
Servings: 14
One pound loaf One/1/2 pound Loaf
1 c Buttermilk 1 1/3 c Buttermilk
4 tb Butter 5 tb Butter
3 tb Molasses 4 tb Molasses
1 1/2 ts Salt 2 ts Salt
1 c Oatmeal 1 1/3 c Oatmeal
2 c Bread flour 2 2/3 c Bread flour
1 1/2 ts Yeast 2 1/2 ts Yeast

Bake according to manufacturer's instructions.

Title: Sour Rye Bread

Categories: Breads
Servings: 1
9 ts Yeast (2 pkg.) 4 ts Caraway Seed (optional)
1 1/2 c Water, warm 1 ts Salt
2 c Rye flour, 1 Egg
- medium or stone ground 3 ts Vegetable oil
1 c Beer, warm 1 Egg white;
6 c Flour, all-purpose (approx) - beaten with 2 Tsp water
1/4 c Sugar

In large mixer bowl, dissolve half of yeast in warm water. Add rye flour; stir until well mixed. Cover bowl tightly w/plastic wrap. Let stand (room temp) for 3 days. Then add remaining yeast & the beer; mix well. Stir in 3 cups of the all purpose flour, sugar, half Caraway seed, salt and the egg, lightly beaten. Beat at moderate speed until smooth, about 2 min. Add oil; beat at high speed for 2 min. Add enough flour to make soft dough. Turn dough out onto a floured board. Knead in remaining flour & knead about 5 min. Place in greased bowl, and let rise until doubled. Punch down and form into 2 braided loaves. Brush with egg white/water, sprinkle with Caraway seeds, and let rise again. Bake at 350, about 40 min. You can vary this by using 3 different seeds on the outside of each braid "rope". Try poppy seed, sesame seed, and caraway, for a change.

Title: CORN DODGERS

Categories: Breads

Servings: 6
-PNewton vkbb14a 2 Large eggs;beaten OR
2 c Cornmeal -egg substitutes
1 ts Baking soda 1 c Nonfat plain yogurt
1/4 c Sugar 1 tb Olive oil
Preheat oven 400F. Sift together cornmeal and baking soda into large bowl; add sugar. Make a well in center and pour in eggs, yogurt and oil. Stir together well and bake for 15 min.

Title: CHEESE STRAWS
Categories: Breads, Cheese
Servings: 1
4 tb Ice water
1 1/2 c Unbleached flour 1 c Grated cheddar cheese;lofat
6 tb All veg shortening Preheat oven 450F. Place flour in large bowl. Cut in shortening until mix is granular. Stirring with fork, work in just enough ice water to form stiff dough. Roll out dough as thinly as possible on floured surface. Spread one-half dough with cheese. Top with other half of dough and roll out. Cut layered dough into 3x1/2" strips and place on baking sheet sprayed with Pam. Bake until golden. Variation: Twist cheese straw dough

Title: Foccaccia,,,,,,
Categories: Italian, Breads
Servings: 1
- G. Granaroli XBRG76A Olive oil
- MM:MK VMXV03A Seasonings
1 lb Pizza dough
Let the dough rise for about 4 hours until double in size. Punch down and roll out to fit a shallow parking pan or

pizza pan. The dough should be about 1 inch thick. Spread olive oil thinly on top. Salt and top with a season of you choice. I love Rosemary. You can also add sun-dried tomatoes, garlic, onions, or any other herbs. Bake at 375 for 25-30 min or until golden. Cut into squares and serve.

Title: Buns Make Shells
Categories: Breads
Servings: 1
Melted butter
Stale hamburger or hot dog Cinnamon sugar-buns Parmesan cheese; grated Small dinner or finger rolls Use buns for small pie shells. For cocktail parties, use smaller rolls. Split in half and hollow into shells by removing part of the soft inside crumbs with the point of a sharp knife. Brush with butter. Sprinkle with a little plain or cinnamon sugar for sweet fillings; leave plain or dust with Parmesan cheese for salty fillings. Arrange on a baking sheet and bake at 350~ until golden and crisp, about 20 to 25 minutes. To serve hot; reheat in the oven, empty and fill with a hot filling just before serving. Source:

Title: Breakfast Bread Pudding with Sausage
Categories: Brunch, Meats, Cheese/eggs, Breads
Servings: 8
1 1/2 c Swiss cheese; shred, divide
3 c French bread; cubed 9 lg Eggs
1/2 lb Bulk pork sausage; crumble 3 c Milk
1 c Onions; chopped 1 ts Dry mustard
2 ts Fresh thymne; chopped or 1 ts Salt
1/2 ts Dried 1/4 ts Freshly ground pepper
10 oz Pk frozen chopped spinach; 1 Plum tomato; diced -thaw squeeze dry Preheat oven to 325~. Arrange bread in 15-1/2x10-1/2" jely-rolly pan. Bake 20 minutes or until crisp. Cool. Meanwhile, brown sausage in large skillet over

medium-high heat; drain on paper towels. Add onions and thyme to skillet; cook until onion is translucent, about 2 minutes. Remove from heat. Stir in sausage and spinach to combine; cool completely. Arrange bread in shallow 3-quart baking dish. Sprinkle 1 cup cheese over top, then layer with sausage mixture and remaining cheese. Beat eggs, milk, mustard, in bowl until well blended. Carefully pour into prepared dish; sprinkle top with tomato. (Can be made ahead. Cover and refrigerate up to 24 hours.) Bake 1 hour or until center is just set. Let stand 10 minutes before serving.

Title: Breakfast Casserole

Categories: Brunch, Eggs, Vegetables, Breads, Meats
Servings: 10

 Salt and pepper to taste
8 oz Loaf Italian bread 1 lg Red pepper; 1/4" slices
3 tb Butter or margarine; melted 1 sm Onion; 1/4" slices
2 lb Hot or sweet Italian sausage 1 sm Zucchini; 1/4" slices
-links 1/2 ts Dried thyme
12 lg Eggs

Preheat oven to 325~. Slice bread into 1/4"-thick diagonal slices. Line bottom of 13x9" baking dish or shallow casserole with bread, overlapping slices if necessary. Brush with butter or margarine. Remove sausage from casings. Cook sausage until well-browned, stirring frequently. Wtih slotted spoon, place cooked sausage on top of bread in baking dish. Discard all but 1 T sausage drippings. In bowl, mix eggs with salt, pepper and 1/3 c water. Pour egg mixture over sausage and bread. Cover baking dish with foil and bake 25 minutes or until eggs are set but still moist. In same skillet, cook veggies with thyme, salt and pepper until tender-crisp and golden brown. To serve, arrange veggies on top of casserole.

Title: DECADENT FRENCH TOAST

Categories: Brunch, Breads, Make ahead, Cheese/eggs, Nuts
Servings: 4

Jean Gaschen 1 ts Vanilla
5 tb Butter French bread
1 c Brown sugar Whipped cream
2 tb Dark Karo) Pecans; chopped
1/2 c Milk Strawberries
5 Egg

Cook corn syrup, butter, and brown sugar until bubbly. Pour into a 13x9 baking dish and generously sprinkle chopped pecans over the syrup mixture. Arrange 2" slices of french bread over the mixture. Beat together eggs, milk, and vanilla. Pour over the bread and refrigerate overnight. Bake at 350 for 45 min. and invert! Serve with cream and strawberries. A nonstick pan makes life easier. Watch closely, you don't want it to get too brown. Can be made the night before.

Title: STRAWBERRY PECAN BREAD

Categories: Breads, Quickbreads, Fruits
Servings: 4

1 1/2 c All-purpose flour 2/3 c Oil
1 c Sugar 2 Eggs; beaten
1 ts Cinnamon 1 c Frozen strawberries
1/2 ts Baking soda 1/2 c (+ 2 T) pecans; chopped Preheat oven to 350F. Generously grease bottom only of a 9x5-inch loaf pan. Combine flour, sugar, cinnamon,and baking soda in a large bowl; mix well. In separate bowl, blend oil and eggs. Slice thawed strawberries and add to oil and egg mixture. Add this mixture to the bowl of dry ingredients. Stir in 1/2 cup of the pecans, blending until dry ingredients are just moistened. Pour bread mixture into loaf pan.

Garnish top with 2 tablespoons chopped pecans. Bake 60-70 minutes, until toothpick comes out clean. Cool 15 minutes; remove from pan. Cool completely before slicing. Adapted from

Title: FLAVORED BUTTERS
Categories: Cheese/eggs, Condiments, Breads, Fruits, Brunch
Servings: 1

--------------CINNAMON BUTTER----------------------------
2 Sticks butter 1 ts Cinnamon
1/2 c Brown sugar -Blend together well.
-----------ORANGE BUTTER-----------------------------
2 Sticks butter 1/8 ts Mace
1 ts Orange rind -Blend together well.
----------STRAWBERRY BUTTER----------------------------
1 Stick butter -ripe; hulled fresh
4 Strawberries Powdered sugar; to taste
-------HONEY-PECAN BUTTER----------------------------
-Spread -beat in
1/3 c Pecans; in a shallow pan. 1/4 c Honey; until well combined.
-Toast in a 350 oven -Then mix in chopped pecans.
-for about 8 minutes; cool. -made ahead; cover an
-Chop toasted pecans finely. -refrigerate. Let stand at
-In a medium bowl; beat -room temperature to soften
1/2 c Butter; until fluffy; -before serving.
We had a brunch potluck at work and I made 4 or 5 different breads with the assorted butters - they make yummy toast!

Title: BANANA SPLIT BREAD

Categories: Bread maker, Breads, Nuts
Servings: 1

 1 ts Vanilla
-Dak Gazette II 4 oz Banana-1 med; sliced
1 pk Yeast -Directly into the
3 c Better for Bread flour -Inner pan
2 tb Gluten 10 Frozen Strawberries; thawed
2 tb Sugar -With their liquid
1 ts -Salt 1/3 c Crushed pineapple; drained
1/8 ts Baking soda -Reserve juice.
1/3 c Instant nonfat dry milk 1/3 c Pineapple juice; from
1/3 c Walnuts; broken -The pineapple-heated
1 Egg 1/2 c Chocolate chips
2 tb Vegetable oil 4 c Maraschino cherries; drained

Place all ingredients (EXCEPT CHOCOLATE CHIPS AND CHERRIES) into the inner pan in the order listed; select white bread and push "Start." Add the chips and cherries when the Auto Bakery "beeps," 88 minutes into the cycle. (33 min. with DAK Turbo II) Delightful whether eaten fresh, chilled or toasted, this soda fountain special is even more spectacular when spread with cream cheese blended with minced maraschinos and their liquid.

Title: SAVORY CORN BREAD PUDDING

Categories: Breads, Side dish, Gourmet
Servings: 10

melted and cooled
1 c All-purpose flour 4 lg Eggs
1 1/2 c Yellow cornmeal 4 c Milk
1 tb Baking powder 1/2 ts Cayenne; or to taste
1 ts -Salt 14 oz Can of tomatoes; drained
1 c Milk -well and chopped
1 lg Egg 6 Scallions; chopped fine

3 tb Unsalted butter;

Make the corn bread: In a bowl, stir together the flour, cornmeal, baking powder and salt. In a small bowl, whisk together the milk, egg and butter and stir the mixture into the cornmeal mixture, stirring until the batter is just combined. Pour the batter into a greased 8-inch square baking pan and bake the corn bread in the middle of a preheated 425 degree F. oven for 20 to 25 minutes, or until a tester comes out clean. Let the corn bread cool in the pan for 5 minutes, invert it onto a rack, and let it cool completely. Crumble the corn bread coarse into 2 shallow baking pans and toast it in the middle of a preheated 325 degree F. oven, stirring occasionally, for 30 to 35 minutes, or until it is dried and deep golden. The crumbled corn bread may be made 3 days in advance and kept in an airtight container. In a large bowl, whisk together the eggs, milk, cayenne and salt to taste, add the crumbled corn bread, tomatoes and scallions and combine the mixture well. Divide the corn bread mixture between 2 greased 9-inch round cake pans, let it stand for 15 minutes and bake the pudding in the middle of a preheated 375 degree F. oven for 40 to 45 minutes, or until it is golden. Cut the pudding into wedges.

Title: Dried Tomato Crostini

Categories: Sun-dried, Breads, Ethnic, Appetizers
Servings: 24

1 1/2 ts Parsley; snipped
12 Sun-dried tomato halves; 1 cl Garlic; minced
-dry pack 1/2 ts Capers; drain, chop
1/4 c Boiling water Cracked black pepper
2 tb Balsamic or red wine vinegar 8 oz Loaf baguette-style French
1 md Tomato; peel, seed, chop -bread
1/4 c Red onion; finely chop Parmesan or Mozzarella;shred

4 Pitted ripe olives; minced Fresh thyme sprigs; optional
1 tb Olive oil

Combine dried tomatoes, water and vinegar. Let stand for 15 to 20 minutes to soften tomatoes. Drain. Discard liquid. Cut dried tomatoes into thin strips; return to bowl. Stir in ripe tomato, onion, olives, oil, parsley, garlic and capers. Season with pepper. Bias-slice bread into 24 pieces, about 1/2" thick. Place bread slices on a baking sheet. Bake in a 350~ oven for 3 to 5 minutes or till light brown. Turn bread over; bake for 3 to 5 minutes more or till light brown. Spoon tomato mixture onto toasted bread and serve immediately. Or, if desired, sprinkle added Parmesan cheese or mozzarella over tomato mixture; return to oven for 3 to 5 minutes more or till cheese is melted. Garnish with fresh thyme sprigs, if desired. Serve

Title: French Bread/Goat Cheese/Sun-Dried Tomato Spre

Categories: Sun-dried, Breads, Spreads, Cheese
Servings: 8
4 ts Fresh thyme; minced or
11 oz Pk Montrachet; or other soft 1 ts Dried thyme; crumbled
-fresh goat cheese 1/4 c Sour cream
2/3 c Walnuts; chopped Fresh thyme; minced
1/2 c Oil-pk sun-dried toms; drain Walnuts; chopped
-chop 2 French bread baguettes;slice Mix cheese, walnuts, tomatoes and thyme. Thin to spreadable consistency with sour cream. Season with generous amount of pepper. Mound cheese in crock or bowl. (Can be prepared 2 days ahead. Cover and chill. Bring to room temperature before serving.) Sprinkle cheese with thyme and walnuts.Serve with bread.

Title: **Banana Muffins**
Categories:, Breads
Servings: 2

6 tb Flour
1 Banana; medium 1 ts Baking powder
1 ts Cinnamon 1/2 c Carrots; grated
1/2 ts Baking soda 2/3 c Powdered milk
2 Eggs 10 pk Sweet and Low
1 ts Vanilla

Mix all ingredients. Spray muffin tin with Pam. Divide equally. Bake at 350 F. for 25 minutes. Makes 12 muffins which is TWO SERVINGS of SIX (yes
6) MUFFINS EACH. For each six (6) muffins the following counts apply: 1 Bread, 1 Fruit, 1 Milk, 1 Protein and 1/2 Vegetable. This is a no fat recipe. You may substitute Egg Beaters for the eggs and Equal for the Sweet and Low. Freeze well.

Title: **BANANA RAISIN WALNUT MUFFINS**
Categories: , Breads, Breakfast
Servings: 12

1 c +2 T. buttermilk
1 c +2 T. flour 1 Egg; lightly beaten
1/2 c Nonfat dry milk powder 1/4 c Less 2 t. vegetable oil
1/4 c Brown sugar; firmly packed 2 tb Sweet whipped butter, melted
2 ts Baking powder 1 Banana; ripe, mashed
1/4 ts Nutmeg 1/2 c Golden raisins; plumped
1/2 ts Baking soda 1 oz Walnuts; chopped

Preheat oven to 400. Spray 12 muffin cups with nonstick spray. In medium mixing bowl cm bean flour, milk powder, sugar, baking powder, baking soda and nutmeg; stir to combine and set aside. In small bowl, combine buttermilk, egg, oil, and butter and stir until blended; stir in dry ingredients. Add banana, raisins, and walnuts and stir to combine (mixture will be lumpy). Fill each baking cup with an equal amount of batter and bake for 15 minutes (until golden brown and a toothpick inserted in center comes out dry). Transfer muffins from pan to wire rack and cool. Makes 12 servings, 1 muffin each. One muffin equals 1/4 protein, 1/2 bread, 1 fat,1/2 fruit, 1/4 milk, 30 optional calories. From Meals in a Minute

Title: Basic Pizza Dough
Categories: Main dish, Breads, Ww
Servings: 8
4 1/2 c All purpose flour 1/2 ts Salt
1 Envelope dry active yeast 1 1/4 c Hot water
In large bowl, combine 2 cups flour, the yeast and salt. With electric mixer, slowly beat in water; beat 2 minutes, occasionally scraping bowl with rubber spatula. With mixer on medium speed, beat in 1/2 cup flour; beat 2 minutes, until dough is stiff. Stir in 1 1/2 cups flour. Sprinkle clean work surface with 1/4 cup flour. Knead dough on floured surface, 6-8 minutes. Spray large bowl with nonstick spray. Place dough in bowl; cover with plastic wrap and kitchen towel. Let rise 1 hour or until doubled in volume. Punch down dough; let rest 15 mintues. Divide dough in half. Sprinkle clean work surface with 2 T flour. Roll 1/2 of dough into 13" round; lift onto a 12" pizza pan. Pinch edges to form a rim. Exchanges: 1 1/2 B. Per serving: 116 cal, 0 gm fat.

Title: Cinnamon Rolls
Categories: Breads, Low-cal,
Servings: 10
1 ts Cinnamon
10 oz Buttermilk Biscuits, Refrig. 1/2 c Raisins; dark

^^(10 biscuits in "tube") 2 tb Raisins; dark
5 ts Margarine; melted 5 ts Powdered sugar; sifted
5 ts Brown sugar; packed, divided 2 ts Water

Preheat oven to 400 F. Spray 8x8x2 inch baking pan; set aside. Separate biscuits; using fingers, flatten each into 3" circle. Brush each circle with an equal amount of the margarine, sprinkle each with 1/4 t brown sugar and an equal amount of cinnamon, then top each with 1T raisins. Roll each circle jelly-roll fashion and arrange in two rows, seam side down, in sprayed pan. Bake until rolls are puffed and golden brown, 8-12 minutes. Transfer pan to wire rack and lets rolls cool in pan. In small brown or cup combine remaining 2 1/2 t brown sugar and the powdered sugar, add water, 1 t at a time, stirring constantly until mixture is smooth and syrupy. Remove rolls to serving platter, brush each with an equal amount of sugar mixture. Makes 10 servings of 1 roll each. Each serving provides: 1 BREAD, 1/2 FAT, 1/2 FRUIT and 20 OPTIONAL CALORIES. Per serving: 143 calories, 5 g fat.

Title: Muffins

Categories: Low-cal, Breads,
Servings: 1

1/4 ts Baking powder
1/2 c Pineapple; crushed 1/3 c Dry powdered milk
1 oz Cornmeal 1 pk Sweet'n Low
1 Egg 1/4 ts Baking soda

Put everything in blender to mix. Bake in muffin tins at 400 for 15 minutes. All 5-6 muffins are ONE serving and provide: 1 fruit, 1 milk and 25 optional calories.

Title: Orange-walnut Muffins

Categories: Ww, Breads
Servings: 6

1 Flour; 1 cup + 2 tbls. 1 Salt; pinch
2 tb Brown Sugar; Lt. (packed) 1/2 c Orange juice
1 1/2 ts Baking powder 2 tb Margarine; melted + cooled
1 ts Lemon Rind; Grated 1 Egg; large
1/2 oz Walnuts; chopped (12 halves)

Preheat oven to 375 degrees F. In medium bowl, stir together flour, sugar, baking powder, lemon rind, walnuts and salt. In small bowl, mix together orange juice, margarine and egg. Add to dry ingredients, mixing with fork until just combined; do not over mix. Spray six 2 1/2 inch muffin cups with nonstick cooking spray; divide batter evenly among the cups. Bake 20 to 25 minutes, or until golden brown. Makes six servings. EACH SERVING PROVIDES: 1 B, 1 F, 60 optional calories. Per serving: 175 calories; 4 g protein, 6 g fat, 25 g carbohydrate, 187 mg sodium, 46 mg cholesterol.

Title: Pancakes

Categories: Breakfast, Breads, Low-cal, Ww
Servings: 1
3 tb Flour 1 Vanilla ALBA 77
1/4 ts Salt 1 Egg
1/2 ts Baking powder 1/2 c Warm water

Mix all ingredients. Makes 4-6 pancakes Exchanges: 1 bread, 1 milk & 1 protein.

Title: Breadstick Dippers

Categories: Appetizers, Breads, Ww
Servings: 12
2 1/4 c Flour; divided 1 c Skim milk
1 tb Sugar 1/4 c Reduced-calorie margarine;
2 ts Baking powder Melted.
1 ts Salt

Preheat oven to 425 degrees. Into medium mixing bowl sift together 2 c flour, the sugar, baking powder; and salt; add milk and, using a wooden sppon, mix to form dough. Using 2 T of the reamining flour, lightly flour work surface; turn dough out onto floured surface and knead, adding remain9ing 2 T flour as needed, until dough becomes smooth and elastic,about 5 minutes. Using rolling pin, roll dough into 12x8" rectangle, about 1/2 " thick. Cut dough in half lengthwise; cut each half crosswise into 18 equal slices. Dip dough slices into margarine; being sure to use all of the margarine; place dough slices on baking sheet, leaving a space of about 1inch between each. Bake until golden brown, 10 to 15 minutes. Makes 12 servings of 3 sticks each. One serving=1 bread; 1/2 fat; 15 cal optional exchange. 114 calories; 3 g protein; 2 g fat; 20 g CHO, 65 mg calcium; 306 mg sodium; 0.4 mg chol.

Title: Dill Cottage Cheese Batter Bread
Categories: Breads, Pat
Servings: 12
1 pk Dry yeast 1 ts Salt
1/2 ts Sugar 1 c Small curd cottage cheese
1/4 c Very warm water -warmed slightly
1 Egg 1/4 ts Baking powder
1 tb Dried instant onions 2 1/2 c Flour
1 tb Butter or margarine Melted butter
2 ts Dill weed

Grease a 1-quart baking dish. Sprinkle yeast and sugar over very warm water in 1-cup glass measure. Stir to dissolve yeast. Let stand until bubbly, about 10 minutes. Beat egg slightly in large bowl. Add dried instant onions, butter, dill weed, salt, cottage cheese and baking powder; beat until well blended. Stir in yeast mixture until well blended. Stir in enough of the flour to make a soft dough. Place dough in prepared baking dish. Cover with buttered wax paper and a towel. Let rise in warm place away from drafts until doubled in bulk, about 1 hour. Bake in preheated moderate oven (350) for 60 minutes or until loaf sounds hollow when topped with fingers. Turn bread out onto wire rack. Brush with melted butter and sprinkle with salt. Serve warm Makes 1 loaf (12 slices). Per slice, 134 calories, 3 g fat.

Title: Overnight Coffee Bread
Categories: Breads, Brunch, Pat
Servings: 10
20 Frozen dinner rolls 1/2 ts Cinnamon
3 oz Box Jello vanilla pudding 1 Stick melted butter
--NOT instant 1/2 c Pecans
1/2 c Brown sugar

Place frozen dinner rolls in a bundt pan. Stir together remaining ingredients and pour on top of rolls. Cover with a towel and leave overnight. The following morning, bake at 350 degrees for 30 minutes. Freeze while hot for fast reheating in microwave.

Title: Benya Banana Fritters
Categories: Fruits, Breads
Servings: 1
3 tb Cinnamon
- MM:MK VMXV03A 2 tb Nutmeg
1 Package of yeast 2 1/2 lb Flour
1 c Hot water 1 1/2 lb Sugar
Sugar Grated rind, med. sz orange
10 Very soft bananas 1/4 ts Salt

Add yeast to hot water ans sprinkle in a little sugar. Cover and let stand to start rising process. Mash bananas throughly in large mixing bowl with yeast. Add cinnamon, nutmeg, flour, sugar, grated orange rind and salt. Mix throughly and let stand overnight. Mixture will rise and triple in amount. Drop by spoonfuls in deep fat; fry until brown. Serve either hot or cold. May be frozen Makes 36 pastries .

Title: APPLE OATMEAL BREAD

Categories: Breads, Fruits
Servings: 1
1 1/2 c Sifted flour 1 c Quick oatmeal
1 ts Baking powder 1 c Chopped nuts
1 ts Baking soda 2 Eggs
1 ts Salt 1/4 c Milk
1 ts Cinnamon 1/4 c Melted margarine,cooled
1/2 ts Nutmeg 2 Apples,cored,coasely shred
2/3 c Packed brown sugar

Preheat oven to 350 F. Lightly grease and flour loaf pan. Sift flour, baking powder, baking soda, salt, cinnamon and nutmeg in large bowl. Stir in brown sugar, oatmeal, and nuts.. Mix eggs, milk and butter in small bowl, add all at once to oatmeal mixture, add apples, stir lightly with fork until liquid is absorbed into mix and it is completely moistened. Spoon into prepared pan. Bake for 1 hour and 5 minutes. Cool in pan on wire rack 10 minutes. Loosen edges with knife, turn out onto rack. Cool completely. Wrap, store overnight.

Title: NUTRITIOUS BREAKFAST BREAD

Categories: Breads, Fruits
Servings: 2
1 c Flour 1/4 c Chopped walnuts
1 c Whole wheat flour 1/2 c Raisins
1/2 ts Salt 1/3 c Chopped prunes
1/2 ts Baking soda 3 Eggs

2 ts Baking powder 1/2 c Oil
2/3 c Dry non-fat milk powder 1/2 c Molasses
1/3 c Oatmeal 3/4 c Orange juice
1/2 c Brown sugar 1 c Mashed banana
1/2 c Chopped peanuts

Preheat oven to 325 F. Combine flour, salt, baking powder, baking soda, milk, oats, sugar, nuts, raisins and prunes in large bowl. Blend with fork. Beat eggs until foamy. Add oil, molasses, juice and bananas. Add mix to dry ingredients. Pour into 2 8x4 greased loaf pans. Bake at 325 F one hour (for muffins, grease tins and fill 2/3 full, bake 350 F for 20 minutes)Cool slightly before removing from pan. You may substitute raw chopped apples, grated carrots, applesauce or grated zucchini for bananas.

Title: BAKING POWDER BISCUITS
Categories: Breads, Rolls
Servings: 12
2 c Flour 1/2 ts Salt
3 ts Baking powder 3/4 c Milk
1/4 c Shortening

Sift dry ingredients into bowl, Cut in shortening until like coarse crumbs. Make a well, pour in milk all at once. Stir quickly with fork just until dough follows fork around bowl, Turn out onto lightly floured work surface.(,,dough is soft) Knead gently 10 or 12 strokes. Roll or pat down 1/2 inch thick. Dip cutter in flour. Bake on ungreased sheet at 450 F for 12-15 minutes.

Title: CHALLAH BREAD
Categories: Breads, Ethnic
Servings: 1
1 pk Active dry yeast Egg

1/4 c Warm water(105-115 F) 1 tb Shortening
1/2 c Lukewarm water 2 3/4 c Flour
1 tb Sugar Egg yolk
1 ts Salt 2 tb Cold water

Dissolve yeast in 115 F water. Stir in lukewarm water, sugar, salt, egg, shortening and 1 1/4 cup flour. Beat until smooth. Mix in remaining flour to make dough easy to handle. Turn dough out on floured work surface, knead until smooth and elastic(5 min) Round up dough in greased bowl, turn over to grease top. Cover, let rise until doubled in bulk, 1 1/2-2 hours. Punch dough down, divide into 3 equal parts. Roll each part into strand 14 inches long. Place strands close together on lightly greased cookie sheet. Braid gently and loosely. Don't stretch. Fasten ends, tuck under securely., Brush braid with shortening. Let rise until doubled in bulk, 40-50 minutes. Beat egg yolk and cold water until blended, brush over braid. Bake at 375 F for 25-30 minutes, or until golden.

Title: WHITE BREAD

Categories: Breads
Servings: 1

1/2 c Lukewarm water(110 F) 1 ts Salt
1 pk Active dry yeast 3 c Flour
1/2 c Hot milk Egg yolk
2 tb Butter 1 tb Milk
1 ts Sugar

Sprinkle yeast over lukewarm water. Leave 5 minutes. Heat milk, stir in butter, sugar and salt. Cool to room temperature. Combine all ingredients. Knead dough until it becomes smooth and elastic, and put into lightly oiled bowl. Cover and rise 1 1/2 hours, Knead again 5 minutes and shape into loaf. Put dough in buttered and floured pan. Rise 1 hour. Preheat oven to 350 F Brush dough with egg yolk and milk mixture. Bake loaf one hour. Remove from pan.

Title: PUMPERNICKLE BREAD
Categories: Breads
Servings: 2

2 pk Active dry yeast 2 c Whole rye flour(100%)
1 1/4 c Warm water 2 1/4 c White flour
2 ts Salt 2 ts Cornmeal
1/3 c Molasses Egg white
1 tb Caraway seeds 3/4 ts Caraway seed
1 tb Shortening

Dissolve yeast in water. Add salt, molasses,caraway seed and shortening. Stir Place rye flour and 2 c white flour in small bowl, blend using large spoon. Gradually add flour to liquid mixture. Use hands to blend in flour at end. Add remaining 1/4 white flour, if necessary to make dough easy to handle. Knead 5-8 minutes on floured work surface until elastic and not sticky. Place in greased bowl, cover and let rise 1-1 1/2 hours. Punch down, divide in two and place on floured surface. Shape each piece into long narrow loaf, about 14 inches long and 1 1/2 inch diameter. Lightly grease inside of French Bread pan. Sprinkle cornmeal in each section. Shake pan to distribute. Place loaves in pan. Make sure loaves do no come any closer than 1 1/2 inch to ends of pan. With sharp knife, make 3-4 diagonal 1/4" deep slashes on the top of each loaf. Brush with egg white, and sprinkle with let over caraway seed. DO NOT COVER! Let rise 30 minutes to double. Bake in preheated 350 F oven for 30-35 minutes. Remove from pan AT ONCE

Title: CINNAMON SWIRL BREAD
Categories: Breads
Servings: 2

1 pk Active dry yeast 1/4 c Shortening

1/2 c Warm water 6 1/4 c Sifted flour
2 c Scalded milk,cooled 1/2 c Sugar
1/3 c Sugar 1 tb Cinnamon
2 ts Salt 1 1/2 ts Water

Soften yeast in water. Combine milk, sugar, salt and shortening. Cool to lukewarm. Stir in 2 cups flour. Beat well. Add yeast, mix. Add enough flour to make moderately stiff dough. Turn out onto floured work surface, knead 8-10 minutes until smooth and satiny. Shape into ball, place in greased bowl, turn once to grease top. Cover, let rise until doubled in bulk, 1 ¼ hours. Punch down. Cut dough into 2 portions, roll dough to two 15x7 inch rectangles. Combine 1/2 sugar, cinnamon, spread half over each bread. Roll into loaves. Place in greased and floured 9x5x3 inch loaf pans. Cover and let rise until doubled in bulk (60 minutes) Bake in preheated 375 F oven for 30 minutes

Title: REFRIGERATOR ROLLS

Categories: Breads, Rolls
Servings: 12
1 pk Active dry yeast 1/4 c Shortening
1/4 c Warm water 1 ts Salt
1 c Scalded milk 3 1/2 c Sifted flour
1/4 c Sugar Egg

Soften yeast in water. Combine milk,sugar,shortening and salt cool to lukewarm. Add 1 1/2 cups flour, beat well. Beat in yeast and egg. Gradually add remaining flour, beating well. Place in greased bowl, turning once to grease surface. Cover, chill at least 2 hours, or up to 4-5 days. About 2 hours before serving, shape dough as desired on floured work surface. Cover, let rise until doubled in bulk.(1 1/4 hours) Bake on greased baking sheet or muffin pans in 400 F oven for 12-15 minutes

Title: TOMATO BREAD

Categories: Breads, Vegetables
Servings: 2

2 c Tomato juice 1 ts Salt
1/2 c Tomato sauce 3/4 ts Oregano
2 tb Olive oil 1/2 ts Dry basil
6 1/2 c Flour 1/4 ts Rosemary
2 pk Active dry yeast 1/4 ts Pepper
3 tb Brown sugar 2 Cloves crushed garlic

Lightly grease large bowl and two loaf pans with olive oil. In small saucepan, heat juice, sauce and 2 tbsp olive oil to 120 F. Combine 3 cups flour with yeast and remaining ingredients. Pour in tomatoe mix and beat 3 minutes. Gradually add remaining flour, mixing by hand, if necessary, until it holds together enough to turn out on floured surface. The dough is quite sticky, and yuou may need to add a little more flour, but not too much, or you will have a dry bread. Knead about 5 minutes, until dough smooths out, place in greased bowl, cover and let rise 1 hour. Punch dough down, let rest 15 minutes, then shape into 2 loaves, and place in pans. Cover pans and let rise 45 minutes.Preheat oven to 375 F Bake loaves 10 minutes, reduce heat to 350 F and bake 30-40 minutes longerBread is done when loaf sounds hollow when thumped with knuckle. Tip loaves out immediately onto wire rack to cool

Title: TRADITIONAL SWEET ROLL DOUGH

Categories: Breads, Rolls
Servings: 1

2 pk Active dry yeast 1 ts Salt
1/2 c Warm water 2 Eggs
1/2 c Scalded milk, cooled to luke 1/2 c Butter or margarine, softene
1/2 c Sugar 5 c Flour

Dissolve yeast in water. Stir in milk, sugar,salt eggs,margarine and 2 ½ cups flour. Beat until smooth. Mix enough flour to make dough easy to handle. Knead 5 minutes. Place in greased bowl, turn greased side up(Dough can be refrigerated 3-4 days) Cover, let rsie until doubled in bulk 2 hours. Punch down and shape into whatever

Title: SWEDISH RYE BREAD

Categories: Breads
Servings: 2
1 pk Active dry yeast 1 1/2 c Hot water
1/4 c Warm water 2 1/2 c Rye flour,stirred
1/4 c Brown sugar 3 tb Caraway seed
1/4 c Light molasses 4 c Sifted flour
1 tb Salt 2 tb Grated orange peel(opt.)
2 tb Shortening

Soften yeast in warm water. In large bowl, combine sugar, molasses,salt and shrotening. Add hot water and stir until sugar dissolves. cool to lukewarm. Stir in rye flour, beat well. Add softened yeast, and caraway or orange peel, mix well. Stir in enough flour to make a moderately stiff dough.Knead on well floured work surface until samooth and satiny (10 minutes) Place dough in greased bowl, turn once to grease top. Cover, let rise until doubled in bulk (2 hours) Punch down. Turn out onto a lightly floured work surface, divide into 2 portions. Shape each into a smooth ball. Cover, let rest 10 minutes. Pat dough in 2 round loaves, place on greased baking sheet. Cover, let rise until doubled in bulk (2 hours) Bake at 375 F for 25-30 minutes. Place foil loosely over tops last 10 minutes. For soft crust, brush with melted butter. Cool on wire racks.

Title: KING ARTHUR'S EASY BEST LOAF

Categories: Breads
Servings: 2
1 tb Sugar 2 c Warm water
1 tb Salt 6 c Flour
1 pk Active dry yeast

Mix yeast,sugar,salt and water together. let stand until salt sugar and yeast are dissolved. Gradually add flour to liquid and mix thouroughly, until dough pulls form bowl sides. Turn ontofloured work surfaceand knead 5 minutes, Let dough rest while you grease bowl. Knead dough again 2-3 minutes, Place dough in bowl, turn once to grease top. Cover with damp towel and keep warm until doubled in bulk(1-2 hours) Punch down dough and knead briefly to get out any air pockets. Cut in half, shape into 2 Italian or french style loafs. Put on cookie sheet sprinkled with cornmeal. Rest 5 minutes. Lightly slash tops 3 times diagonally and brush with cold water. Place on rack in cold oven with roasting pan full of boiling water below.Bake 400 F for 30-45 minutes until crust is golden brown and sounds hollow to the touch,

Title: **FRENCH BREAD**

Categories: Breads
Servings: 2
1 pk Active dry yeast 1 tb Butter
1 1/2 c Water 5 c Flour
1 tb Sugar 2 tb Cornmeal
1 1/2 ts Salt

Dissolve yeast in warm water(110 F) Add sugar and salt, butter (melted) and 2 cups flour, Beat with spoon until mixed. Gradually add remaining flour, until dough is easy to handle. Knead on lightly floured work surface 5 minutes, until elastic, not sticky. Cover, let rise until doubled in bulk. Punch down on floured work surface, divide in half. Shape into loaves. Lightly grease French bread oan, put cornmela in and shake to coat all surfaces. Put each loaf into each section. Make sure loaves don't come any closer than 1 inch of end of pan. With sharp knife, make 3 or 4 diagonal slashes on top of loaves. DO NOT COVER. Let rise in warm place until doubled in bulk. Bake in preheated oven (375 F) 25-30 minutes. Remove from pan AT ONCE!

Title: PEPPERONI BREAD,PAT MCCLAY'S
Categories: Breads, Cheese/eggs
Servings: 1

1 pk Frozen Bread dough (1 loaf) 1/4 lb Provolone cheese
1/2 lb Slicing pepperoni

Split defrosted loaf in half and roll out to about 8x13 inches. Layer
Pepperoni, then provolone on each sheet. Roll up length wise, tucking in ends. Bake 400 F 20-25 minutes .

Title: BREAD STICKS
Categories: Breads
Servings: 24

1 pk Active dry yeast 1 c Lukewarm water
1/4 c Warm water 3 1/2 c Sifted flour
1 1/2 ts Salt Egg white

Soften yeast in water. Combine salt and lukewarm water, beat in 1 cup flour. Blend in softened yeast, stir in 2 1/4 to 2 1/2 cups flour, enough to make a moderatelyu stiff dough. Turn out onto floured work surface, Knead 10-15 minutes, until elastic, Knead in remaining flour. Place dough in lightly greased bowl, turn once to grease top. Let rise until doubled in bulk (60 minutes)Punch down. Let rise until doubled in bulk again.(45Minutes) Divide into 2 portions. Divide each half dough into 12 equal parts. Roll each piece about 12 inches long and 1/2 inch in diameter. Place 1 inch apart on greased baking sheet and brush with a mix of water, slightly beaten egg white. Let rise uncovered until doubled in bulk(60 minutes) Brush again with egg mix. Sprinkle with salt. Place large shallow pan on lower rack oof preheated 400 F Oven, fill with boiling water. Bake dough at 400 F for 15 minutes. Brush again with egg mix, and bake an additional 10-15 minutes.

Title: BANANA BREAD

Categories: Breads, Fruits
Servings: 1
2 tb Shortening 1/2 ts Baking soda
3/4 c Sugar 3 c Flour
1 ts Salt 3 ts Baking poder
1 Egg 2 Mashed bananas
1/2 c Milk

Mix shrotening, sugar and egg together. Stir in milk. Add dry ingredients and beat until smooth. Fold in bananas, then spoon into a greased loaf pan. Bake for 1 hour, at 350 F, or until brown and firm.

Title: BASIC BEER BREAD

Categories: Breads, Quickbreads
Servings: 1
3 c Flour 1 cn Beer
3 3/4 ts Baking powder 1 tb Honeu
2 1/4 ts Salt

Grease loaf pan. Combine flour, baking powder, salt, beer, and honey in large bowl, stir together until well mixed. Bake in preheated 350 F oven for 45 minutes. Turn on rack and cool.

Title: SWEDISH TEA RING

Categories: Breads
Servings: 2
2 CAKES OF YEAST 1 c Milk,scalded, then cooled
1/4 c Lukewarm water 1 ts Lemon rind,grated
1/4 c Shortening 5 c Flour
1/2 c Sugar Melted butter
1 ts Salt Brown Sugar
2 Beaten eggs Cinnamon

Soften yeast cakes in water. Add shortening, sugar and salt to scalded milk, cool to lukewarm. Add yeast, eggs, rind and enough flour to make a stiff batter. Beat well. Add flour to make a soft dough. Turn out on floured work surface, and knead until satiny. Grease bowl, Put dough in bowl, turn to grease top, Cover and rise until doubled in bulk. Punch down. Shape into 2 retangles about 1/4 inch thick. Brush with melted butter. Sprinkle with brown sugar and cinnamon. Roll like jelly roll, and shape into rings. Place on greased baking sheet, cut with scizzors at one inch intervals, ALMOST through rings. Turn slices slightly. Cover and let rise until doubled. Bake in 375 F oven for 25-30 minutes. Cover with Coffee Cake Icing.

Title: WHOLE WHEAT MOLASSES BREAD

Categories: Breads
Servings: 2
2 3/4 c Whole wheat flour 1/4 c Brown sugar
1 c Flour 2 tb Shortening
2 pk Active dry yeast 1 tb Salt
1 3/4 c Water 1 c White flour
1/2 c Dark molasses

In large bowl, combine whole wheat,white flour and yeast. In saucepan,heat water, molasses, brown sugar, shrotening and salt until warm (115 F), stirring constantly. Add to dry mix in bowl. Beat al low speed 1/2 minutes, scraping sides.

Beat 3 minutes high speed. By hand, stir in 1/2-1 cup white flour to make stiff dough. Turn out on light floured work surface, knead until smooth. Shape into ball. Place in greased bowl, turn, cover, let rise until doubled in bulk(1 1/2 hours).Punch down, divide in half. Cover, let rest 10 minutes. Shape into 2 slightly flatten 6 inch balls. Put on greased baking sheet. Cover, let rise until doubled in bulk(45 minutes) Bake at 375 F for 30-35 minutes. For chewy crust, brush each loaf with warm water several times during the last 10-15 minutes of baking. Cool.

Title: BABKAS #1
Categories: Breads, Ethnic
Servings: 2
3/4 c Butter,soft 1 tb Lemon rind
1/2 c Sugar 1 c Milk,room temperature
10 Egg yolks 5 1/2 c Flour
2 pk Active dry yeast 1 c Golden raisins
1/4 c Warm water Confectioner's sugar
1 ts Salt

In large bowl, cream butter and sugar until light and fluffy. Beat in yolk, one at a time, until pale and fluffy. In small bowl, soften yeast in water,beat in egg mix salt,peel, milk and yeast. Slowly beat in 5 1/2 cups of flour until a soft dough forms. Turn out on lightly floured work surface, knead 8-10 minutes, until smooth and elastic. Knead in raisins. Place in greased bowl. Grease top. Let rise 1 hour, or until doubled in bulk. Punch down, divide in half. Place in 2 greased and floured 8 inch fluted pans, let rise until double in bulk (covered) Bake in 350 F oven 25-30 minutes, or until well browned. Invert on rack. Sprinkle with confectioner's sugar. Tastes better eaten within a couple of days. Two Babkas, 10 servings each.

Title: HONEY OATMEAL BREAD

Categories: Breads
Servings: 2

1 1/2 c Water 2 pk Active dry yeast
1/3 c Butter 2 Eggs
1/2 c Honey 1 tb Water
6 1/2 c Flour Egg white
1 c Oats,quick cooking Oatmeal
2 ts Salt

Combine water, honey and butter in small saucepan. Heat over low heat until liquids are very warm(120F)Place 5 cups flour, oats, salt and yeast in Bowl. Attach bowl and dough hook. Turn to speed two and mix 30 seconds. Gradually add warm liquids to flour mixture, about 1 minute. Add eggs and mix an additional minute.Continue on speed two, add remaining flour, ½ cup at a time, until dough clings to hook and cleans sides of bowl. Knead on speed two for 3-5 minutes longer. Place in greased bowl, turning once to grease top. Cover, let rise in warm place , from draft, until doubled in bulk, about 1 hour. Punch down dough and divide in half. Shape each half into a loaf and place in greased loaf pans. Cover, let rise in warm place,free from drafts, until doubled in bulk, about one hour. Combine egg white and water. Brush tops of loaves with mixture. sprinkle with oatmeal, bake at 375 F for 40 minutes. remove from pans immediately, and cool on
wire racks. Yields:two loaves.

Title: CRUSTY PIZZA DOUGH

Categories: Breads, Main dish
Servings: 1

1 pk Active dry yeast 2 ts Olive oil

1 c Warm water 3 1/2 c Flour
1/2 ts Salt Cornmeal

Dissolve yeast in warm water in warmed bowl. Add salt, olive oil and 2 ½ cups flour. Attach bowl and dough hook, Turn to speed 2 and mix 2 minutes. Continuing on speed 2, add remaining flour, 1/2 cup at a time, until dough clings to hook and cleans side of bowl. Knead on speed two for 5 minutes. Place in greased bowl, turning to grease top. Cover, let rise in warm place, free from draft, until doubled in bulk, about 1 hour. Punch dough down. Brush a 14 inch pizza pan with oil, sprinkle with cornmeal. Press dough across bottom of pan, forming a collar around edge to hold filling. Top with desired fillings. Bake at 450 F for 15 to 20 minutes. Yield:one 14 inch pizza.

Title: FOCACCIA

Categories: Breads, Ethnic
Servings: 35

-----------------**DOUGH**----------------------------------

1 pk Active dry yeast 1 1/2 ts Salt
2 c Warm water 3 tb Olive oil
5 1/2 c Flour

-----------------**TOPPINGS**----------------------------------

Olive oil Fresh sage,rosemary+thyme
Kosher or sea salt Sprinkle yeast over 1 cup warm water in large mixer bowl. Stir briefly, the let stand 5 minutes to dissolve. Attach paddle or dough hook to mixer. At low speed,stir in 2 cups flour and salt, beat until smooth.(1 minute) (Or combine ingredients in large bowl and beat vigorously with wooden spoon 2 minutes)Add remaining 1 cup warm water and oil and blend. Add enough flour, 1/2 cup at a time, to make a soft dough that begins to pull away from sides of bowl On lightly floured work surface, knead dough until smooth and elastic, 8-10 minutes. Place in

large, lightly greased bowl, turning once to grease top. Cover with kitchen towel and let rise in a warm, draft-free place, until doubled in bulk, 1-1 1/4 hours. Remove dough from bowl, and gently knead one minute. Lightly oil a 15x10 1/2 inch jelly-roll pan. Shape dough into 12x8 inch rectangle with rolling pin. Carefully transfer to prepared pan, stretching to gently to edges of pan with fingers. Press top of dough with fingertips, leaving 1/2 inch deep indentations. Cover and let rise 30 minutes. Preheat oven to 425 F. Adjust 1 oven rack to lowest position. Place shallow baking pan on top rack of oven. If using a baking stone, place in cold oven and preheat 30 minutes before baking. Press dough again with fingers, and brush with 1 tablespoon olive oil. Sprinkle with 1 teaspoon kosher salt and 2 tablespoons chopped assorted fresh herbs or 1 teaspoon dried herbs. Just before baking, carefully place 1 cup ice cubes in baking pan on top oven rack and immediately place dough on baking stone, or lowest oven rack. Bake 20-30 minutes, until top is golden and bottom sounds hollow when removed from pan and tapped on bottom. Remove Focaccia from pan and transfer to wire rack. While still warm, brush top with another 2 tablespoons olive oil. Cool. Cut into 5x1 1/2 inch pieces. Makes 35

Title: FOUGASSE
Categories: Breads, Ethnic
Servings: 24

----------------FOCACCIA DOUGH--------------------
1 tb Cornmeal Whole sage leaves
1 tb Olive oil 1 ts Kosher salt

Prepare dough as directed for Focaccia. Lightly oil 2 cookie sheets and sprinkle each with 1 tablespoon yellow cornmeal. Divide dough in half, shape each piece into a ball. Stretch each with rolling pin itno 8x4 inch oval. Transfer dough to prepared pans. With small sharp knife, cut 2 ½ inch slit in center of each oval. Cut 8 more slits in circle around center. With fingertips,carefully stretch dough into 12x9 inch oval. Cover and let rise 30 minutes. Preheat oven to 425 F, and prepare oven as directed with Focaccia.Brush each Fougasse with 1 tablespoon olive oil and decorate each with whole sage leaves. Sprinkle each with 1 teaspoon kosher salt. Bake one pan at a time, 18-20 minutes, until golden. Cool on wire racks. Makes two breads,12 slices each.

Title: CINNAMON NUGGETS
Categories: Breads
Servings: 80
1 pk Refrigerated soft breadstick Cinnamon Sugar
(11 ounces)
Preheat oven to 375 F. Unroll dough, cut strips crosswise into 10 pieces. Roll dough in cinnamon sugar. Place on lightly greased baking sheet. Bake at 375 F for 5 minutes. remove from baking sheet immediately. Makes 80 Nuggets To make cinnamon sugar, combine 1 teaspoon ground cinnamon with 3 tablespoons sugar Parmesan Nuggets: Omit cinnamon sugar, roll dough in Parmesan cheese.

Title: RHUBARB BREAD
Categories: Breads, Fruits
Servings: 1
1 c Brown sugar 1 ts Vanilla
1/2 c Sugar 2 1/2 c Flour
2/3 c Oil 1 ts Baking soda
2 Eggs 1/2 ts Nutmeg
1 c Sour milk 2 1/2 c Rhubarb,diced
1 ts Salt
Mix well and pour into 2 greased 9x5 inch loaf pans. Before baking, top

each loaf with 1 tsp melted margarine and sprinklw with 1 tablespoon sugar
over each loaf. Bake at 350 F for about 1 hour

Title: SAUDI ARABIAN PITA BREAD
Categories: Breads
Servings: 12
1 pk Active dry yeast 1 1/2 ts Salt
3 3/4 c Flour 1 1/4 c Warm water
1/4 c Shortening

In large mixer bowl soften yeast in warm water. Add 2 cups flour, shortening and salt. Beat at low speed of electric mixer for 1/2 minute, scraping bowl. Beat 3 minutes at high speed. Stir in as much remaining flour as you can mix in with a spoon. Turn onto lightly floured work surface. Knead in enough remaining flour to make a moderately soft dough that is smoooth and elastic.(5 minutes) Cover, let rest in a warm place about 15 minutes. Divide into 12 equal partions. Roll each between floured hands into a very smooth ball. Cover with a damp cloth, let rest 10 minutes. Using fingers, gently flatten balls. Cover, let rest 10 minutes.(keep dough pieces covered until ready to use.) On well floured surface lightly roll one piece of dough at a time into a circle 7 inches in diameter, turning dough over once. Do not stretch,puncture or crease dough(Work with enough flour so dough does not stick) Place on baking sheet. Bake rounds, 2 at a time, in a 450 F oven about 3 minutes or until dough is puffed and softly set. Turn over with a spatula, bake about 2 more mintes, or until dough is light brown. Repeat with remaining dough, baking one batch before rolling the next batch. To serve, slice bread crosswise, fill pocket with desired filling Makes 12 rounds.

Title: PARKER HOUSE ROLLS

Categories: Breads
Servings: 6
1 pt Milk 2 1/2 pt Flour
4 tb Shortening 1 ts Salt
2 tb Sugar 1 Yeast cake
Scald milk, cool. Dissolve yeast cake in lukewarm milk, add sugar, 1 1/2
pts. flour, and shortening. Rise in warm place untill light. Add salt and rest of flour. Knead well. Place in greased bowl, rise untill double in bulk. Roll 1/2 inch thick. Brush with melted butter, fold over. Let rise untill double in bulk. Bake at 400F for 20 minutes.

Title: ONION PARMESAN BREAD
Categories: Breads, Vegetables, Cheese/eggs
Servings: 2
1 pk Active dry yeast 4 c Flour
1/4 c Warm water 2 tb Butter
1 1/2 ts Salt 3/4 c Chopped onion
2 tb Soft margarine 2 tb Parmesan cheese
1 Egg, slightly beaten 1 ts Poppy seed (opt.)
1 c Scalded milk 1/2 ts Garlic salt
Dissolve yeast in waterIn large bowl, combine yeast, sugar, salt butter, egg, milk and 2 cups flour. Beat with spoon until mixed. Gradually add flour until dough can be handled. Knead 5 minutes or until elastic. Grease bowl, cover douch with plastic, let rise 1 1/4 hour in warm place.
Meanwhile,prepare filling. Melt butter in small saucepan. Add onions, and saute until just tender (5 minutes) Combine cheese, poppy seed,and garlic salt,set both mixtures aside. When dough has risen, punch down, and place on floured work surface. Divide in 2. Roll each piece into a square 12"x12". Spoon half of fillings on each piece of dough.

Spread, roll up like jelly roll, seal. Place loaves, seam side down, on French bread pan. Cover and rise 45 minutes, or until doubled in bulk. Uncover, bake in preheated 350 F oven for 25-30 minutes, until golden. Remove from pan at once~---- YUM!

Title: BOSTON BROWN BREAD (A MUST WITH BAKED BEANS)

Categories: Breads
Servings: 10
1/2 c Flour 3 c Whole wheat flour
3/4 c Sugar 3/4 c Dark molasses
1 1/2 ts Salt 1 Egg
1 1/2 ts Baking soda 2 c Milk
1/2 c Corn Meal 1/2 c Melted shortening
Sift flour, baking soda, sugar, and salt together.
Mix in corn meal and whole wheat flour. Add remaining ingredients, mixing
only untill all flour is moistened. Pour into 2 greased 9x5x3 inch loaf pans. Bake at 300F for 1 hour and 15 minutes. Remove from pans and cool.

Title: KILLER BREAD

Categories: Breads, Ethnic, Cheese/eggs, Sourdough
Servings: 4
1 c Mayonnaise 1 lb Round sourdough bread
1 c Parmesan cheese, grated Butter
1 1/2 ts Garlic, minced 2 tb Fresh basil or 2t dried
Preheat broiler. Halve bread horizontally. Mix mayo, parmesan and garlic in large bowl. Arrange bread cut side up on large baking sheet. Butter bread. Broil until crisp and brown. Spread parmesan mixture over cut sides of bread. Broil until to is puffed and golden brown. Sprinkle with chopped basil. Cut bread into wedges and serve. Source:

Bon Appetit

Title: LIGHT AND FLUFFY WAFFLES
Categories: Breads
Servings: 5
2 EGGS 3/4 c CHOPPED PECANS (OPTIONAL)
2 1/4 c MILK 1 1/2 ts CINNAMON (OPTIONAL)
3/4 c OIL OR MELTED SHORTENING 2 c PEL'D & DICED APPLES (OPT'L)
2 1/2 c FLOUR CRUMBLED BACON (OPTIONAL)
4 ts BAKING POWDER 3 tb COCOA AND
3/4 ts SALT 2 tb CHOC CHIPS (OPTIONAL)
In large bowl beat eggs until light. Stir in milk and vegetable oil or melted shortening. Sift together flour, baking powder and salt and add to milk mixture. Stir until smooth. Stir in either pecans, cinnamon, apples, bacon or cocoa and chocolate chips, if desired. Pour batter onto center of hot waffle iron, cover and bake until steaming stops.

Title: BUCHTA (POPPYSEED BREAD)
Categories: Breads
Servings: 7
1 Cake compressed yeast OR 6 Egg yolks
1 pk Active dry yeast + 1 tsp 1/2 pt Heavy cream (1 cup)
1 c Lukewarm milk 6 c Flour
1/2 lb Butter(1 cup) 1 ts Salt
1/2 c Sugar
-----------**FILLING**---------------------------------
Melted butter 1/2 c Sugar
1 1/2 c Poppyseeds(ground,please) Vanilla
Soften yeast in lukewarm milk. Cream butter, add sugar gradually, beating until light and fluffy. Add egg yolks, and beat. Add uyeast-milk mixture and heavy cream;blend. Sift

together flour and salt and add to egg yolk mixture. Knead until the dough no longer sticks to your hands.(this can be done in a mixer with a dough hook too.)Put the dough in a greased bowl, cover and let rise until doubled in bulk. Divide dough into 7 balls. On a floured surface, roll each ball into a rectangle 1/4" thick. Spread with your favorite filling and roll up as you would a jelly roll. Place the rolls on a greased cookie sheet(1 roll per pan), cover and let rise until doubled. Bake at 325 F for 30 minutes. Filling: After you roll out the dough, brush with melted butter then mix poppyseeds and sugar together and spread over the dough. Drizzle with melted butter to which some vanilla has been added and then roll up.

Title: PENNSYLVANIA DUTCH PRETZELS

Categories: Breads
Servings: 12
4 c Unsifted flour 1 qt Water
1 ts Sugar 3 tb Baking soda
1 pk Active dry yeast Coarse salt
1 1/2 c Very warm water (120F-130F)

In large bowl of mixer, mix 1 1/2 cups flour, the yeast, sugar and 1/2 tsp salt. With mixer at low, add 1 1/2 cups very warm water.Beat 3 minutes at medium. Gradually add the rest of the flour. Turn out onto floured board and knead 5 minutes.,Place in a greased bowl, turn greased side up. Cvover, let rise 45 minutes to an hour. Punch down, turn out onto board. Roll pieces of dough out into pencil shapeds and knot, forming preztel shape. Cover, and let rise on floured obard for 30 minutes. Boil 1 quart water and the baking soda in a skillet. Put each preztel in the water and simmer 20 seconds. Place on well greased cookie sheet, salt and bake at 400 F for 15 minutes.

Title: OLD MILWAUKEE RYE

Categories: Breads
Servings: 2

-----------------**SPONGE**-----------------------------------

1 pk Active dry yeast 2 c Rye flour
1 1/2 c Warm water 2 tb Caraway seed

---------------**BREAD**-----------------------------------

1 pk Active dry yeast 1 tb Salt
1 c Warm water 1 c Rye flour
1/4 c Molasses 6 c Bread flour
1 Egg 3 tb Butter

SPONGE PREPARATION: Dissolve 1 pk yeast in the warm water. Stir in rye flour and caraway seed. Cover bowl snugly with plastic wrap and let stand for 1-3 days. BAKE DAY PREPARATION: Sprinkle the remaining package of yeast and remaining 1 cup water on the sponge mixture, blend well. Add molasses, caraway seeds,egg,salt and rye flour and 2 cups of the bread flour. Beat until smooth. add butter. Stir in remaining flour and mix well either with your hands or in a mixer with dough hooks. Knead for 5-10 minutes. Put in a greased bowl and let rise until doubled in bulk (about 1 hour) Punch down and let rest 10 minutes. Shape into loaves or put into loaf pans, cover and let rise until doubled. Carefully make slashes on the top of each loaf with a sharp knife or a razor blade, and brush with a beaten egg mixed with a tablespoon of milk. Bake at 375 F for about 40 minutes. this will make 2 large loaves or 3 smaller ones.

Title: QUICK RYE-BATTER BUNS

Categories: Breads
Servings: 24

3 c Flour 1 Eggs
2 pk Quick-rising yeast 1 tb Caraway seed

2 c Milk 2 c Rye flour
1/2 c Dark brown sugar Milk
3 tb Cooking oil Caraway seed (optional)
1 1/2 ts Salt

1. In a large mixer bowl, combine the flour and yeast.
2. In a saucepan, heat the 2 c milk, brown sugar, oil and salt until warm (120-130 degrees), stirring constantly. Add to the flour mixture. Add the eggs and the caraway seed. 3. Beat the batter with electric mixer on low speed for 30 seconds, scraping sides of bowl. Beat the batter on high speed for 3 minutes. Return to low speed and beat in rye flour. 4. Fill the greased muffin pans half full. cover and let the dough rise until double, about 25 minutes. 5. Bake in 400 degree oven for 10 minutes. Brush the buns with milk. Sprinkle the tops with caraway seed, if desired. Bake for 5 to 10 minutes more or until done. Remove the buns from the pans; cool. Makes about 24.

Title: ANGEL ROLLS
Categories: Breads, Rolls
Servings: 18
2 pk Yeast;dry active 4 c Flour
1/2 c Oil 1 ts Salt
2 tb Sugar 1/2 ts Soda
1 1/2 c Buttermilk

Sift dry ingredients together into a mixing bowl. Add the softened yeast. milk and oil. Beat well. let rise punch down shape into rolls let rise till doubled and bake 350 for 15 to 20 minutes.

Title: KAVRINGS
Categories: Breads, Ethnic
Servings: 24
4 ts Baking soda

1 c Butter 5 3/4 c Flour
1/2 c Sugar 10 Cardamon;seeds crushed
1 c Milk:whole 1/2 ts Salt
1 Egg

Method; Cream butter and sugar; add slightly beaten egg, then the milk and lastly the dry ingredients, which have been sifted together. stir as little as possible. turn the dough out onto a floured board, shape into small buns and bake 10 minutes in hot oven (425) when done cut each roll in half and return to oven. bake in a slow oven(200) till light browned. these rusks are delicious served with hot fruit soup. This is a recipe from grandma cookbook published in 1920

Title: SWEDISH SCONES

Categories: Breads, Ethnic
Servings: 12
4 c Flour
1 pk Yeast 5 tb Butter
1 c Milk 1 ts Salt
3 Eggs 1/2 c Sugar

METHOD:Dissolve yeast in 1 tbl warm milk with 1 t of sugar. Scald milk, add butter, sugar and salt. When luke warm add to yeast. Add beaten eggs, then add 2 cups flour and beat thoroughly. add rest of flour gradually. Cover and place in ice box over night. Four hours before baking remove from fridge. Divide dough into 4 parts roll each 1/4 inch thick. Brush with melted butter. cut into segments like a pie, roll each strip up begining at wide end and roll to point. Place on greased baking sheet, cover and let rise 4 hours. Bake in moderate oven(350)for 20 minutes or till golden brown. this is from Grandma 1920

Title: CUBAN BREAD

Categories: Breads, Ethnic

Servings: 1

5 c To 6 cups bread flour aprox. 2 1/2 c Hot water,120 to 130 degs.

2 pk Dry yeast Corn meal

1 tb Salt Water

2 tb Sugar

Sprinkle the cornmeal on a non stick baking sheet. Place 4 cups of flour in large mixing bowl,add yeast,salt,and sugar.Stir until all are well blended.Pour in the hot water and beat 100 strong strokes or three minutes with mixer dough hook. Gradually work enough of the remaining flour,using fingers if necessary,1/2 cup at a time,that the dough takes shape an no longer sticky. Sprinkle work surface with some of the remaining flour.Place dough on work surface,working in flour as you knead. Keep a dusting of flour between dough and working surface.Knead for 8 minutes by hand or with dough hook of mixer until it feels alive under your hands. Place dough in a greased bowl.Cover with plastic wrap and put in a warm place,80 to 100 degs,until double in bulk,about 15 minutes. Punch down dough,turn it out on work surface,cut into 2 pieces.Shape each piece into a round. Place on non stick baking sheet sprinkled with corn meal. With a sharpe knife or razor slash an x on each loaf: brush with water. Place baking sheets on middle shelf of cold oven.Place a large pan of hot water on shelf below. Heat oven to 400 deg.After 1/2 hour reduce oven to 375 deg. The bread will continue to rise while oven is heating. Bake for a total of 45 minutes.(Timing starts when you turn on the oven.) Loaves should sound hollow when baked.Cool before slicing.Bread will not keepbeyond a day or two,but freezes well and makes excellent toast when old.....

Title: PEPPERONI PIZZA BREAD

Categories: Breads, Ethnic
Servings: 2

1 tb Oil 1 ts Dried oregano, crumbled
2 lb Pkg frozen bread dough, thaw 1 ts Dehydrated onion flakes
1/2 lb Pepperoni, sliced 1/2 c Parmesan, grated
1 lb Mozzarella, grated Egg, beaten
1 tb Garlic powder Sesame seeds
1 ts Dried basil, crumbled

Makes 2 loaves. Brush 2 11x17" cookie sheets with oil. Divide dough in half. Roll 1 dough piece out to edges of 1 cookie sheet. Place half of pepperoni slices in crosswise rows on dough, leaving 1/2" borders at ends. Sprinkle with 1/2 mozzarella, 1/2 garlic, 1/2 basil, 1/2 oregano, ½ onion. Top with 1/2 parmesan. Starting at short end, roll up jelly roll fashion and turn seam side down on cookie sheet. Brush with egg. Slice crosswise slits in top of dough. Sprinkle with sesame seeds. Repeat with remaining ingredients. Preheat oven 400 deg. Bake until golden, about 25 mins. Slice loaves, serve hot. Can be prepared 1 week ahead. Wrap tightly and freeze. Thaw before baking. Source: Bon Appetit

Title: BAGELS

Categories: Breads
Servings: 12

1 pk Active dry yeast 1 c Milk
1/3 c Warm water 1 Egg; beaten with a little
1 ts Salt - water for glaze
4 c All-purpose flour Coarse salt, or poppy seeds
2 tb Sugar

Sprinkle the yeast over the warm water, stir, and let dissolve. Put the salt, flour, and 4 teaspoons of the sugar in the bowl of a food processor equipped with the dough blade. Pulse the mixture several times to mix it well. (This action aerates the ingredients. Combine the yeast mixture and milk in a measuring cup. With the motor running, pour the mixture through the feed tube. Knead until the mixture balls together and is no longer sticky, about 60 seconds. Lightly flour a large plastic bag, place the dough in it, squeeze out the air, and close the end of the bag with a twist tie. Let the dough rise until doubled, about 45 minutes. Punch it down. (At this point, the dough can be refrigerated for up to 4 days. Bring it to room temperature before proceeding.) Let the dough rest for 10 minutes. Pull off pieces of dough to form 12 2-inch balls. Poke a finger through the ball, making a hole the size of a golf ball. With your fingers, shape the bagel evenly. Put the bagels on a tray or cookie sheet, cover them with oiled plastic wrap, and let them rise until puffy, about 30 minutes. Preheat the oven to 400F. Bring 4 quarts of water to the boil in a wide pot. Add the remaining 2 tsp of sugar. Poach the bagels, 3 or 4 at a time, for 30 seconds. Turn them and poach for 30 seconds more. Remove them with a slotted spoon, let them drip briefly on a towel held under the spoon, and place them 1 inch apart on baking sheets. Brush each bagel with a little of the egg glaze. (At this point you may sprinkle on coarse salt, or poppy or sesame seeds). Bake until golden, about 15 minutes. Let cool on racks.

Title: GARLIC BUBBLE LOAF
Categories: Breads
Servings: 6

3 c Flour 2 tb Shortening
1 pk Instant dry yeast 1 Egg
1 tb Sugar 1/4 c Butter; melted
1 ts Salt 1 ts Paprika
1/2 c Milk 1/2 ts Garlic powder

1/2 c Water 1 tb Sesame seed
In lg. mixer bowl, combine 1 1/2 c. flour, yeast, sugar and salt; mix well. In saucepan heat milk, water and shortening until warm (shortening does not need to melt); add to flour mixture. Add egg. Blend at low speed until moistened; beat 3 minutes at med. speed. By hand, gradually stir in remaining flour to make a soft dough. Knead on floured surface 25-30 strokes. Divide dough into 12 parts; shape into balls. Combine melted butter, paprika and garlic powder; mix well. Dip balls into butter mixture; place in greased 9x5" loaf pan, using 6 balls on each layer. Sprinkle with seame seed. Cover; let rise in warm place until light and doubled, about 45 minutes. Bake at 375 for 40-45 minutes, until golden brown. Remove from pan; serve warm. This is a one-rise, garlic bread in a pull-apart bubble loaf. Makes 1 loaf.

Title: LANGOS- HUNGARIAN FRIED BREAD

Categories: Breads, Ethnic
Servings: 4
200 g Flour 1 tb Oil
2 Cooked, baked potato, mashed 1 ts Sugar
1/2 ts Salt 1 c Milk, lukewarm
1 pk Active dry yeast 1 c Oil, to fry

Let the yeast grow in 1/2 cup of lukewarm sweetned milk for 10 minutes. Add mixturte to the flour. Add one tablespoon of oil. Add the mashed potatoes. Add salt. Add as much warm milk as needed to make a soft bread dough. Work the dough well, for at least 15 minutes, until smooth. On a warm place let it rise for one hour(or until doubled in bulk) Make little balls from the dough and then flatten them in your hand by pulling it to the size of a large saucer. fry then in hot oil. Toppings: Sour cream, or grated cheese, or Feta cheese with fresh dill and sour cream. Or if you like sweet toppings, mashed strawberries with whipped cream, or vanilla custard, or apple sauce,etc.

Title: EPISCOPALIAN BANANA BREAD

Categories: Breads, Fruits
Servings: 1
1 1/2 c Flour 1/4 c Brown sugar
3 ts Baking powder 3/4 c Oatmeal
1/3 c Oil 1/2 ts Baking soda
2 ts Cinnamon 1/4 c Milk
1/2 c Sugar OR 2 c Mashed bananas
2 Eggs, well beaten

Mix everything in one bowl and stir it up. In greased and floured bread pan, cook at 350 F for 50-60 minutes. This is really better if left to sit overnight before eating, it's almost too moist to eat right away.

Title: BAHAMA BREAD

Categories: Breads, Fruits
Servings: 8
Tmbg12a 1/3 c MILK
2 c FLOUR 1 ts LEMON JUICE OR
1 ts BAKING SODA 1/2 ts VANILLA EXTRACT
1/2 ts SALT 1/2 c CHOPPED NUTS; OPTIONAL.
1/2 c BUTTER 2 Bananas; mashed
1 c SUGAR Banana; could use four
2 EGGS

PREHEAT OVEN TO 350 COMBINE FLOUR, BAKING SODA, AND SALT IN A BOWL. CREAM THE BUTTER IN A MIXING BOWL. GRADUALLY ADD THE SUGAR AND MIX TO WELL BLENDED. ADD THE EGGS AND THE BANANA MIX UNTIL WELL BLENDED. COMBINE THE MILK AND LEMON JUICE IN A LARGE BOWL. ALTERNATELY MIX THE

FLOUR MIXTURE INTO THE BANANA MIXTURE. ADD A LITTLE AT A TIME, BEGINNING AND ENDING WITH THE DRY INGREDIENTS. BLEND WELL AFTER EACH ADDITION. ADD NUTS. TURN THE BATTER INTO A HEAVILY BUTTERED 9 X 5 X 3 INCH LOAF PAN. BAKE FOR ONE HOUR OR UNTIL BREAD IS GOLDEN AND SPRINGS BACK WHEN TOUCHED. COOL IN PAN FOR TEN MINUTES. TAKE BREAD OUT OF PAN AND COOL COMPLETELY.

Title: BOSTON BAKED BROWN BREAD
Categories: Breads
Servings: 8
2 c Buttermilk,,1 c Whole wheat flour
1 c All-purpose flour 2 ts Baking soda
1 c Cornmeal 1 c Raisins
3/4 c Molasses
,,(or 2 C milk and 1 T lemon juice) Beat all ingredients in large mixing bowl for 2 minutes on medium speed. Pour into greased angel food pan. (I use a Bundt pan.) Bake in 325 F oven for 1 hour.

Title: WARM SPRINGS FRIED BREAD
Categories: Breads
Servings: 6
3 c Sifted all-purpose flour 1 ts Salt
1 tb Butter 2 tb Melted butter
2 ts Baking powder 1 ts Sugar
3/4 c (to 1c) Warm milk Fat for deep frying
Combine dry ingredients; cut in butter. Add enough warm milk to make a soft dough, easy to handle. Knead on floured board until dough is very smooth and soft but elastic. Do

not use a lot of extra flour. Divide dough into 6-8 balls and brush the tops with melted butter. Cover and let stand 30-45 minutes. Pat out each ball into a round, 5 or 6 inches in diameter and ¼ inch thick. Fry in deep fat (preheated to 365 degrees). Dough should rise immediately to surface. Cook until brown on one side, turn, and brown on other side being careful to not pierce crust. Drain on absorbent paper and serve hot.

Title: WHOLE WHEAT BATTER BREAD
Categories: Breads
Servings: 1
8 c Whole wheat flour 3 tb Soya flour
4 tb Honey-molasses 3 c Corn oil
3 tb Wheat germ 3 pk Yeast
3 1/2 c Very warm water 2 tb Salt

This recipe is for 2 loaves of bread. If one loaf is desired, use 2 packages yeast instead of 3 and cut all other ingredients in half. Wheat germ and soya flour may be omitted. Put flour in oven to warm, at lowest heat. In a VERY large bowl, dissolve yeast in 3/4 cup of very warm water. Add honey to yeast. Coat loaf pans well with margarine and flour. Add oil, 2-1/2 cups warm water, and 2T salt yeast. Add about 4c flour mixture and beat at medium speed for 2 minutes. Gradually add more flour, beating well. Dough should be sticky - if runny, add more flour. Put in pans, smoothing top and making sure dough is pushed into corners. Cover with hot, wet towel and let rise in warm place. Check bread in about 20 minutes and keep checking to be sure dough doesn't rise over lip of pan. When dough has risen ALMOST to lip of pan, bake at 450 degrees for about 40 mins. Remove from pan immediately and cool on rack.

Title: CORN LIGHTBREAD
Categories: Breads, Vegetables
Servings: 1
2 c Cornmeal 1 ts Salt
1 c All purpose flour 2 c Buttermilk or sour milk
1/2 c Sugar 3 tb Oil or bacon drippings
1 ts Baking soda

Combine dry ingredients; blend in milk and oil. Spoon into lightly greased 9" X 5" loaf pan. Let stand 10 minutes. Bake at 375 degrees for 35-40 mins; let cool 5 mins before removing from pan.

Title: CRANBERRY NUT BREAD
Categories: Breads, Quickbreads, Holidays, Fruits
Servings: 1
1 ts Salt
2 c Flour; sifted 1/2 ts Baking powder
3/4 c Orange juice 1/4 c Walnuts; chopped
1 c Sugar 1/4 c Shortening
1 tb Orange rind; grated 1 tb Flour
5 1/2 ts Baking powder 1 Egg; beaten
1 c Cranberries; chopped

Sift together 2C. flour; sugar, baking powder, salt and baking soda in a bowl. Cut in shortening until mixtuore resembles coarse meal. Combine egg, o.j. and orange rind in small bowl. Add to fry ingredients all at once; stir just till moistened. Combine cranberries, walnuts, and 1 tblsp. flour; stir into batter. Pout inyo greased and waxed-paper-lined 9x5x3" loaf pan. Bake in 350F oven 1 hour or until bread tests done. Cool in pan on rack 10 minutes. Remove from pan; cool on rack.. Makes 1 loaf.

Title: Sweet Bread, Portuguese
Categories: Breads, Hawaii

Servings: 2
1/4 c Water; warm 1/2 c Margerine
1 c Milk; scalded and cooled 5 c Flour
3/4 c Sugar 1 Eggs
1 ts Salt 2 pk Yeast
3 Eggs 1 ts Sugar

„DISSOLVE YEAST IN WARM WATER IN A LARGE BOWL. STIR IN MILK, 3/4 CUP SUGAR, SALT, 3 EGGS, MARGERINE, AND 3 CUPS FLOUR. BEAT UNTIL SMOOTH. STIR IN REMAINING FLOUR (MAY NEED UP TO A CUP MORE THAN CALLED FOR) UNTIL YOU HAVE A EASILY MANAGABLE DOUGH. „TURN OUT DOUGH ON FLOURED SURFACE; KNEAD 5 MINUTES. PLACE IN GREASED BOWL; TURN GREASED SIDE UP; COVER AND LET RISE 1 1/2 TO 2 HOURS. „PUNCH DOWN DOUGH AND DIVIDE IN TWO. SHAPE EACH INTO A ROUND, SLIGHTLY FLAT LOAD. PLACE EACH LOAF IN ROUND LAYER PAN (9X10 1/2 INCHES) THAT HAS BEEN GREASED. COVER AND LET RISE UNTIL DOUBLE (ABOUT 1 HOUR). HEAT OVEN TO 350 DEGREES. BEAT 1 EGG SLIGHTLY AND BRUSH OVER LOAVES. SPRINKLE WITH 1 TSP. SUGAR. BAKE UNTIL LOAVES ARE GOLDEN BROWN (35-45 MINUTES). MAKES 2 LOAVES.

Title: Coco-Carmel Toast
Categories: Breakfast, Breads, Kids
Servings: 4
1 tb Soft butter or margarine
2 tb Brown sugar 4 sl White, whole wheat, or
2 tb Flaked coconut -raisin bread
1. Heat oven to 325 degrees.

2. Mix brown sugar, flaked coconut, and soft butter in bowl.
3. Toast slices of bread. Spread with the brown sugar mixture. Place on
unreleased cookie sheet.
4. Bake in 325 degree oven for 10 minutes.

Title: Log Cabin Toast

Categories: Breakfast, Breads, Kids
Servings: 1
2 sl White or whole wheat bread
1/4 c Sugar Soft butter or margarine
2 ts Cinnamon
1. Mix sugar and cinnamon in custard cup
2. Toast slices of bread. Spread with soft butter. Sprinkle with
sugar-cinnamon mixture.
3. Cut each slice of toast into 4 strips. Put them together on plate like stacked logs to make the walls of a log cabin. Start from the top and eat all the logs.

Title: BEATEN BISCUITS

Categories: Colonial, Breads, Biscuits
Servings: 24
---------OLD YANKEE -FARMER'S ALMANAC-------------
2 c Flour 1/3 c Shortening
1 ts Salt Milk
Sift flour with salt and cut shrotening in thoroughly. Add enough milk
to make stiff dough. Work dough for 20 minutes on floured board by beating
dough with mallet or rolling pin, folding it, then beating and

folding agin
over and over until the dough is blistered and pops. roll of 1/3 inch thick
and cut with 2-inch round cutter. prick with fork. Bake on ungreased cooke
sheet for about 15 minutes at 400 F. Makes approximately 2 dozen.

Title: Apple-Nut Bread
Categories: Apples, Breads
Servings: 20
2 c Sugar 1 c Salad oil
4 Eggs, beaten 1/4 c Commercial sour cream
4 c All purpose flour 2 c Apples, peeled and chopped
2 ts Baking soda 1 c Pecans, chopped
1 ts Salt 1 ts Vanilla

Gradually add sugar to eggs; beat until light and fluffy. Combine dry ingredients; add to sugar mixture alternately with oil and sour cream, beating well after each addition. Stir in apples, pecans and vanilla. Spoon batter into 2 greased and floured 9x5x3 inch loaf pans. Bake at 350~ for 1 hour or until toothpick inserted in center comes out clean. Let cool in pans 5 minutes; turn out on wire racks to finish cooling.

Title: Fresh Apple Bread
Categories: Apples, Breads
Servings: 10
1 c Sugar 1 ts Baking soda
1/2 c Shortening 1 c Broken pecan pieces
2 Eggs, beaten 1 1/2 tb Buttermilk
1 c Tart apples,ground or grated 1/2 ts Vanilla

2 c All purpose flour, sifted 3 tb Sugar
1/2 ts Salt 1 ts Cinnamon
Cream sugar and shortening; add eggs and apples. Sift dry ingredients together. Mix with sugar mixture; add pecans. Stir in buttermilk and vanilla. Pour into greased 10x6x3 inch loaf pan. Mix sugar and cinnamon;sprinkle over top. Bake for 1 hour at 350~.

Title: Apple Butterscotch Muffins
Categories: Apples, Breads, Muffins
Servings: 18
3 c Self rising flour 1/3 c Salad oil
1/4 c Sugar 6 oz Butterscotch chips
2 Eggs, beaten 1 c Apples, peeled and diced
1 1/2 c Milk
Combine flour and sugar. Combine remaining ingredients; add all at once to flour mixture, stirring only until flour is moistened. Fill greased muffin cups 2/3 full. Bake at 425~ for 20 to 25 minutes, or until golden brown.

Title: Apple Pan Bread
Categories: Apples, Breads, Bars
Servings: 9
1 c All purpose flour, sifted 1 Egg
2 1/2 ts Baking powder 1/4 c Soft vegetable shortening
1/2 ts Salt 1/2 c Sugar
1/4 c Sugar 1/2 ts Cinnamon
2 c Raisin bran flakes 2 c Cooking apples, pared and
2/3 c Milk -thinly sliced
Sift together flour, baking powder, salt and 1/4 cup sugar. Set aside. Combine bran flakes and milk, add egg and shortening; beat well. Add sifted dry ingredients; stir only until blended, but do not beat. Spread in a greased 8x8x2 inch pan. Mix together 1/2 cup sugar and 1/2 ts cinnamon.

Dip apple slices in mixture; arrange on top of batter. Sprinkle any remaining sugar mixture over apple slices. Bake at 400~ about 30 minutes. Cut in squares and serve warm.

Title: Apple-Cheese Bread
Categories: Apples, Breads, Cheese
Servings: 10
1/2 c Shortening 1/2 ts Salt
1/2 c Sugar 2 tb Milk
2 Eggs 3/4 c Rolled oats, uncooked
1 1/2 c All purpose flour, sifted 1 c Raw apples, finely chopped
1 ts Baking powder 2/3 c Cheese, coarsely grated
1 ts Baking soda 1/2 c Nut meats, chopped

Beat shortening until creamy; gradually add sugar. Add eggs; beat well. Sift together flour, baking powder, soda and salt. Add to egg mixture with milk and stir only until blended. Add oats, apples, cheese and nut meats, all at once. Stir lightly. Batter will be very stiff. Place in greased pound loaf pan. Bake at 350~ about 50 minutes.

Title: Apple-Dapple Loaf
Categories: Apples, Breads
Servings: 10
1/4 c Shortening 1 ts Soda
2/3 c Sugar 1 ts Salt
2 Eggs 2 c Raw apples, grated
2 c All purpose flour 1/2 c Nuts, chopped
1 ts Baking powder

Beat shortening, sugar and eggs together until light and fluffy. Sift dry
ingredients together; add alternately with grated apples. Add nuts. The
batter will be stiff. Turn into greased and floured loaf pan.

Bake at 350~
for about 1 hour.

Title: Autumn Apple Bread
Categories: Apples, Breads
Servings: 10
1/4 c Shortening 1 ts Salt
2/3 c Sugar 2 c Apples, coarsely grated,
2 Eggs, beaten -peeled raw
2 c All purpose flour, sifted 1 tb Grated lemon peel
1 ts Baking powder 2/3 c Nuts, chopped Cream shortening
and sugar until light and fluffy; beat in eggs. Sift next
4 ingredients. Add alternately with apples to egg mixture.
Stir in lemon rind and nuts. Bake in floured, greased 9x5x3
inch loaf pan in preheated 350~ oven for approximately 40
to 50 minutes. Cool before slicing.

Title: Mini Corn Muffins with Smoked Turkey
Categories: Appetizers, Martha s, Entertain, Tvg, Breads
Servings: 36
3/4 c Butter, melted, cooled
1 1/2 c Yellow cornmeal 2 Eggs, slightly beaten
1 c Flour, sifted all-purpose 1/2 lb Smoked turkey breast,
1/3 c Sugar -thinly sliced
1 tb Baking powder 1/2 c Cranberry relish
1 ts Salt -or honey mustard
1 1/2 c Milk
Preheat oven to 400 degrees. Butter mini-muffin tins.
Combine cornmeal, flour, sugar, baking powder and salt in
large bowl. Mix milk, butter and eggs together in medium
bowl. Stir milk mixture into cornmeal mixture until just
moistened. Spoon batter into mini muffin tins. Bake until

golden, 14-16 minutes. Let cool on wire rack for five minutes. Remove from pans and let cool completely. To serve, put a small amoung of smoked turkey on a sliced muffin that's been spread with cranberry relish or honey mustard.

Title: CHOCOLATE MINT BREAD
Categories: Breadmaker, Breads, Chocolate
Servings: 15
1 pk Yeast 1 1/2 ts Salt
2 1/2 c Better for Bread flour 1 tb Vegetable oil
1/2 c Wheat flour 2 tb White Creme de Menthe
1 tb Gluten 1 c Very warm water;+ 1 tb.
1/4 c Instant nonfat dry milk 1 c Mint-chocolate morsels
3 tb Sugar

Add all ingredients (EXCEPT CHOCOLATE MORSELS) into the pan in the order listed. Select white bread and push "Start." Add the chocolate at the "beep," 88 minutesinto the cycle. (33 minutes with Dak Turbo II) For a funtastic dessert or sweet treat,spread quarter-round slices with cream cheese blended with the syrup from green maraschino cherries plus a few drops of mint extract, then top with a halved cherry.

Title: BEER BREAD
Categories: Breads
Servings: 8
3 c Flour, unsifted 1 tb Honey
3 3/4 ts Baking powder 12 oz Beer
2 1/4 ts Salt

Grease 9x5x3" loaf pan. Combine flour, beer, and honey in large bowl, stir together until well mixed. Spread batter in prepared pan. Bake at 350f for 45 min or until browned and a wooden pick comes out clean. Turn out on rack. Cool before slicing.

Title: APPLESAUCE TEA BREAD
Categories: Breads
Servings: 20
2 1/2 c White flour 1 tb Cinnamon
2 ts Baking powder 8 oz Applesauce
1/2 ts Salt 1 Egg
1/2 c Sugar 1 c Skim milk
Mix the dry ingredients together and add the applesauce, then the egg and milk. Pour into nonstick loaf pan and bake at 350F for 50 min. Remove and cool.
Cal: 77 (slice); Fat: 1/10g.

Title: BATTER ROLLS
Categories: Breads
Servings: 18
1 ts Granulated sugar 1/4 c Shortening
1/2 c Warm water 2 ts Salt
1 pk Dry yeast 2 Egg
1 1/2 c Milk 3 3/4 c Flour
1/4 c Granulated sugar
Disolve 1 tsp sugar in warm water in lrge bowl. Sprinkle in yeast. let stand 10 minutes, then stir well. Combine milk, ¼ cup sugar, shortening and salt in saucepan. Heat until lukewarm and shortening is melted. Stir well. Add to yeast mixture. Add 2 3/4 cups flour and beat vigorously with wooden spoon or electric mixer until smooth. Gradually stir in remaining 1 c flour. Batter will be soft. Cover with tea towel. Let rise in warm place until doubled about 1 hour. Stir down dough and let stand 10 minutes.

Fill greased muffin cups 1/2 full. Let rise until doubled 45 minutes. Bake at 375 degrees for 20-25 minutes or until golden. Turn out of pans immediately. Serve warm and cool. Makes about 18 rolls.

Title: BROWN SEED BREAD

Categories: Breads

Servings: 1

2 c Flour, all purpose 1 tb Baking powder

1 c Whole wheat flour 1 1/2 ts Baking soda

1 c Natural bran 1 ts Salt

1 c Quick cooking rolled oats 1/4 c Liquid honey

2 tb Sesame seeds 2 c Plain yogurt

2 tb Poppy seeds

In large bowl, combine all-purpose and whole wheat flours, natural bran, rolled oats, sesame and poppy seeds, baking powder, baking soda and salt; stir in honey. Add enough of the yogurt to make sticky dough. Knead lightly in bowl until dough is well blended. Fit dough into one greased 9x5 in. (2L) loaf pan. Bake in 375F oven for 40 min., or until tester comes out clean.

Title: CHEDDER CHEESE CASSEROLE BREAD

Categories: Breads

Servings: 2

1 ts Sugar 1 Egg beaten

1 c Warm water 4 c Flour

1 pk Dry yeast 2 c Shredded sharp chedder

1 c Warm milk 1 tb Salt

2 tb Butter

Dissolve sugar in warm water in large mixer bowl. Sprinkle in yeast. Let stand 10 minutes, then stir well. Stir in warm milk, butter and beaten egg. Combine 2 cups flour, cheese and salt. Stir well to blend. Add flour cheese mixture and beat with electric mixer on medium speed for 5 minutes. Add remaining flour, beating well with wooden spoon. Cover and let rise in warm place until doubled (about 45 minutes). Stir down and turn into two well greased 1 quart casseroles. Let rise until doubled (about 30 minutes). Bake at 375 degrees for 30-40 minutes. Remove from casseroles immediately and cool on wire racks. Makes 2 round loaves.

Title: MOLASSES BROWN BREAD

Categories: Breads
Servings: 4
2 1/2 c Whole-wheat flour 1 c Raisins; mixed dark & light
1 1/2 c Wheat germ 2 ts Baking soda
1/3 c Brown sugar 1 7/8 c Buttermilk
1/2 ts Salt 1/3 c Molasses

Preheat oven to 325 degrees F. Grease a 9 X 5 X 3-inch pan. Combine flour, wheat germ, brown sugar, salt and raisins in a mixing bowl. Mix well. In a second mixing bowl, mix baking soda, buttermilk and molasses, using a wooden spoon. This misture will start to bubble. Immediately mix it into the dry ingredients. Spoon the batter into the greased pan. Bake at once. The bread is done when a toothpick comes out clean, about 1 hour. Turn out of the pan and cool on a wire rack. Makes 1 loaf.

Title: MINIATURE FRENCH BREAKFAST PUFFS

Categories: Breads, Rolls
Servings: 42
1/3 c Soft shortening/butter mix 1/3 c Butter, melted
1/2 c Sugar 1 1/2 ts Baking powder
1/4 ts Nutmeg 1/2 c Sugar

1 Egg 1/2 ts Salt
1/2 c Milk 1 ts Cinnamon
1 1/2 c Sifted flour

Heat oven to 350 degrees. Grease bottoms of 48 small muffin cups. Mix shortening, 1/2 c sugar, and egg thoroughly. Sift together flour, baking powder, salt and nutmeg. Stir flour mixture and milk alternately into sugar/shortening mixture. Fill greased muffin cups 2/3 full. Bake 15 minutes or until golden brown. Dip immediately in melted butter, then in mixture of cinnamon/sugar. Serve hot. Makes 3-1/2 to 4 dozen.

Title: FUNNEL CAKE
Categories: Breads
Servings: 8

1/2 ts Salt
2 c Flour 2 Eggs
1 ts Baking powder 1 1/2 c Milk.

Mix the ingredients together: Heat cooking oil in a deep fryer or skillet until very hot. Put batter into a funnel (be sure to cover the spout with one finger), then, holding the funnel over the hot oil (use extreme caution when cooking with hot oil), release some of the batter in circular motions to form one funnel cake. The funnel cake will rise quickly and expand, so be careful about how much batter you use for the first one until you get the "feel" for cooking it. Cook to a light golden brown on both sides, then remove from the oil and place on paper towels to drain.. Sprinkle with powdered sugar and serve while still warm! Mmmm, mmm, good"

Title: PARMESAN CROUTONS
Categories: Cheese/eggs, Breads
Servings: 2

1 Slice Whole Wheat Bread 1 tb Grated Parmesan Cheese
1 tb Butter Or Margarine

Trim crust from bread. Cut bread slice into quarters, making squares. Diagonally cut each square in to halves, making triangles. Arrange bread triangles in a shallow baking dish or pie plate. Micro-cook, uncovered, on 100% power for 1 to 1 1/2 minutes or till the bread is dry. Remove the bread from the microwave oven. In a custard cup micro-cook butter or margarine, uncovered, on 100% power for 40 to 50 seconds or till melted. Drizzle over bread triangles. Sprinkle with grated parmesan cheese.

Title: BERMUDA BANANA BREAD
Categories: Breads, Fruits
Servings: 6

1/2 c Butter or margarine 2 c Flour
1 c Brown sugar 1 ts Baking soda
2 x Eggs 1 ts Salt
1 c Mashed bananas 1/2 c Chopped walnuts
1 ts Vanilla

Cream butter and sugar. Gradually add eggs, then bananas and vanilla. Fold in dry ingredients that have been sifted together. Add nuts. Bake in buttered loaf pan, at 350 degrees, for 1 1/4 hours or until loaf tests done. Cool in pan for 10 minutes and then turn out to cool completely.

Title: WW CINNAMON ROLLS
Categories: Ww, Low-cal, Breads
Servings: 10

10 oz Buttermilk Biscuits, Refrig. 1/2 c Raisins; dark
^^(10 biscuits in "tube") 2 tb Raisins; dark
5 ts Margarine; melted 5 ts Powdered sugar; sifted
5 ts Brown sugar; packed, divided 2 ts Water
1 ts Cinnamon

Preheat oven to 400 F. Spray 8x8x2 inch baking pan; set aside. Separate biscuits; using fingers, flatten each into 3" circle. Brush each circle with an equal amount of the margarine, sprinkle each with 1/4 t brown sugar and an equal amount of cinnamon, then top each with 1T raisins. Roll each circle jelly-roll fashion and arrange in two rows, seam side down, in sprayed pan. Bake until rolls are puffed and golden brown, 8-12 minutes. Transfer pan to wire rack and lets rolls cool in pan. In small bowl or cup combine remaining 2 1/2 t brown sugar and the powdered sugar, add water, 1 t at a time, stirring constantly until mixture is smooth and syrupy. Remove rolls to serving platter, brush each with an equal amount of sugar mixture. Makes 10 servings of 1 roll each.

Each serving provides: 1 BREAD, 1/2 FAT, 1/2 FRUIT and 20 OPTIONAL CALORIES. Per serving: 143 calories, 5 g fat.

Favorite Recipes (1986).

Title: TSOUREKI

Categories: Breads, Ethnic
Servings: 1

----------**GREEK EASTER BREAD**----------------

1/2 ts Salt 1 Egg yolk;with 1 T water
2 Eggs 1/4 c Sugar
1 ts Vanilla 1/4 c Butter
1 pk Yeast;dry active 1/2 c Milk
1 1/2 ts Lemon peel;grated 3 c Flour;all purpose
5 Eggs;hard boiled colored at

In pan add salt,sugar, butter,and milk warm to 125 in a lg bowl combine 1 c flour with yeast add warm milk mixture, eggs,vanilla, and lemon peel. Beat low speed for 5 minutes then with a spoon beat in the rest of the flour to make stiff dough knead for 20 minutes let rise 45 minutes punch down and divide into 3 equal parts roll into ropes place in greased baking sheet. Th braid at evenly spaced intervals press colored eggs into dough cover let ri 30 minutes press eggs in again if necessary. Brush egg yolk mixture over braid do not touch eggs with yolk bake 350 for 25to35 minutes till golden brown cool on rack. dough can be made in BM. Greek Easter bread wraps around colorful hard cooked eggs. The greeks favor bright red eggs- but because the dye seeps into the dough, you may prefer pastel shades that tinge it less.

Title: JO GOLDENBERG'S BAGELS
Categories: Breads
Servings: 12
3/4 pt Warm water 1 tb Sugar
2 Envelopes dry yeast 1 Egg white; beaten
1 1/2 oz Sugar Salt; -=OR=-
1/2 oz Salt -Sesame, Poppy -=OR=-
3 1/2 c Bread flour -Caraway seeds
2 qt Boiling water - (optional)

This is the bagel recipe taught at the New York Cooking School. PREHEAT OVEN TO 450F. Mix yeast, 1 1/2 ounces sugar and warm water. Let stand 2-or-3 minutes. Mix 2 cups flour and the salt and add to the yeast mixture. Add remaining 1 1/2 cups flour. Knead for 5 minutes, adding flour if dough sticks to the table. Bagel dough should be firm. Place dough in a clean, greased bowl. Cover and let rise until double. Bring water to a boil and add 1 tablespoon sugar. Divide dough into 12 pieces and shape each into a ball. Allow the dough to relax 3-to-4 minutes. Flatten with your palm. With your thumb, press deep into the center of the bagel and tear open with your fingers. Pull the hole open. Place bagels on a sheet and cover for about 10 minutes. Put 2-or-3 bagels at a time into simmering water for about 45 seconds, turning once. Drain and place on greased baking sheets. Brush with beaten egg white and sprinkle with salt, sesame, poppy or caraway seeds. Bake for 35 minutes, turning over when bagels are light brown. Bagels are done when they are brown and shiny. Cool on a rack.

Title: STRAWBERRY BREAD

Categories: Breads, Fruits
Servings: 5

1 1/2 c. flour 2 eggs, well beaten
1/2 tsp salt 1/2 c. oil
1/2 tsp soda 10 oz frozen strawberries
1/2 tbsp cinnamon 1/2 c chopped nuts
1 c sugar

Combine flour, salt, soda, cinnamon and sugar. Make a well in center of dry ingredients. Add eggs and oil stirring only until dry ingredients are moistened. Stir in strawberries and pecans. Spoon batter into lightly greased 9 x 5 x 3 inch loaf pan. Bake 350 degree oven for 1 hour.

Title: MAPLE SYRUP AND BROWN SUGAR BANANA BREAD

Categories: Breads
Servings: 1

1 c Brown Sugar; dk or light 1/8 c Milk
1/2 c Margarine 2 c Flour
2 Eggs; unbeaten 1 ts Baking Soda
1 c Ripe Bananas; mashed 1/2 ts Baking Powder
1/8 c Maple Syrup 1/8 ts Salt

Cream sugar with butter. Add and mix the next 3 ingred. Sift and add the dry ingred. and mix thoroughly. Put mixture in 6x10 greased loaf pan. Bake 40-45 min. in 350 oven. Sift some confectioners' sugar on bread when cooled.

Title: JELLO ROLLS

Categories: Breads
Servings: 48
Mary Bowles DNSR31A 1 ts Sugar
2 c Boiling Water 6 c Flour (about)
2 tb Butter 1 ts Salt
1/4 c Sugar 1/4 c Lukewarm Water
2 pk Dry Yeast

------------------**FILLING**--------------------------------

1 pk Red Jello--dry 1/4 c Butter, melted
1 c Pecans 3/4 c Sugar

-------------**GLAZE**----------------------------------

1 c Powdered Sugar 1 1/2 ts Milk

Mix boiling water, butter, 1/4 cup sugar, salt. Cool to lukewarm. Put yeast in lukewarm water. Add 1 tsp. sugar. Mix with cooled butter mixture. Mix half of flour, 1 cup at a time, in electric mixer. Blend well. By hand, stir in enough remaining flour to make dough. Knead into a smooth ball. Cover and let rise until double in bulk. (May refrigerate overnight at this point if you want these for breakfast). Roll dough 1/8 inch thick. Cover with melted butter. Mix jello and sugar and sprinkle over. Sprinkle nuts on top. Roll up as for jelly roll. Cut into 1/2 inch slices and place on well buttered pan, well apart. Let rise until double, about 1 hour. Bake at 400 degrees for 20 minutes. Mix glaze and drizzle over hot rolls.

Title: HONEY "RISIN" BREAD

Categories: Breads
Servings: 12
Mary Bowles DNSR31A 1/4 c Sugar
1 pk Yeast 1 3/4 c Flour
3 tb Warm Water 1 ts Baking Powder

1 ts Sugar 1/2 ts Ginger
1 1/3 c Honey 1/2 ts Cinnamon
1/4 c Butter; softened 1/2 ts Nutmeg
3 Eggs; beaten 1/4 ts Salt

Mix yeast, water and 1 teaspoon sugar. Let set 15 minutes or until foamy. Heat 1 cup honey to boil. Pour in bowl and cool 3 minutes. Add butter and beat smooth. Beat eggs and sugar until lemony colored and add honey butter and yeast. Stir in 3/4 cup flour. Sift together 1 cup flour, baking powder, spices and salt. Add to honey mixture and mix well. Turn into well-buttered and floured loaf pan and bake at 350 degrees for 50 minutes. Cool in pan for 10 minutes. Turn onto rack and brush with 1/3 cup honey.

Title: SAVORY BREAD STICKS

Categories: Breads, Quickbreads
Servings: 8

1 ts Garlic Powder
1 lg Pkg Day-old Hot Dog Buns 1 ts Paprika
1 c Butter; melted 1/2 ts Cayenne Pepper or to taste
2 tb Italian Seasonings

Slice hot dog buns into fourths lengthwise. Dip bread in melted butter and arrange on a baking sheet. Mix spices and sprinkle over bread sticks. Bake at 350 degrees for 20 minutes or until crunchy, but not brown. Serve hot or cold. Let cool well before covering. Stores well in air-tight containers. This was invented by a friend to use up left-over buns from a weiner roast, but it is too delicious to wait for left-overs. It is great
with stew, spaghetti, or by themselves for snacks!

Title: POPEYE'S BISCUITS

Categories: Breads, Rolls
Servings: 12
-JEANNETTE DABBS (RFNR19B) 8 oz Sour cream
4 c Pioneer biscuit mix 6 oz 7-up
Cut sour cream in biscuit mix, add 7-up. Roll on floured surface. Cut or shape with hands . Bake 6 -8 mins 400`. Delicious!!!!

Title: PISKOTA FANK-(HUNGARIAN DOUGHNUTS WITH CREAM)

Categories: Breads, Doughnuts
Servings: 1

--------**THE ART OF HUNGARIAN COOKING**-------

1/2 lb Sweet butter 4 Egg yolks
4 Whole eggs 5 tb Sour cream
5 tb Sugar 2 c Flour
1 Yeast cake dissolved in 1 Egg
1/2 c Warm milk

--------**CREAM MIX**--------------------------------

1/2 pt Milk 2 tb Sugar
4 Egg yolks

Beat butter until creamy, beat in 4 whole eggs, beat in 4 egg yolks, add sugar and sour cream, add flour and the yeast mixutre. Beat until smooth, set aside to rest and rise until doubled in size. Place on board that has been dusted with flour. Roll out to 3/4 inch thickness, cut with doughnut cutter. Put in greased pan, lat raise 40 minutes. Brust top with beaten egg. Bake in 350 F oven for 1/2 hour. For cream mix; cook milk, egg yolks and sura over low heat, in double boiler until mixture is smooth. Stirring all the while, cool and pour over doughnuts and serve.

Title: FARSANGI FANK- HUNGARIAN PLAIN DOUGHNUTS

Categories: Breads, Doughnuts
Servings: 1

------THE ART OF HUNGARIAN COOKING----------

3 c Flour 1/4 c Milk
1/2 ts Salt 1/8 lb Sweet butter, melted
1 tb Sugar 2 Yeast cakes (dissolved in
5 Egg yolks -1/4 cup warm milk)

Sift the flour and salt into bowl, add yeast mixutre, add egg yolks and melted butter slowly ot flour mixutre. Beat with wooden spoon until smooth and dough falls off the spoon, this dough should be rather soft. Put dough on lightly floured board. Roll to 1/2 inch thickness. Cut with round cookie cutter, that has been dipped in flour. Put in warm place to rise until doubled in size. Fry in deep fat until light brown. Sprinkle with powdered.sugar.

Title: BASIL & SAGE BREAD

Categories: Breads, Wine
Servings: 1

1 Yeast; dry; envelope 1/4 ts Sage; crumbled dried
1 c Water; warm (105-115~) 1/2 c Dry white wine
5 1/2 c All purpose flour 1 3/4 ts Salt
1/4 c Olive oil 1/4 ts Pepper; freshly ground
4 ts Basil; crumbled dried 1/2 c Water; warm (105-115~)

(Makes 2 baguettes.) Sprinkle yeast over 1 cup water in bowl of heavy-duty electric mixer; stir to dissolve. Let stand 5 minutes. Thoroughly mix in 1 1/2 cups flour. Sprinkle 1/2 cup flour over dough. Cover with towel. Let rise in warm draft-free area until doubled, about 1 1/2 hours. Heat oil in heavy small skillet over low heat. Add basil and sage and stir until aromatic, about 1 minute. Cool. Blend 1 cup flour, oil mixture, wine, salt and pepper into dough, using dough hook. Slowly add remaining 1/2 cup water. Stir in 2 1/2 cups flour 1/2 cup at a time. Knead dough in mixer until smooth and resilient, about 10 minutes, adding more all purpose flour if sticky. Grease large bowl. Add dough, turning to coat entire surface. Cover bowl. Let dough rise in warm draft-free area until doubled, about 1 1/4 hours. Grease two baking sheets. Punch dough down. Divide in half. Form´each piece into 14-inch-long loaf. Place on prepared sheets, seam side down. Let rise in warm draft-free area until almost doubled, about 1 hour. Preheat oven to 400~. Slash tops of loaves with sharp knife. Bake until breads sound hollow when tapped on bottom, about 50 minutes. Cool on wire racks before serving.

Title: PORTUGUESE SWEET BREAD

Categories: Breads
Servings: 1

3 Yeast; fresh cakes 6 Eggs; room temperature
1/2 c Water;warm (105-115~) 1 c Sugar
1 c Milk c All purpose flour; sifted
1/2 c Butter; cut into pieces 2 tb Butter; melted
2 ts Salt

Crumble yeast cakes into large bowl. Stir in water. Let mixture stand until foamy, about 5 minutes. Scald milk. Add butter and salt and stir until butter melts. Cool to lukewarm. Using electric mixer, beat eggs until frothy. Add sugar and beat until creamy, about 3 minutes. Blend in milk mixture. Stir into yeast mixture. Stir in 7 cups flour 1 cup at a time; dough should be soft and pull away from sides of bowl. Turn dough out onto well-floured surface, sprinkle with 1 cup flour and knead until smooth and elastic, adding up to 1 cup more flour as necessary to prevent stickiness, about 10 minutes. Grease large bowl. Add dough. turning to coat entire surface. Cover and let rise in warm draft-free area until doubled in volume, about 2 hours. Punch dough down. Let rest 10 minutes. Grease two 9-inch round cake pans. Divide dough in half. Press each half into pan. Cover and let rise in warm draft-free area until doubled in volume, about 1 hour. Preheat oven to 350~. Bake until loaves are golden brown and sound hollow when tapped on bottom, about 30 minutes. Brush tops immediately with melted butter. Serve warm. Makes 2 loaves.

Title: CSOROGE-HUNGARIAN CRISPY CRULLERS

Categories: Breads, Doughnuts
Servings: 1

-----**THE ART OF HUNGARIAN COOKING**-----------

6 Egg yolks 1 tb Vinegar
1 ts Salt 2 1/2 c Flour
2 tb Sugar 1/2 c Sour cream
1 ts Brandy

Add all or enough of flour to egg yolks and sour cream to make a soft dough. Add sugar, salt, brandy and vinegar. Knead until smooth. Roll out very thin. Cut into diamond shapes. Make a slit in center and pull one end through slit. fry in deep fat until light brown. Drain on absorbent paper. Sprinkle generously with powdered sugar.

Title: PICKLE JUICE RYE

Categories: Breads, Vegetables
Servings: 2

Frances Nossen (SWTK50B) 1 EGG, LARGE,ROOM TEMP
From Bread in Half the Time 2 ts SALT
3 c FLOUR, BREAD 1 tb DILL WEED, DRY
3 pk YEAST, DRY 1 1/2 c FLOUR, MEDIUM RYE
1 c BRINE, SOUR DILL 1 1/2 ts CARAWAY SEEDS
3/4 c WATER, 120 DEGREES ,,,,,,,,,,,GLAZE:

2 tb CRISCO 1 EGG
2 tb SUGAR 1 tb MILK
COMBINE BREAD FLOUR AND YEAST IN MIXER BOWL. ADD PICKLE BRINE (AT LEAST AT ROOM TEMP) AND MIX. ADD REMAINING INGREDIENTS AND MIX, ADDING MORE BREAD FLOUR AS NEEDED UNTIL DOUGH CLEANS SIDE OF BOWL. LET RISE UNTIL DOUBLE IN BULK. PUNCH DOWN AND KNEAD FOR A FEW SECONDS. LET DOUGH REST FOR 10 MINUTES. GREASE YOUR LARGEST BAKING SHEET WITH CRISCO. FORM DOUGH INTO A BALL AND PLACE ON BAKING SHEET. MAKE A FEW PARALLEL SLITS IN THE TOP, BRUSH WITH THE GLAZE, AND SPRINKLE WITH ADDITIONAL DILL WEED IF DESIRED. LET RISE UNTIL DOUBLE IN BULK. BAKE ABOUT 50 MINUTES 375 OR UNTIL LOAF SOUNDS HOLLOW WHEN TAPPED. COOL ON RACK. FOR CHEWIER CRUST, BRUSH WITH WATER WHILE STILL HOT.

Title: Garlic Monkey Bread Ring ,,
Categories: Breads
Servings: 1

1 pk Active dry yeast 1/4 c Butter or margarine; melted
1 c Water; warm (105~ - 115~) 1 lg Garlic clove; minced
1 ts Sugar 1 ts Dried parsley
1 ts Salt 1/4 ts Salt
2 1/2 c To 3 c all purpose flour 1/8 ts Fresh ground black pepper

In mixing bowl, dissolve yeast in water. Add sugar. Stir to dissolve. Let stand 3-5 minutes or until yeast bubbles. Add salt. Slowly stir in flour. After half the flour is added, beat until very smooth and satiny. Then stir in enough flour to make a stiff dough. Turn out onto lightly floured boars. Cover and let rest about 10 minutes. Knead about 5 minutes until smooth and satiny. Place dough in a bowl that has been greased. Turn dough over. Cover and let rise for 1 hour or until doubled. Meanwhile, in small bowl, mix melted butter, garlic, parsley, salt and black pepper. Turn risen dough out onto counter. Cut in walnut sized pieces. Dip into butter mix. Place into buttered 10" ring mold (1-1/2 qt size). Make even layer. Let rise about 1 hour or until doubled. Bake at 375~ for 25-30 minutes or until golden.

Title: Tomato Barbecue Rolls ,,
Categories: Breads, Rolls
Servings: 12
2 c To 2 1/2 cups unbleached 1 pk Active dry yeast
- all purpase flour 3/4 c Tomato juice (good quality)
1 tb Sugar 1/4 c Water
1/2 ts Seasoned salt 2 tb Butter or margarine
1/2 ts Italian seasoning 1 ts Instant minced onion
1/8 ts Pepper

In medium bowl, mix 1 cup flour, sugar, seasoned salt, Italian seasoning, pepper and yeast. In small saucepan, heat the tomato juice, water, butter and onion, until warmed (butter need not be melted). Add to dry ingredients. Beat at medium speed of mixer for 2 minutes. Add 1/2 cup more flour. Beat at high speed for 2 minutes. Stir in enough to make a soft dough that clears the bowl. Turn out onto lightly floured surface. Knead 5-10 minutes or until smooth and elastic. Put into greased bowl, turning to grease top. Cover dough lightly with plastic wrap. Let rise in warm (85~) area for 30 minutes or until doubled. Punch down. Shape dough into 12 even balls. Arrange 6 on each of 2 greased baking sheets. Flatten with hand to 1/2" thickness. Let rise for 20 minutes or until light. Bake at 350~ for 20 minutes or until golden. Remove to wire rack to cool.

Title: San Francisco Sour Dough Bread ,,
Categories: Breads
Servings: 2

--------------**STARTER**---------------------------------
1 pk Active dry yeast 2 c All purpose flour
2 c Water; warm (105~-115~)

--------------**DOUGH**----------------------------------
1 pk Active dry yeast 2 ts Sugar
2 tb Water; lukewarm 2 ts Salt
pn Sugar 1/2 ts Baking soda
1 1/2 c Water; warm (105~-115~) 2 c Unsifted all purpose flour
1 c Starter 1 tb Cornmeal
4 c All purpose flour

STARTER: In large bowl mix yeast with warm water and flour. Beat until smooth. Cover and let stand at room temperature for 48 hours, stirring mix 4 times during the 2 days. DOUGH: In a cup soften yeast in warm water with a pinch of sugar for 5 minutes. Pour 1-1/2 cups warm water into mixing bowl. Stir in the yeast mix and starter. Stir in flour, sugar and salt. Mix vigorously for 3 minutes. Turn into greased bowl. Cover. Let rise in warm place until doubled. Mix baking soda with 1 cup remaining flour. Add to dough. Turn onto floured board. Knead, adding remaing flour little by little until smooth and satiny. Divide dough in half. Shape into 2 loaves on a gresed and cornmeal dusted baking sheet. Cover. Let rise until doubled. Brush loaves with water. Slash diagonally with sharp knife. Place a shallow pan of hot water in bottom of oven. Bake loaves at 400~ for about 45 minutes or until crust is golden. For a crisper crust, remove loaves from oven after 35 minutes. Brush with salted water. Bake for another 10 minutes.

TIP: Store starter in refrigerator for future use. Bring to room temperature for 4 hours before using.

Title: Honey Whole Wheat Bread or Dinner Rolls ,,

Categories: Breads, Rolls
Servings: 1

1 pk Active dry yeast 1/4 c Lard; melted
1 1/2 c Water; warm (105~-115~) 2 c Whole wheat flour
2 Eggs 4 c All purpose flour;
1/4 c Honey - to 4 1/2 cups
2 ts Salt

Dissolve yeast in the water in large mixing bowl. Let stand 5 minutes. Stir in eggs, honey, salt and cooled, melted lard. Add whole wheat flour. Stir well. Add all purpose flour gradually, beating to make a smooth lump-free batter. Continue adding flour until stiff dough forms. Turn out onto lightly floured board and kneed for 10 minutes. Place dough into bowl to rise. Cover lightly with plastic wrap. Let rise in warm place (85~) until doubled, about 1-1/2 hours. Turn dough out onto oiled board. Shape into 2 loaves or 24 dinner rolls. Place loaves into lightly greased sheets. Let rise until doubled. Bake at 375~ for 40-45 minutes for loaves, 15-20 minutes for dinner rolls.

Title: Herbed Ring Bread ,,

Categories: Breads, Ready-rolls
Servings: 1

1/2 c Butter or margarine; melted 1 tb Parsley; chopped
1/3 c Green onions; chopped Garlic salt
1/4 ts Dried oregano 2 cn Refrigerator biscuits
1/2 ts Dried tarragon

Melt butter in saucepan. Add onions, oregano, tarragon, parsley and garlic salt to taste. Cut each biscuit in half lengthwise. Dip each piece in the butter-herb mix. Layer in

5-cup ring mold. Drizzle any remaining butter over the top. Bake at 375~ for 30-40 minutes or until bread is a deep golden brown. Unmold and serve immediately.

Title: Quick Parsley-Garlic Rolls ,,
Categories: Breads, Rolls
Servings: 12
1 lb Loaf frozen bread dough 1 Garlic clove; minced Flour Dried parsley leaves
3 tb Butter or margarine; melted

Thaw frozen bread at room temperature about 2-3 hours. Place on lightly floured surface and with a knife dipped into flour, cut the loaf in half lengthwise. Then cut each half into 6 or 7 pieces. Roll out each piece to about 1/4" thickness. Combine melted butter and garlic, mixing well. Brush dough with the mixture. Lightly sprinkle with the parsley leaves. Roll up each piece jelly-roll fashion. Place, end up, into lighlty oiled muffin tins. Set in warm place to rise for 1 to 1-1/2 hours or until doubled. Bake at 400~ for 12-15 minutes or until rolls are golden brown.

Title: Herb Crusted Parmesan Bread ,,
Categories: Breads
Servings: 1
1 lb Loaf frozen bread dough 3 tb Parmesan cheese
Butter or margarine; melted 1 ts Dried chevril leaves
Flour 1/2 ts Caraway seeds

Brush frozen loaf with melted butter to prevent surface from drying. Cover and thaw at room temperature for 2-3 hours. Cut dough into thirds. On lightly floured surface, roll each portion into a long strand. Braid strands. Coil braid into a spiral on greased baking sheet. Brush with more melted butter. Sprinkle with cheese, chevril and caraway seeds. Let rise about 1 hour in warm place, until doubled. Bake at 375~ for 25-30 minutes or until golden brown. Remove from pan. Cool on rack. VARIATIONS: Sprinkle bread with mix of 2 tbls dried minced onions, 1 tsp dried rosemary and 1/2 tsp dried thyme and 1/2 tsp marjoram. A second variation is to mix 1/2 cup grated cheddar cheese and 1-1/2 tbls poppy seeds into the dough before rolling the strands. Can really do almost anything you want with herbs and spices and this bread.

Title: Peanut Butter Loaf „
Categories: Breads, Sweet bread
Servings: 1
4 c Flour 2 Eggs; well beaten
1/3 c Sugar 1 3/4 c Milk
2 tb Baking powder 1 tb Grated lemon rind
1 ts Salt 1 tb Lemon juice
1 c Chunky peanut butter 1/2 c Peanuts; chopped (opt)
In mixing bowl, combine the flour, sugar, baking powder and salt. Cut in peanut butter with pastry blender or use food processor; blend until mix resembles coarse crumbs. In separate bowl, mix the eggs and milk. Add lemon rind, lemon juice and peanuts, if used. Stir into flour mix only until blended. Pour batter into greased 9x5" loaf pan. Bake at 350~ for 1 hour or until tested done. Remove from pan to wire rack to cool. Wrap and store overnight before serving.

Title: Swiss Cheese Gougere „
Categories: Breads, Cheese
Servings: 1
1 c Water ds Pepper

1/4 c Butter or margarine 1 c All purpose flour
1 ts Oregano 4 Eggs
1/2 ts Salt 1 c Swiss cheese; shredded

In 2 qt saucepan, combine water, butter, oregano, salt and pepper. Bring to a roiling boil. Stir until butter is melted. Add flour, all at once. Stir to make a thick ball of dough that clings together. Beat in eggs, one at a time. Beat until dough is satiny smooth. Mix in cheese. Generously grease a baking sheet. Spoon 6 mounds of dough onto sheet in a ring formation, close enough so that they touch each other. Bake at 375~ for 55-60 minutes or until golden brown. Serve hot with sweet butter. For breakfast serve with jam or preserves.

Title: Extra Good Cheese Bread

Categories: Breads, Cheese
Servings: 1

2 tb Butter or margarine 1/4 c Oil
1/2 c Onion; minced 1/2 c Milk
1 1/4 c All purpose flour 1/2 c Cottage cheese
2 ts Baking powder 1/2 c Cheddar cheese; grated
3/4 ts Salt 1 tb Poppy seeds
1 Egg; lightly beaten

Melt butter in skillet. Add onion. Saute until tender. Stir together flour, baking powder and salt. Blend egg, oil and milk. Stir into flour mixture, blending lightly. Stir in cottage cheese and sauteed onions. Turn into buttered 9" round cake pan. Sprinkle with cheddar cheese and poppy seeds. Bake at 425~ for 25 minutes or until golden brown. Serve hot, cut in wedges.

Title: Rosemary-Olive Focaccia

Categories: Sun-dried, Breads
Servings: 4

6 Kalamata olives; pit,quarter
1 lb Frozen bread dough; thawed 4 Oil-pk dried tomatoes;

drain
3 tb Olive oil -cut in strips
1 tb Fresh rosemary; minced or 2 lb Cloves garlic; thinly sliced
1 ts Dried rosemary Fresh rosemary sprigs; opt
3/4 c Parmesan

Preheat oven to 450~. Place dough in bowl. Add 1T oil and minced rosemary. Season generously with pepper. Knead dough until ingredients are dombined. Roll dough out on lightly floured work surface to 9x6" rectangle. Transfer to baking sheet. Flatten and press dough into 12x9" rectange. Rub 1 T oil over. Sprinkle 1/2 C Parmesan over; press gently into dough. Bake until bread is almost cooked through and cheese begins to brown, about 12 minutes. Arrange olives, tomatoes and garlic atop bread. Sprinkle enough remaining Parmesan over to cover lightly. Drizzle remaining 1 T olive oil over. Top with rosemary sprigs. Continue baking until cheese melts and bread is cooked through, about 5 minutes. Cut into squares or wedges and serve.

Title: POPPY SEED OATMEAL BREAD

Categories: Breads
Servings: 16

1 c Flour, all purpose 2 ts Poppy seeds
1 c Flour, whole wheat 1 1/2 c Buttermilk
1 1/4 c Oatmeal, quick-cooking 1/4 c Honey, liquid
1 tb Baking powder 1 Egg
1/4 ts Salt 1 ts Butter, melted

In large bowl, combine all-purpose and whole wheat flours, oatmeal, baking powder, salt and poppy seeds. In separate bowl, whisk together buttermilk, honey and egg. Add all at once to dry ingredients; mix quickly, just until combined. Spoon batter into greased 8 x 4 in (1.5L) loaf pan. Brush top with melted butter. Bake in 350F (180C) oven 45 to 50 minutes or until cake tester inserted in centre of loaf comes out clean. Let cool 5 minutes in pan. Turn out onto wire rack.

Title: SWEET POTATO BISCUITS
Categories: Breads, Vegetables
Servings: 1
1 c Flour 2 1/2 ts (to 3) baking powder
1 c Sweet potatoes, cooked/mashed 3 tb Sugar (or more, to taste)
Salt 1/4 c Shortening
Sift dry ingredients. Add shortening and potato and mix thoroughly. Knead dough; cut with biscuit cutter (you may need more flour, as dough is sticky). Bake in 400 degree oven 12 to 15 minutes.

Title: BISQUICK MIX
Categories: Breads, Mixes
Servings: 13
-Diana Lewis-VGWN37A 1 ts Cream of tartar
9 c All-purpose flour 1/4 c Sugar
1/3 c Double-acting baking powder 2 c Shortening; like crisco
1 tb Salt
sift baking powder, salt, cream of tarter, sugar with flour 3 times. Cut in shortening until mix is consistency of cornmeal store in covered containers and store at room temp. (I put the shortening in my fresser for 30 minutes then put it in the processor with the flour works great.

Title: GINGERBREAD-BISQUICK
Categories: Breads, Mixes

Servings: 1
-Madeline Whalley BWPG01A 2 tb Sugar
1 c Bisquick; mix 1 Yolk;or half egg
1/4 ts Cinnamon 1/4 c Molasses
1/4 ts Cloves 1/4 c -water
1/4 ts Ginger

Stir in sugar and spices into mix. Add water, egg, and Molasses. Stir half
into mix beat 2 minutes. Add remainer and beat 1 minute. Bake in a 4 X 6
inch pan that has been greased and floured at 350 for about 40 minutes. Or
bake in a waffle Iron for gingerbread waffles top waffles with whipped
cream and chopped bananas for something special.

Title: PEACH BREAD

Categories: Breads, Peaches
Servings: 2

3 c Fresh peaches 1 ts Gr. cinnamon
6 tb Sugar 1 1/2 c Sugar
2 c Flour 1/2 c Shortening
1 ts Baking soda 2 Eggs
1 ts Baking powder 1 c Pecans; finely chopped
1/4 ts Salt 1 ts Vanilla extract

Puree peaches with 6 tb sugar. (should yield 2 1/4 c.) Combine flour
baking powder, soda, salt and cinnamon. Set aside. Combine 1 1/2 c. sugar
and shortening - cream together. Add eggs and mix. Add puree and dry
ingred. Mix til moist. Stir in nuts and vanilla. Spoon into well greased

9x5x3" loaf pans (2). Bake @ 325 for 55-60 min. Cool 10 min. in pan. Turn
out on rack and cool completely. I have used 1/2 peaches and 1/2 pears for
a variation. It turned out very good.

Title: APPLE-CINNAMON SWIRL LOAF

Categories: Breads, Cake mix, Fruits
Servings: 2

1 pk Active dry yeast 2 1/2 c Apples,chopped and peeled
1 1/4 c Very warm water 1/3 c Sugar
1 Egg 1/3 c Pecans, chopped
1 pk 1-layer-size white cake mix 2 ts Cinnamon
1 ts Salt 1/4 c Butter, melted
3 3/4 c Flour
Light cream 1/2 ts Vanilla
1 c Confectioner's sugar, sifted ds Salt

In bowl dissolve yeast in 1-1/4 cups warm water(115-120 F) Add egg, cake mix and salt, beat until smooth. By hand, stir in enough flour to make a soft dough. Knead on floured surface until smooth (dough will be sticy) Place in greased bowl; turn once. Cover, let rise until doubled in bulk, 1-1/4 hours. Punch down, divide in half. Cover, let rest 10 minutes. Mix apples, sugar, pecans and cinnamon. Roll half of dough to 12x8" rectangle. Brush surface of dough with some of the butter. Sprinkle with half of the apple mixture. Starting a short end, roll as for jelly roll. Seal side and ends. Place in a greased 8-1/2x4-1/2x2-1/2" loaf pan. Brush top with more butter. Repeat with remaining dough, filling and butter. Cover, let rise in warm place until doubled (1 hour) Bake in 375 F oven for 30-35 minutes. remove from pans; cool. Drizzle with Confectioner's icing (recipe follows) Sprinkle with chopped pecans if desired. Makes

two.
CONFECTIONER'S ICING:
Blend enough light cream into 1 cup sifted confectioner's sugar to make of spreading consistency. Blend in vanilla andsalt.

Title: PUMPKIN COFFEE LOAF
Categories: Breads, Vegetables
Servings: 1

1/3 c Shortening 2 1/2 ts Baking powder
1 c Brown sugar, packed 1/2 ts Salt
2 Eggs 1/2 ts Ginger
1 c Canned pumpkin 1/2 ts Cinnamon
1/4 c Milk 1/2 ts Baking soda
1 c Flour 1/4 ts Ground cloves
1 c Whole wheat flour 1/3 c Pumpkin seeds, chopped

Cream shortening and sugar. add eggs, one at a time, beat well after each. Stir in pumpkin and milk. Stir together dry ingredients. add to pumpkin mixture. Beat 1 minutes with electric mixer. stir in seeds. Bake in greased loaf pan at 350 F for 55-60 minutes. Cool 10 minutes. remove from pan. Cool. Wrap, store overnight. Makes 1.

Title: CHUNKY PEANUT BUTTER BREAD
Categories: Breads, Pnut butter
Servings: 18

-FHMN87A Phill Bower 1 c Chunky Peanut butter
2 c Flour 1 c Milk
1/2 c Sugar 1 Egg; beaten
2 ts Baking powder 2 ts Vanilla
1/4 ts Salt

Preheat oven to 350. Combine flour, sugar, baking powder andf salt into a large bowl. Add the peanut butter, milk, egg and vanilla. Mix well. Pour into a greased loaf pan and bake for 50 to 60 minutes.

Title: Apricot Braid
Categories: Breads
Servings: 4
-Jo Ferry cmsj69b 17 oz Can apricot halves in
1 lb Loaf frozen dough -heavy syrup
4 tb Margarine; softened 3/4 c Miniature marshmallows
4 tb Brown sugar 1 ts Cinnamon
Let bread dough completely thaw. On a lightly floured surface, roll thawed loaf into a rectangle approximately 14 by 8". Place rectangle of dough on a greased sheet pan. Spread with 2 tablespoons margarine and 2 tablespoons brown sugar (save remaining margarine and sugar for glaze). Drain the apricots, reserving the liquid for the glaze. Place drained apricot halves lengthwise down center of rectangle. Sprinkle with marshmallows and cinnamon. With sharp knife or scissors, cut dough into strips lengthwise down eachside of rectangle. Make strips 1" wide an 2" deep (or cut in until it almost hits the filling). Gently stretch each strip and criss-cross over filling. Let rise in warm area until puffy, 30 to 60 minutes (see note). While rising make glaze. For glaze, combine remaining sugar and margarine with reserved apricot syrup in a medium sauce pan. Bring to a boil. Let boil for 5 minutes. Remove form heat. Set aside. When twist has risen, bake in a preheated 350 oven for 25 minutes. Remove from oven and brush with glaze. Return twist to oven and bake 10 to 15 minutes longer. Remove from oven, brush with additional glaze. Remove twist from sheet pan to cool on a wire rack. When cool, slice and serve. Note: Twist can be assembled in the evening to rise in the refrigeratior

overnight. This enables you to quickly bake it for breakfast in the morning. Simply brush the unrisen twist with some melted margarine and cover with plastic wrap to keep from drying out while in the refrigerator. In the morning, proceed with remaining recipe instructions.

Title: Sausage Cornbread
Categories: Pork, Breads, Microwave
Servings: 6
1 lb Bulk pork sausage 1/2 ts Salt
3/4 c Flour 2 Eggs; beaten
3/4 c Cornmeal 1/2 c Milk
1 tb Sugar 1/3 c Sausage drippings
1 tb Baking powder

Crumble sausage over bottom of 9" round baking dish. Microwave on high setting for 4 1/2 to 7 minutes, stirring after half the time. Drain off fat and reserve 1/3 cup of it for cornbread. In another dish reserve half of the cooked sausage. Combine remaining ingredients in mixing bowl. Stir only till smooth. Pour over sausage in baking dish. Crumble reserved sausage over top. Center dish on inverted saucer in oven. Microwave on medium 6 minutes, rotating every 2 minutes. Check for doneness by looking into the bottom of the dish to be sure there is no raw batter. Let stand for 10 minutes before serving.

Title: English Muffin in a loaf (2 loaves)
Categories: Breads
Servings: 2
-RCXX09B G.Mulhorn 1 tb Sugar
2 c Milk 1 ts Salt
1/2 c Water 2 pk Active dry yeast

2 3/4 c Flour 1/4 ts Baking soda
1/4 c Cornmeal

Heat until very warm (120-130F) the milk and water. Combine the other ingredients in a large bowl. Add hot liquids to dry mix; beat well; stir in 3 cups flour to make stiff batter. Spoon into 2 bread pans, greased and sprinkled with cornmeal and sprinkle tops. Cover. Let rise in a warm place 45 minutes. Bake 400F for 25 minutes. Remove from pans immediately and cool. (I rub top crust with oleo.) Slice, toast and enjoy.

Title: Skillet Sizzled Cornbread

Categories: Breads
Servings: 6

1 c Stone ground yellow 1/4 ts Baking soda
-cornmeal 1 1/4 c Buttermilk
1 c Unbleached all purpose 1 Egg
-flour 2 tb Sugar
1 tb Baking powder 1/4 c Vegetable oil
1/4 ts Salt 3 tb Butter

Preheat oven to 375 degrees. In a large bowl, combine cornmeal, flour, baking powder and salt. In a small bowl, stir the baking soda into the buttermilk. In another bowl, whisk together the egg, sugar to taste, and the oil, then whisk this mixture into the buttermilk mixture. Spray an 8 or 9 inch cast-iron skillet with vegetable cooking spray. Put the skillet over medium high heat. Add butter; heat until butter melts and is just starting to sizzle. Tilt the pan to coat the bottom and sides. Add buttermilk mixture to cornmeal mixture; quickly stir together, using only as many strokes as needed to combine the mixtures. Scrape the batter into the hot, buttery skillet. Immediately put the skillet into the preheated oven and bake about 25 minutes, or until cornbread is golden brown. Cut into wedges to serve. (For a decandent cornbread, substitute 1 3/4 cups sour cream for the 1 1/4 cups buttermilk.)

Title: Pane Di Mattina Alla Siciliana
Categories: Breads, Italy
Servings: 2

1 ts Olive oil 1/3 c Marsala
1 pk Active dry yeast 1/2 c Unsalted butter
1/2 c +1ts sugar 3 tb Shortening
1 1/3 c Scalded milk cool to 100F 1 1/2 ts Fennel seeds
6 1/2 c Unbleached flour;approximate 4 Eggs
1/4 c Dried currents 1 tb Grated lemon rind
1/3 c Golden raisins 1/2 ts Salt

-------------**EGG WASH**---------------------------------
1 tb Whipping cream 1/2 tb Marsala
1 Egg yolk

brush olive oil over surface of a large stainless steel bowl. Put yeast and 1 teaspoon sugar in bottom of bowl add 1 cup of scalded milk and stir to disolve the yeast. Set aside for 10 minutes then add 1-1/2 cups flour and remaining milk. Knead by hand or with mixer and dough hook till dough is soft and silky, about 7 or 8 minutes. Cover and let rise for 5 hours. While dough rises soak currents and raisins in Marsala for at least 1 hour. In a small sauce pan over low heat, melt butter and add 2 tablespoons shortening. add fennel seed, remove from heat and let stand till cool. Add eggs one at a time to the fennel seed mixture and mix after each addition then add lemon rind and remaining sugar. Set aside. when dough has risen 5 hours add fennel seed mixture and mix well. add salt and begin adding remaining flour, 1/2 cup at a time. when dough is firm enough to knead turn out onto a lightly floured board and knead till soft and smooth about 10 to 15 minutes, adding as much additional flour as necessary to keep it from sticking. During final 5 minutes knead in raisins and currents. form dough into 2 loaves. use remaining shortening 2 grease 2 nine inch pans place dough in pans cover and let rise till doubled in bulk. this may take as long as 3 hours. preheat oven to 375 brush egg wash on bread 5 minutes before baking. brush again immediately before baking. Bake until loaves are golden brown and sound hollow when tapped about 35 minutes turn out and cool. this is Sicily's answer to the moring danish. recipe

Title: Merenda Fiorentina (Florentine snack bread)

Categories: Breads, Italy
Servings: 1

1 pk Dry active yeast The crust
1 ts Salt 1 tb Minced garlic
3 c Unbleached flour Cornmeal for dusting
1 c Warm water (105F) Coarse salt
3 tb Olive oil + oil for brushing 1 ts Minced fresh rosemary:option

combine yeast, salt and flour in large bowl. combine water and oil in a small bowl add liquid to dry ingredients and mix till they form a rough mass. Knead mixture in a bowl with your hands till it holds together then turn out onto a lightly flour surface and knead in garlic. Continue till dough is smooth and elastic about 8 minutes form ball and let rest on a lightly floured surface covered for 1 hour. {Preheat oven to 375F Preheat oven to 375 roll dough into 12 X 14 inch rectangle and transfer to baking sheet sprinkled with cornmeal. Use finger tips to make indentations in the dough at 2 inch intervals sprinkle dough lightly with coarse salt and drizzle olive oil over the top. Sprinkle with rosemary if used bake till golden brown about 25 minutes remove from oven and brush with a little more oil cool slightly serve warm. to serve cut into thin slices and pack along with a picnic lunch with roast chicken roasted red peppers and red

wine. recipe from "Italian"

Title: Pane Giallo (Polenta Bread)
Categories: Breads, Italy
Servings: 8

5 tb Unsalted bread 3 Eggs;separated
2 tb Minced garlic 2 c Milk
1 c Polenta (coarse yellow corn 1/2 c Half and half
Meal) 1 c Roasted red peppers;minced
1 1/2 ts Salt Olive oil
1 ts Fresh ground black pepper

in small skillet over moderatly low heat, melt 2 tablespoons of butter. Add garlic and saute until fragrant. remove from heat. combine polenta, salt and pepper in a bowl and set aside. Put egg yolks, milk and half and half in a saucepan and wisk well. Bring to a boil, whisking constantly. Add cornmeal mixture gradually, then add garlic and red peppers. cook 2 minutes stirring constantly with wooden spoon. Add remaining butter and cook an additional 2 minutes. Preheat oven to 375 brush souffle dish or casserole with olive oil. Place dish in oven for 5 minutes to warm it. Beat egg whites with a pinch of salt until stiff peaks form. Gently fold whites into thickened cornmeal. Pour mixture into hot souffle dish. Bake until puffed and golden about 30 minutes. Serve immediately.

Title: Pizza Dough
Categories: Breads, Ethnic, Genie
Servings: 1

1 tb Fast rising yeast 1/2 ts Salt
1 c Flour 1/2 ts Sugar
1 c Luke warm water 2 1/4 c Flour
2 tb Vegetable oil

In a large bowl mix yeast and 1 cup of flour, then mix in

water, oil, salt and sugar. Add 2 to 2-1/4 cups of flour or enough to make a soft dough. Knead until smooth and elastic. Place in a lightly greased bowl, turning dough to grease all over. Cover with a tea towel and let rise in a warm place for 1 to 1-1/2 hours or until dough doubles in size. Punch down and divide dough in half. Preheat oven to 425 F. Grease pizza pans and roll out dough on lightly floured surface into a 12" circle. Place on pan. Let rise for 10 minutes. Put on topping and bake according to recipe directions. OPTION: For a crustier bottom, precook dough slightly (about 10 minutes or until edges are lightly browned). Then put on topping and cook another ten minutes until cheese is golden brown. TO FREEZE DOUGH: Spread dough onto pans, cover with plastic wrap and freeze. Once frozen, put in plastic freezer bag. Keeps well for one month. Thaw in refrigerator.

Title: Bill's Pizza Crust

Categories: Breads, Ethnic, Genie
Servings: 1
2 1/2 c Unbleached Flour 1 1/4 c Pastry Flour
1 pk Active Yeast: 2 1/4 ts Salt
-dissolved in: 1 1/4 c Tepid water
1/3 c Water

Mix until massed, add 3 t Olive Oil Knead, & let rise to 3X size Knead again & let rise again to 3X size Cut in half, roll out every 2 minutes until expanded to 14 inches. Add toppings and bake at 450 for 12-15 minutes. Bill was attempting to find the perfect pizza crust. He developed this over a period of time through trial and error. This should produce a thin firm crust for your pizza. 1980

Title: **Herb Pizza Dough**
Categories: Breads, Ethnic, Genie
Servings: 1
1 pk Active dry yeast 2 1/4 c All-purpose flour
1 ts Sugar 1/2 ts Salt
7/8 c Warm water, 1 tb Garlic olive oil,
-110 degrees -more as needed ,,,,
1/4 c Chopped herbs, Oil and cornmeal for pan -optional ,,
Stir together the yeast, sugar and warm water. Let stand until foamy, about 10 minutes. In the work bowl of a food processor fitted with the steel blade, chop the herbs. Turn off machine. Add flour and salt. Turn the machine on and off a couple of times. While the machine is running, add yeast. Process until the dough forms a ball at the side of the bowl. Add garlic, olive oil and process for 30 to 40 seconds more. Transfer dough to a bowl that has been oiled with olive oil. Turn the dough until the entire surface has been coated with the oil. Cover bowl with a damp towel and allow to rise in a warm draft free place for 1 hour or until doubled. Roll out on a lightly floured surface and if dough is too elastic, try tossing it from hand to hand to flatten it out. Lightly grease the pizza pan with a little oil and sprinkle with cornmeal. Place the dough on the pizza pan and trim the edges. Bake for 10 minutes 425 degrees. Remove from oven, lightly brush the crust with a little more oil and proceed with recipe. Makes enough dough for one 12" crust. ,,Try basil, thyme, Italian flat leaf parsley, oregano, rosemary, cilantro.

Title: **Pizza Dough #1**
Categories: Breads, Ethnic, Genie
Servings: 1
1 pk Active dry yeast 1/2 ts Salt
3/4 c Warm water 2 tb Olive or vegetable oil
1/2 ts Sugar 2 c All-purpose flour

Dissolve the yeast in the water. Stir in sugar, salt, oil and one and ¾ cups of the flour. Turn onto a well-floured board and knead until smooth and elastic. This should take about five minutes. Knead in enough of the remaining flour to prevent sticking.

Title: Whole Wheat Pizza Crust
Categories: Breads, Ethnic, Genie
Servings: 2
1 pk Dry yeast 3/4 c Whole wheat flour
1 c Warm water 2 ts Salt
-(105 to 115 F) 4 ts Cornmeal (optional)
2 1/2 c All-purpose flour
Stir yeast into warm water and set aside for 5 to 10 minutes. Combine
the flours and salt in a mixer bowl; add yeast mixture. Mix until dough
begins to pull away from side of bowl. (Add a little more flour if dough
sticks to side.) Divide dough in half. On a floured surface with floured
rolling pin, roll each half into a 15-inch circle (dough should overlap pan
by 1 inch all around). If dough resists rolling, let it rest a few minutes
and try again. Dough can be refrigerated or frozen before rolling. Thaw
thoroughly before attempting to roll out.
Coat two nonstick 14-inch pizza pans with cooking spray and sprinkle
with cornmeal (optional). Arrange each crust in a prepared pan and top as
desired.

Title: New Classic Pizza Dough

Categories: Breads, Ethnic, Genie
Servings: 1
1 pk Dry Active Yeast 3/4 c Cold milk
1/2 c Warm water 2 tb Olive Oil
-(105-115F) 3 c All-Purpose flour
1/8 ts Sugar 1 1/2 ts Salt

For two 16 inch crusts (Food Processor Directions)
Mix the yeast and 1/4 tsp sugar in the 1/2 cup of warm water. Let stand for 10 minutes, until bubbly. Measure the DRY ingredients into the bowl of the processor. Stir the 3/4 cup milk into the finished yeast mixture. Turn on the processor and pour in the yeast mixture, then the oil, stop the machine when the dough has massed on the blade. The dough will be soft. Allow it to rest 5 minutes. Turn on the processor for a few seconds more (no more than 5) Turn the dough out onto a lightly floured surface and knead by hand about 60 strokes. Let the dough rise in a covered bowl until doubled (about 1 hr.) Divide the dough in half. The dough may be kept covered in a cool
place (up to an hour) Use it immediately, refrigerated it or even freeze it.

Title: Mama Lorraine's Pizza Dough

Categories: Breads, Ethnic, Main dish, Genie
Servings: 1
1 pk Yeast 1 1/3 c Lukewarm water
1/3 c Honey 3 c Flour (mix white &
1/3 c Cooking oil -whole wheat)
Salt

In a very large mixing bowl, add water and yeast. Dissolve

yeast. Add honey and oil. Stir well. Add flour, one cup at a time until dissolved, then add rest to make a bread dough consistency. Take dough from bowl and on floured surface, knead for about five minutes. Roll into ball and in greated bowl put into a warm oven for an hour to rise. After an hour, grease a cookie sheet and flatted dough evenly all over, make edges come up on sides. Turn oven to 350F, place dough on cookie sheet in oven for 15 minutes. Take out, add toppings and sauce, then cook for 20 more minutes at 370-375F. Watch closely. If cheese browns too fast, cook longer at a lower temperature. 1975.

Title: Pizza Dough #2

Categories: Breads, Ethnic, Genie
Servings: 1

----------**IN A LARGE BOWL MIX**--------------------------
1 pk Dry yeast 1 3/4 c Hot tap water

---------**STIR UNTIL YEAST IS DISSOLVE**--------
1/2 ts Salt 2 c Flour

Now with a mixer mix (if hand-held mixer) 2 minutes high speed or (if you have a regular mixer) 2 minutes medium speed. Then add: 1 cup flour And carefully mix high speed for one more minute. Then add by hand kneeding for 5 minutes minimum: 1 cup flour (or more if dough is too sticky) Kneed this until the dough is soft but easily handlable without being too sticky. Place in a bowl greased with olive oil in a warme (but turned off!) oven covered with a cloth and let the dough rise until it is doubled ~ takes about 1 1/2 hours or so. When dough has risen punch it down and separate it into either 2 for 2 thick crust pizzas or 4 for 4 thin crust pizzas and carefully, by spinning and tossing the dough shape it into olive oil greased (lightly) pans. Be careful you don't toss it too high! Place on top your favorite sauce and fixings and bake for 20 minutes or until edges look done (baking time depends on the oven) at 375 f

Title: Sarah's Pizza Crust
Categories: Breads, Ethnic, Genie
Servings: 1
1 tb Yeast -110 to 115 degrees
1 tb Sugar 3 c Flour
1 c Warm water

Disolve yeast and sugar in water. Stir in flour 1/2 cup at a time. Knead 10 mins or so. Rise. Punch down, rest 10 mins. Pat into lightly oiled pizza pan. Finish as usual.

Title: Traditional Pizza Dough 1
Categories: Breads, Ethnic, Genie
Servings: 1
1/4 c Water (110 to 115 F.) -115 Degrees F.)
1/2 ts Sugar 1 tb Olive Oil (Room Temperature)
1/2 ts Salt 1 1/2 c Unbleached Flour
1/2 pk Dry Yeast Additional Flour
1/4 c Warm Water (110 to Additional Water

HAND METHOD:

Pour the first 1/4 Cup of water into a medium bowl and add the sugar and salt, stirring to dissolve the sugar. Sprinkle the yeast over the water mixture, stirring once to blend and let sit for 5 minutes until the top is bubbly and the yeast has bloomed. Stir in the remaining warm water and the oil. Place the flour in a large bowl and add the water and oil mixture to it. Stir, adding enough flour to make a soft dough that will pull away from the sides of the bowl. If it is too dry, add a little water a tbls at a time. Turn the dough out on a well-floured work surface, sprinkle the top with a little additional flour. Knead until it become very springy, elastic and very smooth. It should be light in weight, if it is heavy, you have use too much flour and it will not raise properly. Form into a smooth ball and let rest on the work surface while you wash and clean the large bowl. Spray with a non-stick spray. Put the ball of dough into the bowl and turn it over to get some of the spray on the top. Cover with plastic wrap or a warm, damp, clean dishtowel. Let the dough rise in a warm, draft free place until double in volume, about 1 1/2 to 2 hours. If the dough rises before you are ready, punch it down in the bowl by kneading making sure all of the air is gone. Turn it over and reshape it into a ball and let rise again. If the top is dry, use a little olive oil to grease it. You can punch the dough down and cover the bowl and keep the dough refrigerated for up to two days before letting it rise at room temperature. For a thin, crisp pizza crust punch the dough down and turn out and spread over a pizza pan or baking sheet or a bakers peel. Cover with filling and topping, baking at once. For thicker, softer pizza crust punch the dough down and turn out shaping as above and then cover lightly with a clean dishtowel. Let rise about 30 minutes before covering with filling and topping. Makes enough dough for one 12 to 14 inch round pizza, two 7 to 8- inch round pizzas or one oblong pizza, or one dozen appetizer-sized pizzas.

Title: HERB PARMESAN BREAD
Categories: Breads, Breadmaker
Servings: 1
--------**1-POUND LOAF-**------------------------------
2 c All-purpose flour 1 tb Milk
2 tb Sugar 3/4 c -Water; lukewarm
1/2 ts Salt 1 1/2 ts Active dry yeast
1 tb Butter or margarine;softened 1/4 c Parmesan cheese; grated(or shortening, softened) 1 tb Italian-style herbs

Title: ENGLISH MUFFIN LOAF
Categories: Breads

Servings: 2
2 pk Active dry yeast 2 c Milk
6 c Flour; unsifted 1/4 ts Baking soda
1 tb Sugar 1/2 c Water
2 ts Salt Corn meal
,,makes 2 loaves

Combine 3 cups flour, yeast, sugar, salt, and baking soda. Heat liquids until very warm. Add to dry mixture; beat well. Stir in rest of flour to make a stiff batter. Spoon into two 8-1/2 x 4-1/2 inch pans that have been greased and sprinkled with cornmeal. Sprinkle tops with cornmeal. Cover; let rise in warm place for 45 minutes. Bake at 400-degrees for 25 minutes. Remove from pans immediately and let cool.

Title: **Deluxe Jalepeno Cornbread**
Categories: Breads, Ethnic, Genie
Servings: 9
1 c Yellow cornmeal Pimento
17 oz Whole kernel corn -chopped
1/2 ts Baking soda 1/2 c Margarine
3/4 ts Salt -melted
1 Jalepeno peppers 1 c Cheddar cheese
-chopped -grated
2 Eggs 1 md Onion
-beaten -chopped
1 c Buttermilk

Mix all ingredients except cheese. Pour into a well-greased 9x9" pan. Place the 1 C. cheese on top. Bake at 350^ for 45 minutes. Serves 4-6 people.

Title: **Antipasto Bread**
Categories: Breads, Ethnic, Genie
Servings: 2
2 Loaves frozen bread dough 1/2 lb Provolone

-thawed -sliced
1 Jar mixed colored peppers 1/4 lb Salami
-in oil 1/4 lb Pepperoni
1 Egg Oregano
-slightly beaten

On a lightly floured surface, roll bread dough out, 1 at a time, to 14x8 inch rectangles. Brush rolled dough with beaten egg. Use half of the ingredients per loaf. Arrange ingredients on bread doutyh. Stretch dough and bring down top; bring up bottom of dough and roll in jelly-roll fashion. Seal edges and ends with egg wash. Place on baking sheet. Repeat second loaf. Cool loaves loosely with towel and let rise about 30 minutes. Brush and seal with egg wash. Bake 30 minutes at 350F.

Title: Peppy Pizza Pie
Categories: Main dish, Breads, Ethnic, Genie
Servings: 6

1 lb Lean Ground Beef 8 oz Tomato Sauce; 1 Cn
2 oz Pepperoni; Chopped, 8 oz Mushroom Stems &
Pieces; „
-1/3 C Abt 1/4 c Ripe Olives; Pitted,
1/3 c Bread Crumbs; Dry -Sliced
1 Egg; Lg 1 c Mozzarella Cheese;
1/2 ts Oregano Leaves -Shredded
1/4 ts Salt

„Use 1 8-oz can of Mushroom Stems and Pieces that has been drained. Heat the oven to 400 degrees F. Mix the meats, bread crumbs, egg, oregano leaves, salt and half of the tomato sauce. Press the mixture evenly against the bottom and sides of an ungreased 10-inch pie pan. Sprinkle the mushrooms and olives in the meat line pan then pour the remaining tomato sauce over the vegetables. Bake uncovered for 25 minutes. The pepperoni gives a red-flecked appearance to the meat. Sprinkle the pie with the shredded cheese and bake an additional 5 minutes. Cool for 5 minutes then cut into 6 wedges. NOTE: If a 10-inch pie pan is not available, use a 9-inch one but put a pan under it to catch the run off of juices. Also you can use an 8 oz can of cut green beans or whole kernel corn in place of the mushrooms if desired.

Title: AMISH BREAD W/OATMEAL

Categories: Breads
Servings: 12
1 c Sourdough starter 3 Eggs
1/2 c Oil 2 ts Baking powder
1 c Light brown sugar 1/2 ts Baking soda
3/4 c Flour 1 1/2 ts Cinnamon
3/4 c Oatmeal (quick) 1/2 ts Nutmeg
Mix all ingredients together. Bake at 350-degrees for 40 minutes.

Title: HERMAN WHEAT'N'HONEY STARTER ,,

Categories: Breads, Sourdough, Herman
Servings: 1
2 tb Dry yeast
1 tb Ginger 2 c Milk
1/2 c Honey;or brown sugar 1 c Whole wheat flour
1/3 c Warm water 1 c Flour white;or unbleached
Sprinkle ginger and 1 T honey or brown sugar over warm water. Sprinkle yeast over this and stir. Let stand in warm place about 10 minutes till doubled in size. Mix milk, rest of honey or brown sugar, flours into yeast mixture in a glass container about the size of a gallon pyrex jar. Stir, using only a wooden spoon, since metal objects will retard herman's

growth. Leave the cover on lossely or place a glass plate over the top of the container. So Herman can breathe. Herman doubles, enen tripples at time of vigorous rising. Place Herman in a warm place overnight. Next day refridgerate, Lossely covered and stir each day. This is very important with wheat and honey starter as more gasses form in the container and are released during stirring. Formation of this gas may cause the starter to appear darker on the top than on the bottom. But this is okay. On the 5 th day measure out 1 cup herman for baking and another to give to a friend if you wish. Then feed what herman you have left thusly:
FEEDING HERMAN 1/2
CUP WHOLE WHEAT 1/2 C WHITE FLOUR 1 C MILK 1/4 C HONEY;OR BROWN SUGAR 1/4 T

Title: INSTANT POTATO STARTER „

Categories: Sourdough, Breads
Servings: 1
-------------**STARTER**--------------------------------
1 pk Dry yeast, 2 tb Salt
1/2 c Sugar 1/2 c Instant potato flakes
2 c Warm water,
---------------**FEED**------------------------------
3/4 c Sugar, 1 ts Instant potato flakes
1 c Warm water,
---------------**BREAD**-----------------------------
1 c Starter, 1/4 c Sugar
1 1/2 c Lukewarm water 1/2 c Oil,
1 ts Salt, 6 c Flour
STARTER: Dissolve yeast in 1/2 C. of warm water. Add remaining ingred. and
stir well. Place in glass jar, covered loosely with foil, plastic wrap, etc. (to allow for gas expansion). Keep at room

temperature for 24 hrs. Then place starter in frig. for 3-5 days. Feed: After starter has been refrigerated 3-5 days, take out and feed it above mixture. Let stand out (loosely covered) all day (8-10 hrs.). Take out 1 C. to use in making bread and return remaining starter to frig. Keep refrigerated from 3-5 days; feed again. After feeding, take out 1 C. to use in making bread, or give 1 C. to a friend, or throw 1 C. away. Starter must be fed again in 3-5 days. Bread: Mix first 5 ingred. together. Add in flour 1 C. at a time until thoroughly mixed. Knead until good "elastic" consistency, but don't over knead. Place approx. 2 Tbl. oil in bottom of large boowl; turn dough over so oiled side is facing up. Cover with dish towl; let rise until double - about 8-10 hrs. Punch down, knead again only a few times, mixing in flour until good consistency. Divide dough in half, shape into loaves. Place in ungreased loaf pans; let rise again (4-6 hrs.). Bake 350 for 25-35 min. until golden brown and loaves sound hollow when tapped. Cinnamon Bread: Before placing dough in loaf pans to rise, roll out, brush with melted butter, sprinkle with cinnamon and sugar. Roll up and place in loaf pan to rise. This is a great receipe - I've enjoyed it for years! Your starter should bubble a little after it has set out for the day (before you feed it). If not, I have added yeast to the warm water of the "feed" and added it in and the starter has recovered just fine!

Title: AUNT CORA'S SOURDOUGH BISCUITS ,,

Categories: Breads, Sourdough
Servings: 4
1 1/2 c Sifted Unbleached Flour 2 tb Sugar
3 ts Baking Powder 1/4 c Shortening, Melted
1 ts Salt 1 1/2 c Sourdough Starter
1 1/2 ts Baking Soda ,,

,,More Baking Soda may be added if the starter if very sour. Place flour in bowl, add starter in a well, then add melted shortening and dry ingredients. Mix lightly and turn out onto a lightly floured board and knead until the consistency of bread dough, or of a satiny finish. Pat or roll out dough to 1/2 inch thickness, cut and put on a greased pan. Coat all sides of biscuits with melted butter. Let rise over boiling water for 1/2 hour. Bake at 425 degrees F for 15 to 20 minutes.

Title: Fruit Bread With Grape-nuts Tspn00b

Categories: Breads

Servings: 10

2 c Milk; scalded 1 c Plus 3 tb. sugar

1 c Grape-nuts 1 Egg; well-beaten

3 c Sifted flour 3 tb Butter

4 ts Baking powder 1 c Currants or raisins

1 1/2 ts Salt 1 tb Orange rind; grated

Pour the scalded milk over the grape-nuts and set aside to cool. Sift

baking powder, salt, sugar, and flour together, and then twice more. Add

the beaten egg and butter to the grape-nuts and milk mixture and blend

well. Add flour, stirring gently until blended. Mix in raisins and orange

rind. Turn into a well-buttered loaf pan, and let stand for 1/2 hour. Bake

in 350 oven for an hour and 25 minutes.

Title: Apple Cinnamon Bread

Categories: Abm, Breads

Servings: 1
-----------**SMALL**----------------------------------
1/2 c ;water 1/4 ts ;salt
2 1/2 tb Apple juice concentrate 1 c Flour,whole wheat
1/4 c Applesauce 1 1/2 tb Vital gluten;optional
1/2 ts Cinnamon 1 c Flour,bread
2 ts Sugar,brown 1 ts Yeast
-----------**MEDIUM**----------------------------------
3/4 c ;water 1/3 ts ;salt
3 3/4 tb Apple juice cocentrate 1 1/2 c Flour,whole wheat
1/3 c Applesauce 2 tb Vital gluten;optional
3/4 ts Cinnamon 1 1/2 c Flour,bread
1 tb Sugar,brown 1 1/2 ts Yeast
----------------**LARGE**----------------------------------
1 c ;water 1/2 ts ;salt
5 tb Apple juice concentrate 2 c Flour,whole wheat
1/2 c Applesauce 3 tb Vital gluten
1 ts Cinnamon 2 c Flour,bread
1 1/3 tb Sugar,brown 2 ts Yeast

Pats comments.... "This bread is really good. It can be used on the timer. On my Panasonic I use the regular cycle, but with the light crust due to all the juices in it. Makes a beautiful high rising loaf with a warm cinnamon color. Definitely use the vital gluten as it rises much better. I use frozen apple juice concentrate. You could also add raisins or chopped apples, either fresh or dried, or even nuts might be nice. Fits McD beautifully, don't you think?!"

Title: Sausage Bread,,,,,,
Categories: Italian, Breads
Servings: 2
- G. Granaroli XBRG76A 1/4 lb Shredded mozzarella
- MM:MK VMXV03A 1/4 c Grated cheese
1 lb Pizza dough Salt and pepper

4 Sausage links Egg wash (1 egg whipped
1 lg Onion chopped With 1 tb water)
1 lg Pepper

Let dough rise until double in size. (about 4 hrs) Squeeze sausage meat from skin and crumble. Sautee with onion and chopped pepper. Drain well. Punch down dough and cut in half. Roll into a rectangle. Top with half meat and cheeses. Roll up and place in shallow baking pan seam side down. Repeat with other dogh. Brush egg wash over both loaves. Cut 3 slits 1" in each loaf. Bake at 375 for 25-30 min. Serve warm.

Title: All-Bran Seed Loaf

Categories: Breads
Servings: 10

3/4 c Whole wheat flour 3/4 c Orange juice
3/4 c Flour, all-purpose 1/4 c Honey
1 tb Baking powder 2 Eggs
1/2 ts Salt 1/4 c Vegatable oil
1/3 c Sesame seeds 1/2 c Bran cereal
2 ts Poppy seeds

Stir together flour, baking powder, salt and seeds. In large bowl, beat together orange juice, honey, eggs and cereal. Let stand 2 min. Add flour mixture, stirring only until well combined. Spread evenly in greased 8.5 x 4.5 x 2" loaf pan. Bake at 350f about 40 min. Let cool 10 min and remove from pan. Cool completely before slicing.

Title: Bagel Thins, Lo Cal, Lo Salt

Categories: Appetizers, Breads, Low-cal
Servings: 20

1 Bagel 1 ts Oregano, dried

2 ts Soft margarine, melted

Using a very sharp serrated knife, slice bagel into very thin rounds.

Arrange in single layer on baking sheet; brush with margarine. Sprinkle

with oregano. Bake in 350F oven for 12 minutes. Let cool and store in

airtight container for up to 1 week. Per 1 piece serving: 14 cal; .5g fat,

0 cholesterol, 15 mg salt.

Title: BRAN MUFFINS

Categories: Breads
Servings: 12
1 c White flour 1 1/4 c Skim milk
2 c Bran 1/2 c Molasses
1/4 c Cornmeal 1 ts Baking soda, dissolved in wa
1 ts Salt 1 c Raisins (optional)

Mix all ingredients together and pour into a muffin tin, using either nonstick pan or paper liners. Bake 325F for 25 min.

Title: CARROT OR ZUCCHINI MUFFINS

Categories: Breads
Servings: 24
1 1/2 c Whole-wheat flour 2 Eggs
1 ts Salt 1/4 c Vegetable oil
1 1/2 ts Baking soda 1 1/2 c Skim milk or orange juice
1 ts Cinnamon 2 tb Vinegar
1/2 ts Nutmeg 1/2 c Honey
1 1/2 c Natural bran 1/4 c Molasses
3 Carrots, 1c grated 1/2 c Raisins

Blend flour, salt, baking soda, cinnamon, nutmeg, and bran

together in food processor, 4 to 5 seconds. Pour into large mixing bowl. Process carrots until pureed and add to dry ingredients. Process the eggs and oil for 2 – 3 seconds and add to bowl along with the milk, vinegar, honey, molasses, and raisins. Stir with a wooden spoon until just blended; do not over mix. Spoon the batter into paper-lined muffin tins and bake at 375F for 20 to 25
min.

Title: Corn Muffins
Categories: Muffins, Breads
Servings: 2
1/3 c Unbleached flour 1 Large beaten egg
1/3 c Yellow cornmeal 1/4 c Milk
2 tb Sugar 4 ts Cooking oil
1 1/2 ts Baking powder Yellow corn meal
1/4 ts Salt

In a small bowl sift together flour, 1/3 c of yellow cornmeal, sugar,baking powder, and salt. Make a well in the center of the dry ingredients. Stir together beaten egg, milk and cooking oil. Add all at once to the dry ingredients, stirring just till moistened. Line four 6-oz custard cups with paper baking cups. Fill 2/3rds full. Sprinkle a little additional cornmeal atop muffins. Micro-cook, uncovered, on 100% power about 1 1/2 minutes or till done, rearranging twice. (When done, the surface may appear moist but a wooden pick inserted near the center should come out clean.)

Title: PINEAPPLE-BRAN WHOLE-WHEAT MUFFINS
Categories: Breads

Servings: 12
1 c Whole wheat flour 1 c 100% all-bran cereal
1 tb Baking powder 1/3 c Skim milk
1/4 ts Salt 1/4 c Vegetable oil
1 1/2 tb Brown sugar 8 oz Can crushed pineapple w juic
1 Egg

Mix the flour, baking powder, salt, and sugar. Beat the egg slightly. Add cereal, milk, and oil to the egg. Stir to combine. Let stand for 2 min. or until the cereal has softened. Stir the pineapple, including the juice, into the mixture. Add flour mixture, stirring only until combined. Spoon the batter evenly into a paper-lined muffin tin and bake at 400F for about 25 min. Serve warm. Cal: 100, Fat: 1g.

Title: Potato Farls (Irish)
Categories: Breads, Appetizers
Servings: 8
1 1/4 lb Potatoes (3 or 4) 1/2 ts Salt
2 tb Butter, melted 4 ts Vegetable oil
1 c Flour, all purpose

Peel and halve potatoes; put in large saucepan with enough water to cover. Bring to boil; simmer, covered, 20 to 30 minutes, until fork-tender. Drain well; return to saucepan over low heat. Add butter; mash potatoes well. Stir in flour and salt. Gather mixture into a ball; turn onto lightly floured surface. Knead lightly until smooth. Divide dough in half. Roll out one half into an 8 in. (20 cm) circle, about 1/4 in. thick. Cut into quarters; set aside. Repeat with remaining dough. In large nonstick skillet, heat half the oil over medium-high heat. Cook dough quarters in batches, 2 minutes on each side or until golden brown, adding more oil as necessary. Serve warm.

Title: Rhubarb-Pecan Muffins

Categories: Breads
Servings: 12

2 c Flour 1 Egg, large
3/4 c Sugar 1/4 c Vegetable oil
1 1/2 ts Baking powder 2 ts Grated orange peel
1/2 ts Baking soda 3/4 c Orange juice
1 ts Salt 1 1/4 c Rhubarb, fresh fine chopped
3/4 c Chopped pecans

Combine all dry ingredients. Beat egg and oil; add orange juice. Add to
flour mix. Add rhubarb. Bake 350F 25-30 min.

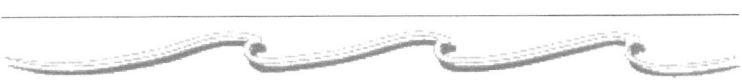

Title: Soda Bread (Irish whisky soda)

Categories: Breads
Servings: 8

-----------bread------------ 1/2 c Honey, liquid
4 c Flour, all purpose 1/4 c Irish whisky or buttermilk
1 ts Salt -----------glaze------------
1 ts Baking soda 2 ts Irish whisky
1/4 c Butter, chilled 2 Ilk
1 c Raisins or currants (option)

BREAD: In large bowl, combine flour, salt and baking soda. With pastry blender or two knives, cut in butter until mixture resembles coarse crumbs. Stir in raisins or currants (if using). In separate bowl, combine buttermilk, honey and whisky. Add all at once to dry ingredients; stir just until no dry spots remain. Turn dough out onto lightly floured surface. Knead lightly 1 minute (too much handling will toughen loaves, while too little will inhibit rising.) Divide dough in half and shape each half into an 8 in (20 cm) round. Place in two greased 8 in (1.2 L) round cake pans. With floured knife, cut a cross 1/2 in deep in each loaf.
GLAZE: In small bowl, combine whisky and milk. Brush

loaves with glaze. Bake in 350F (180C) oven 35 to 40 minutes or until loaves sound hollow when tapped on bottoms. Remove from pans; let cool on wire racks. Cut into wedges.

Title: Spaetzle Cheese Noodles

Categories: German, Breads, Cheese
Servings: 4

3 tb Butter or margarine 1 ts Dry mustard
3 Onions;sliced in small rings 2 c Spaetzle noodles
3 oz Emmenthaler cheese; grated 2 tb Chives; chopped

Heat butter in frypan, add onions, and brown lightly. Toss cheese with dry mustard. Add cooked noodles to cooked onions and cheese; mix well. Place mixture in an ovenproof casserole. Bake at 300 degrees F. for 20 to 30 minutes or until hot and bubbly. Sprinkle top with chopped chives before serving.

Title: Toasty Walnut Muffins

Categories: Muffins, Breads
Servings: 2

1/4 c Quick-cooking rolled oats 2 tb Milk
1/2 c Unbleached flour 1/4 c Broken walnuts, toasted
2 tb Sugar 2 tb Raisins
1/2 ts Baking powder 2 ts Unbleached flour
Dash ground cinnamon 1 ts Brown sugar
1 Large beaten egg yolk 1 ts Butter or margarine
2 tb Cooking oil

Stir together oats and 2 T warm water, let stand for 5 minutes. Meanwhile stir together 1/2 cup flour, sugar, baking powder, cinnamon and a DASH of salt. Stir egg yolk, oil and milk into oat mixture; add to dry ingredients, stirring just till moistened. Fold in 3 T of the walnuts and the raisins.

Line four 6-ounce custard cups with paper baking cups. Fill 2/3rds full. Combine 2 t flour , brown sugar, butter, and remaining walnuts. Sprinkle atop muffins. Micro-cook, uncovered, on 100% power for 1 1/2 to 2 1/2 minutes or till done, rearranging twice. (When done, surface may still appear moist but a wooden pick inserted near the center should come out clean.) Remove from custard cups. Let stand on a wire rack for 5 minutes. Serve warm.

Title: Tomato Brushetta, Lo Cal
Categories: Appetizers, Breads, Low-cal
Servings: 4
8 Slices fr or italian bread 1 Tomato, diced
2 Garlic cloves, halved 1 pn Oregano,dried
1 ts Olive oil 1 pn Ground pepper
2 tb Onion, minced 2 ts Parmesan cheese, optional
Toast bread. Rub one side of hot toast with cut side of garlic. Heat oil in nonstick skillet over medium-high heat; add onion and cook, stirring until tender. Add tomato, oregano and pepper, stir. Spoon tomato mixture over garlic side of hot toast and serve immediately. Alternatively, sprinkle with Parmesan and broil for 1 minute. Per serving (2 slices): 105 cal; 2 g fat; 1 mg cholesterol; 190 mg salt.

Title: Wheaten Bread (Maddybenny, Irish)
Categories: Breads
Servings: 1
3 c Flour, whole wheat 1/2 ts Nutmeg, grated
1 c Flour, all purpose 2 c Buttermilk
1 ts Baking soda 1 ts Orange rind, grated
1/2 ts Salt
In large bowl, stir together whole wheat and all-purpose flours, baking soda, salt and nutmeg. Make a well in centre; add buttermilk and orange rind. Mix just until dough is soft

but not sticky. Turn dough out onto lightly floured surface. Knead 10 times. Put dough into greased 8 x 4 in (1.5 L) loaf pan. Bake in 350F (180C) oven 20 minutes. Reduce temperature to 300F (150C); bake 25 to 30 minutes longer or until a cake tester inserted in centre of loaf comes out clean. Turn out onto wire rack.

Title: Wild Onion Bread
Categories: Breads
Servings: 1
1 1/2 oz Package onion soup mix 3/4 c Hot water
1 pk Dry yeast 2 tb Sugar
2 tb Warm water Egg
2 x Recipies Dry Baking Mix 1 c Sourdough Starter
Add soup mix to 3/4 cup hot water;let stand until lukewarm. In a separate container, soften yeast and sugar with 2 tablespoons warm water.Beat soup mixture and yeast mixture together with egg, 1 cup Dry Baking Mix and Sourdough Starter. Stir in remaining Dry Baking Mix to make a stiff dough. Place on a floured surface;knead until smooth and elastic. Place in a greased bowl, turning to grease top. Cover and let rise for 2 hrs. Shape into a round loaf. Place on a greased pan, cover and let rise 45 mins. Bake in a 375 Deg. oven for 35 mins.

Title: Cream Biscuits
Categories: Breads, Londontowne
Servings: 1
4 c Flour 1 ts Salt
3 ts Cream of tartar 1 1/2 ts Baking soda
1/4 c Butter 2 c Cream or "Half and Half"
Sift dry ingredients. Cut in 1/4 cup of butter. Add the cream. Roll out on a floured board. Cut with a 2-inch cutter. Bake on an ungreased pan in a hot oven of 400 degrees for

12 to 15 minutes or until golden brown.

Title: Corn Fritters
Categories: Breads, Londontowne
Servings: 16
1 1/2 c Sifted flour 1 1/2 ts Baking powder
1 ts Salt 16 oz Can cream style corn
1 Egg, slightly beaten 1 c Corn oil
Powdered sugar Sift together dry ingredients. Mix together corn and egg. Add dry ingredients. Stir slowly. Heat oil in large skillet over medium heat. Drop batter by tablespoonfuls into hot oil, one layer at a time. Fry about 2 minutes on each side until golden brown. Drain on absorbent paper, and dust with powdered sugar if desired. Makes 16 fritters.

Title: Frances Cook's Bread & Rolls
Categories: Breads, Londontowne
Servings: 24
3/4 c Milk 1 Fresh cake yeast
1/4 c Sugar 3 tb Shortening
1 ts Salt 1 Egg
3 1/2 c Flour 1/4 c Lukewarm water
Scald milk and pour over sugar, shortening, & salt. Let it cool to lukewarm while softening yeast in a small bowl with the warm water. When soft, add the egg and beat together slightly. Pour the yeast/egg mixture into the milk mixture and stir them together. The flour may be sifted or poured into the liquid. With a large spoon, stir until flour/milk is well mixed. You should have a firm, but not stiff dough. Without removing it from the bowl, cover the dough with a plate or towel and set aside to rise until double in bulk (about 2 hrs depending on the temperature in the kitchen). Instead of letting the dough rise at this point you may put it

in the refrigerator and use it later, or the next day. Watch to make sure it doesn't spill out of the bowl. If it starts to spill before you're ready to use it, punch it back down. Refrigerated dough is easier to handle but takes longer to rise. BREAD: If you want to make bread, dump the dough out of the bowl onto a floured surface and with more flour as needed to keep it from sticking, knead it until springy and easy to handle. This dough does not require a lot of kneading; only enough to make it easy to handle. For 2 medium size loaves cut the dough in half and knead/shape each into loaves and put into greased baking pans. Allow about 2 hours for the dough to double again. Bake in a 375 degree oven until lightly browned on top (if uncertain whether or not bread is done, tip out of pan and see if bottom is browned too). ROLLS: To make rolls, work and knead dough until springy and easily handled. Roll out with a rolling pin and cut with a biscuit cutter and foldover and place on a greased cookie sheet (Parkerhouse rolls), or break dough into small pieces, make into little balls and place 3 in each section of a greased muffin pan (Cloverleaf rolls). SWEET ROLLS: For Christmas bread or sweet rolls, roll out dough as for Parkerhouse rolls, except trying to make an oblong instead of a round. Spread it with raisins and sprinkle with cinnamon and sugar. Dot with butter and roll as for a jelly roll. Slice and place on a greased pan or make into a circle and make slashes through the dough at intervals. Let rise and bake as for loaves. Top with an icing made of confectioners' sugar, melted butter, milk, and vanilla or rum flavoring and drizzle over the bread or rolls while hot. Decorate with nuts or fruits. If you want to make a whole wheat bread, use half white and half whole wheat flour, and use brown sugar instead of white. The amounts above will yield 1 large or 2 medium loaves of bread, or 2 dozen large rolls.

Title: Angel Biscuits (no rising necessary)
Categories: Breads, Londontowne
Servings: 1

1 Cake yeast 3 ts Baking powder
2 tb Lukewarm water 4 tb Sugar
5 c Plain flour 1 ts Salt
1 ts Soda 1 c Shortening
2 c Buttermilk

Dissolve yeast in water. Into a bowl, sift flour with other dry ingredients. Cut in shortening, add buttermilk, then add yeast mixture. Stir until all flour is dampened. Knead on floured board a minute, roll to desired thickness, and cut with a biscuit cutter. Bake at 400 degrees about 12 minutes. Dough may be kept refrigerated and used about a week.

Title: Old Time Cornbread
Categories: Breads, Londontowne
Servings: 1

2 Eggs 1 1/2 c Buttermilk
1 ts Salt 3/4 ts Soda
1 1/2 c Cornmeal 3 tb Lard, melted
1 c Flour

Beat eggs, milk, and lard together. Add remaining ingredients and mix well. Pour into greased 11" X 7" X 2" and bake in hot (400) oven about 30 minutes.

Title: Irish Bread
Categories: Breads, Londontowne
Servings: 1

1/4 lb Butter 2 1/2 ts Baking powder
1/2 c Sugar 1/4 ts Salt
2 Eggs 1 c Milk
2 1/2 c Flour 1 c Raisins

Cream butter and sugar. Mix flour, salt, baking powder, and

add to buttermixture alternately with milk. Add raisins. Pour into 8" X 8" pan. Bake at 350 degrees one hour.

Title: Yorkshire Pudding

Categories: Breads, Londontowne
Servings: 2
2 Eggs 1 1/2 c Flour
Salt, pinch Milk
2 tb Beef fat

Beat eggs and salt slightly with fork. Add flour gradually, beat, add milk a little at a time until smooth. Add more milk to make a batter like a rather thin pancake batter. Let stand 1 hour. Put 2 tablespoons beef fat in baking pan and heat in oven. Pour batter on hot fat. Bake 20 minutes in 425 degree oven. The PERFECT accompaniment to Rib Roast!

Title: Tex-mex Cornbread

Categories: Breads, Spicy, Tex-mex
Servings: 8
2 Egg 1 tb Baking Powder
2/3 c Salad oil 1 1/2 ts Salt
1 c Sour cream 2 Green Onion Tops chopped fin
1 c Corn meal, yellow 4 Jalapeno Peppers sm chpped
3/4 c Cream style corn 1 c Cheddar cheese, grated
Combine all ingredients except cheese...add half the cheese..pour into a
well greased 8/12 pan and rest of cheese bake 425 20-25 min from"Deep in the Heart of Texas"

Title: ITALIAN LOAF

Categories: Meats, Breads, Italian
Servings: 8
1 cn Refrigerated prepared pizza 1 pk Frozen spinach; (10 oz)

- crust dough (10 oz) - thawed and drained
4 c Mozzarella cheese; grated 1 Egg; lightly beaten
1 lb Spicy pork sausage, browned 1 7 oz jar diced pimientos,
- and drained - drained
1/2 c Tomato sauce 1 pk Sliced pepperoni; 3 oz
1 ts Oregano flakes 12 Large pimiento-stuffed green
1/2 ts Basil flakes - olives, cut in half

Preheat oven to 400F. Unroll dough and cut off one-fourth of dough crosswise; set aside. Line a greased 9 1/4x5 1/4x2 1/2-inch loaf pan with the large piece of dough. Moisten the dough with water at corners and press to seal. Place one-half of the cheese on the bottom of the dough and top with sausage. Spoon tomato sauce over sausage and sprinkle with oregano and basil. Combine spinach with egg and spread over tomato sauce. Layer pimientos on top of spinach and top with remaining cheese. Arrange the pepperoni on top of the cheese layer. Top with olive halves. Cover filling with reserved dough and crimp edges of dough to seal. Cut slits in top of dough to allow steam to escape. Bake 50 minutes or until crust is well browned (if crust browns too quickly, cover loosely with aluminum foil).Allow to cool 10 minutes before removing from pan and cutting into slices.

Title: Pumpkin Bread with Streusel Topping

Categories: Breads, Echo
Servings: 1

1 2/3 c All-purpose flour, sifted 1 1/3 c Granulated sugar
1/4 ts Baking powder 1/2 ts Vanilla
1 ts Baking soda 2 Eggs
1/8 ts Salt 1 c Pumpkin puree
1/2 ts Cinnamon 1/3 c Sherry
1/2 ts Nutmeg Orange slices, for garnish
1/3 c Butter, softened

---------**STREUSEL TOPPING**---------------------------
2/3 c Brown sugar, packed 1/2 ts Ground ginger
2 tb Butter 1/4 c Chopped walnuts
3 1/2 tb All-purpose flour
Makes one 9-by-5-inch loaf
Preparation time: 30 min. Baking time: 50 to 60 min. Oven Temperature: 350
degrees F.
1. Sift together dry ingredients. Set aside.
2. Cream butter with sugar until light and fluffy. Add vanilla, eggs and
pumpkin puree. Beat well.
3. Mix pumpkin mixture with flour mixture and sherry. Blend just until
ingredients are combined.
4. Pour into a greased and floured 9-by-5-inch loaf.
5. For streusel, cream butter with sugar. Add flour and ginger. Blend with
hands to form small crumbles. Add walnuts.
6. Sprinkle streusel topping evenly over batter.
7. Bake at 350 degrees F for 50 to 60 minutes.
8. Cool on rack for 10 minutes. Remove from pan. Serve warm or at room temperature. Garnish with orange slices, if desired. The "LARK"

Title: CRANBERRY RAISIN BREAD

Categories: Breads, Holidays, Christmas, California, Echo
Servings: 4
Cranberry Raisin Bread Serve this bread warm topped with Cranberry Butter (below) on Christmas morning.
4 cups flour 1.3/4 cups sugar 1 Tablespoon baking powder 1.1/2 teaspoons salt 1 teaspoon baking soda 1/2 cup unsalted butter 2 large eggs 1.1/2 cups orange juice 1 Tablespoon finely grated orange peel 2 cups fresh cranberries, washed, stemmed and copped (or frozen

cranberries, thawed and patted dry) 1 cup raisins
Preheat the oven to 350 degrees. In a large bowl, combine flour, sugar, baking powder, salt and baking soda. With a pastry blender or fork, cut in butter until the mixture makes coarse crumbs. In another bowl beat eggs, orange juice, and orange peel until well blended. Stir in flour mixture. Gently fold in cranberries and raisins. Pour batter into 2 buttered 9-inch x 5-inch-x 3-inch loaf pans and bake for 1 hour and 10 minutes, or until a toothpick inserted in center comes out clean. Cool in pans on rack for 10-15 minutes before removing from pans. Cranberry Butter: 1 cup fresh cranberries, washed and stemmed (or frozen cranberries, thawed and patted dry) 1.1/2 cups powdered sugar 1/2 cup unsalted butter, softened 1 Tablespoon lemon juice In a food processor puree the cranberries with the sugar. Add the butter and lemon juice, and blend until smooth. Transfer to a serving bowl and chill, covered, until firm

Title: Maple Biscuits
Categories: Breads, Echo
Servings: 16
2 c Sifted flour   5 tb Shortening
3 ts Baking powder 2/3 c Milk (about)
1/2 ts Salt

Sift flour with baking powder and salt. Cut in shortening until mixture is as fine as corn meal. Add milk, mixing until a soft dough is formed. Knead lightly on floured board for about 20 seconds. Roll to about 1/4 inch thickness and spread well with soft butter. Now spread one half of the dough very generously with maple sugar which has been scraped from the pail. Fold the other half of buttered dough over the sugared half. Cut in 1 inch squares and place thightly together in buttered baking pan. Bake quickly in 450 F. for 15 minutes.

Title: Truly Yeast Bread (gluten Free)
Categories: Celiac, Breads
Servings: 6

3 c GF Flour Mix (recipe 1/2 c Lukewarm water
-follows) 1 1/2 Yeast cakes, or 1 1/2
1/4 c Sugar -tablespoons yeast granules
3 1/2 ts Xanthan gum 1/4 c Shortening
2/3 c Dry milk powder 1 1/4 c Water
1 1/2 ts Salt 1 ts Vinegar
2 ts Sugar 3 Eggs

It is not easy to turn out a yeast bread recipe without wheat that smells, slices and tastes like wheat bread. This recipe is adapted from the nutrition dept. of the Univ. of Washington School of Medicine. Combine flour, sugar, xanthan gum, milk powder, and salt in bowl of heavy duty mixer. Use your strongest beaters. Dissolve the 2 teaspoons of sugar in the 1/2 cup of lukewarm water and mix in the yeast. Set aside while you combine the shortening and 1 1/4 cups water in saucepan and heat until shortening melts. Turn mixer on low. Blend dry ingredients and slowly add shortening and water mixture and the vinegar. Blend, then add the eggs. This mixture should feel slightly warm. Pour the yeast mixture into the ingredients in the bowl and beat at highest speed for 2 minutes. Place mixing bowl in a warm place, cover with plastic wrap and a towel, and let the dough rise approximately 1 to 1 1/2 hours or until doubled. Return to mixer and beat on high for 3 minutes. Spoon the dough into 3 small (2 1/2" x 5") greased loaf pans or 1 large one. Use muffin tins and bake any remaining as small rolls. Or make all rolls (approximately 18). Let rise until the dough is slightly above the top of pan. Bake in preheated 400 degree oven for 10 minutes. Place foil over bread and bake large loaves 50

minutes longer, small loaves slightly less time, and rolls about 25 minutes.
NOTES: The dough texture will seem more like cookie dough than bread dough, so don't be alarmed. Bread is better when baked in small loaf pans and delicious in rolls. I have successfully doubled the recipe to turn out 2 large loaves plus 18 rolls in the muffin tins or 3 small 2 1/2" x 5" loaves plus 24 rolls. This bread freezes well. For convenience, slice before freezing. This bread may be made with either brown or white rice flour in the GF flour mix.
GF flour mix: 2 parts white rice flour 2/3 part potato starch flour 1/3 part tapioca flour The Gluten-Free Gourmet

Title: Buttermilk Biscuits
Categories: Breads, Biscuits
Servings: 18
3 c Flour,all-purpose,sifted 2/3 c Shortening
1 ts Salt 1 c Buttermilk
1/2 ts Baking soda 4 tb Butter (opt)
3 ts Baking powder
1. Preheat oven to 450'F.
2. Sift flour, salt, soda, and baking powder into mixing bowl. Cut in shortening, using 2 knives, a pastry cutteror your hands dusted with flour. Add sufficient buttermilk to make a soft dough. Knead lightly and turn out onto a lightly floured board. Roll out to 1/2" thickness and cut with biscuit cutter into rounds. Place rounds not touching - for crisper biscuits - or close together - for softer biscuits - on ungreased baking sheet. Brush with melted butter if desired and bake in preheated oven 12-15 minutes, or until firm and lightly browned.

Title: Annie Mae Jones' Sweet Potato Biscuits
Categories: Breads, Biscuits

Servings: 14
1 c Flour,all-purpose 2 tb Shortening
3 ts Baking powder 1 c Sweet potatoes,mashed
1 ts Salt 1/2 c Milk

1. Preheat oven to 400'F.
2. Sift flour, baking powder, and salt into mixing bowl. Cut in shortening.Add potatoes and mix thoroughly, then add enough milk to make a soft dough. Turn out onto a lightly floured board and roll out to about 1/2" in thickness. Cut into squares. 3. Place squares not touching on ungreased baking sheet bake in preheated oven for 12-15 mimutes.
4. Serve warm, split, and spread with room-temperature butter.

Title: Peanut Putter Biscuits

Categories: Breads, Biscuits
Servings: 9
2/3 c Milk 2 c Biscuit mix
1/4 c Peanut butter 3 Bacon slices,,
,,- cooked crisp, drained, and crumbled.

1. Preheat oven to 400'F.
2. Place milk and peanut butter in a deep bowl or blender container and beat at high speed until smooth and well blended. Combine biscuit mix and bacon; stir lightly. Add milk and peanut butter mixture all at once and
stir with a fork until dough clings together. Turn out on a lightly floured board and knead gently a few times, then pat out to about 3/4" thickness. Cut into 2" rounds. Bake on an ungreased cookie sheet for 10-15 minutes, or until lightly browned.

Title: Garlic Cheese Biscuits

Categories: Breads, Lrk, Echo
Servings: 12
1/4 c Butter
2 c Bisquick -melted
2/3 c Milk   1 Garlic clove -=OR=-
1/2 c Cheddar cheese -minced fine
-shredded (2oz)   1/2 ts -garlic powder

Pre-heat oven to 450 degrees
Melt butter with garlic. Set aside and keep warm.
Mix baking mix, milk, chives and cheese until a soft dough forms- beat vigorously 30 seconds. Drop dough by spoonfuls onto ungreased cookie sheet. Bake 8 to 10 minutes or until golden brown. Brush garlic/butter mix over warm biscuits before removing from cookie sheet. Makes 10 to 12 biscuits. (Unless ya like 'em real big)

Title: Cranberry-Orange Nut Bread
Categories: Breads, Holiday, Lrk, Echo
Servings: 2
4 c Flour   2 ts Grated orange peel
1 1/2 c Sugar   1 1/2 c Orange juice
3 ts Baking powder 2 Egg
1 1/2 ts Salt   2 c Cranberries
1 ts Baking soda   -chopped
1/2 c Butter   1 c Nuts
-or margarine, softened   -chopped

Preheat oven to 350F. Grease bottom of 9x5 inch loaf pan. In large bowl, combine flour, sugar, baking powder, salt and baking soda. With pastry blender or fork, mix in butter until mixture is crjmbly. Stir in orange peel, orange juice and egg just until flour is moistened. Stir in cranberries and nuts. Spread batter in prepared pan. Bake 55-65 minutes, or until wooden toothpick inserted in center comes out clean. With spatula, loosen edges of loaf; remove from pan to wire rack to cool completely. Slice to serve. Best Ideas of Christmas

Title: STICKY ORANGE MUFFINS

Categories: Breads, Cunningham, Both, Breakfasts, Echo
Servings: 12

2 Oranges 1 ts Salt
1/4 c Honey 1/2 c Sugar
2 c Flour 2 Eggs; slightly beaten
1/2 c Uncooked oatmeal 2/3 c Milk
-(not instant) 5 1/2 tb Butter; melted
1 tb Baking powder

PREHEAT OVEN TO 400F. Either grease the muffin pans or line them with paper baking cups. Using the small side of the grater, grate the rind from the oranges, removing only the bright orange part, and set aside. With a small, sharp knife, remove all the remaining peel and, if necessary, trim the oranges all around so that the slices will fit into the bottom of your muffin pans. Cut the oranges into slices about 1/4-inch thick, pick out all the seeds and set the slices aside. Put about 1 teaspoon honey in the bottom of each muffin cup, and place an orange slice on top. Combine the flour, oatmeal, baking powder, salt and sugar in a large mixing bowl, and stir with a fork or wire whisk to mix. Add the reserved grated orange rind, the eggs, milk, and melted butter, and stir just until mixed. Spoon the batter over the orange slices, filling each cup about 2/3 full. Bake for 15-to-20 minutes, or until a toothpick inserted in the center of a muffin comes out clean. Remove from the oven and serve warm.

Title: Ada's Molasses Nut Bread

Categories: Breads, Holiday, Both, Echo
Servings: 1

2 3/4 c Flour; sifted all-purpose 1/2 c Seedless raisins
2 ts Baking powder 3/4 c Molasses
1/4 ts Soda 1 Egg; beaten
1/2 ts Salt 1/4 c Shortening; melted or oil
1/4 c Sugar 2 ts Grated orange rind
1/2 c Nut meats; chopped

Mix together and sift flour, baking powder, soda, salt and sugar into a mixing bowl; add nut meats and raisins and mix together. Combine the milk, molasses, egg, shortening and orange rind; add to dry mixture and stir only enough to dampen flour. Bake in a greased bread pan, 10x5x3 inch, in a moderate oven, 350 degrees F., for 1 1/4 hours. This recipe makes a large loaf of fruit bread.

Title: Oatcakes (not Sweet)
Categories: Breads, Scottish, Mine
Servings: 1
3 1/2 c Oats; quick 1/2 c Shortening
1 ts -salt 1/2 c -water ,approx.
2 tb Flour

Combine the oats, salt and flour. Cut in the shortening and add enough water to dampen and form a ball. (A food processor does the work in a jiffy). Leave to swell for ten minutes. Divide the dough and roll each part to 1/8" thickness; slide onto ungreased cookie sheet, indent in squares with a pastry wheel or knife. Bake in 350F for about 1/2 hour but watch that they don't turn brown. Sweet Oatcake: Add 1 cup sugar to recipe.

Title: Pictou County Oatcakes
Categories: Breads, Scottish, Mine
Servings: 1
2 c Oatmeal 3/4 c Shortening
1 c Flour 1/4 ts Baking soda

1 c Brown sugar 1/4 c -boiling water
1 ts -Salt

Combine dry ingredients and cut in shortening. Dissolve baking soda in the boiling water and add, continuing to mix with a knife. Mold with the hands and shape into a long wedge. Slice off and bake in a 400F oven for 10 minutes. This recipe comes from the county where the Scots first landed in Canada (and where my dad was born.) To quote the author, "Our Scottish ancestors used "real" oatmeal when they made their favorite oatcakes.However sugar did creep in, as indicated by this 75 year old recipe. (1894.) Out of Old Nova Scotia Kitchens

Title: PASTA DOUGH (Manual Pasta Machines ONLY)

Categories: Italian, Breads
Servings: 1
2 1/3 c All purpose flour 2 lg Eggs
(for better pasta, use 1 tb Olive oil
1 1/3 c AP flour and 1/2 ts Salt
1 c Semolina flour) 1/3 c Water

Mix 2 cups flour and salt in bowl, reserve 1/3 cup for later. Make a well in the center Mix eggs, olive oil and water and pour into well. Stir flour into egg mixture until dough forms into a ball. Turn out onto floured surface and kneed for about 10 minutes, adding extra flour if too moist. Kneed until dough is smooth and elastic. Cover with towel and rest for 30 minutes. Cut into 4 portions, keep pieces covered until used. Get out your machine and set dial on widest setting (1 on the Atlas). Flatten dough ball and run through rollers several times until smooth (you may add a bit of flour here too). Move rollers to next setting and roll again once. Continue to roll until pasta is the proper thickness (5 or 6 on the Atlas). You may cut sheet in half if it's too long.

Continue with other pieces and then put the finished sheet aside to dry for about 3 minutes. Attach desired pasta cutters and run the sheets through. You can use right away or spread out the pasta to dry overnight and then freeze extra. To cook, drop into large pot of boiling water with a bit of salt and oil. Cook until al dente, which should only take about 2 minutes for fresh. A tip - be sure the dough is fairly dry, otherwise it won't cut into separate strands. Another tip - You can substitute heavy cream for the 1/3 c water for a richer pasta. Great for fettuchini alfredo.

Title: BRENDA'S ITALIAN BREAD
Categories: Breads
Servings: 2
5 1/2 c Unsifted flour (120 to 130 degrees)
1 tb Salt Cornmeal
1 tb Sugat Corn or other vegetable oil
1 tb Butter or margerine 1 Egg white
2 Pkgs active dry yeast 1 tb Cold water
1 3/4 c Very warm tap water

With the metal blade in place, add 3 cups flour, salt, sugar, butter and yeast to bowl of processor. Turn machine on and off rapidly 2 or 3 times or until butter is thoroughly cut into dry ingredients. Add half the water and turn processor on and off 4 times. Add 1 1/2 cups flour and remaining water. Repeat on/off turns 4 times, then let processor run until a ball of dough formson the blades. If the dough is too sticky (wet), add remaining flour a few tablespoons at a time. When correct consistency, let processor run 40 to 60 seconds to knead dough. Turn dough out onto a lightly floured board and knead several times to form a smooth ball. Cover with plastic wrap and a towel. Let rest 20 minutes. Divide dough in half. Roll each half into an oblong 15 x 10 inches. Beginning at wide side, roll tightly Pinch seam to seal and taper ends by rolling gently back and forth. Place on greased baking sheets sprinkled with cornmeal. Brush dough with corn oil. Cover loosely with plastic wrap. Refrigerate 2 to 24 hours. When ready to bake, remove from refrigerator. Uncover dough carefully and let stand at room temperature for 10 minutes. Make 3 ro 4 cuts on top of each loaf with edge of metal blade or sharp knife. Bake at 425 degrees for 20 minutes. Remove from oven and brush with egg white beaten with cold water. Return to oven and bake 5 to 10 minutes longer or until golden brown. Remove from oven and cool on a wire rack.

Title: BASIL-PARMESAN SCONES

Categories: Breads, Appetizers
Servings: 4
1 Recipe buttermilk bisquits Dash garlic & onion
1/2 c Parmesan Powder, black pepper
1 tb Basil

There's a bakery near me called Aunt Mary's (are you listening, Sallie?) and they have the most wonderful basil-parmesan scones. One day I experimented and was pleased to find a pretty good facsimile. Just add the above ingredients along with all the other dry ingredients and proceed as above. These are a nice change of pace from Italian or garlic bread. Or cut with smaller cutter and serve as appetizer (don't forget to reduce baking time if smaller).

Title: Bacon And Onion Muffins

Categories: Breads, Main dish, Breakfast
Servings: 6
1/2 lb Bacon, Diced 1/2 ts Salt
1/4 c Chopped Onion 2 Large Eggs, Slightly Beaten

2 1/4 c Unbleached Flour, Sifted 1/3 c Milk
3 ts Baking Powder 1 c Dairy Sour Cream
1/2 ts Baking Soda Sesame Seeds

Fry bacon until crisp in skillet. Remove with slotted spoon and drain on paper towels. Saute onion in 1 T bacon drippings until tender (do not brown). Set aside to cool. Sift together flour, baking powder, baking soda and salt in large mixing bowl. Combine eggs, milk and sour cream in small bowl; blend well. Add all at once to dry ingredients, stirring just enough to moisten. Stir in bacon and sauteed onion. Spoon batter into greased 2 1/2-inch muffin-pan cups, fill 2/3rds full. Sprinkle with sesame seeds. Bake in 375 degree F. Oven 18 to 20 minutes or until golden brown. Serve hot with homemade jelly or jam.

Title: Banana Nut Muffins

Categories: Main dish, Breakfast, Breads
Servings: 6

2 c Unbleached Flour, Sifted 1 c Sugar
3 ts Baking Powder 2 Large Eggs
1/2 ts Salt 1 1/3 c Mashed Ripe bananas (3 Med.)
1/2 c Shortening 1 c Chopped Walnuts

Sift together flour, baking powder and salt; set aside. Cream together shortening and sugar in bowl until light and fluffy, using electric mixer at medium speed. Beat in eggs, one at a time, blending well after each addition. Stir in mashed bananas. Add dry ingredients all at once, stirring just enough to moisten. Gently mix in chopped nuts. Spoon batter into greased 3-inch muffin-pan cups, filling 2/3rds full. Bake in 350 degree F. oven 20 minutes or until golden brown. Serve hot with homemade jam or jelly.

Title: Heirloom Raisin Muffins

Categories: Breads, Breakfast
Servings: 4
1 c Raisins 2 Large Eggs
1 c Water 1 1/2 c Unbleached Flour, Sifted
1/2 c Butter/Regular Margarine 1 ts Baking Powder
1/4 c Sugar

Combine raisins and water in saucepan. Bring to a boil, reduce heat and cover. Simmer 20 minutes. Drain raisins, reserving liquid. Add enough water to reserved liquid to make 1/2 cup. Cool well. Cream together butter and sugar in bowl until light and fluffy, using electric mixer at medium speed. Add eggs, beat 2 more minutes. Sift together flour and baking powder. Add flour mixture alternately with 1/2 cup of reserved raisin liquid into creamed mixture, mixing well after each addition. Stir in raisins. Spoon batter into greased 3-inch muffin-pan cups, filling 2/3rds full. Bake in 400 degree F. oven 18 minutes or until golden brown. Serve hot with homemade jam or jelly.

Title: Country Bran Muffins
Categories: Breads, Breakfast, Main dish
Servings: 8
1 c 40% Bran Flakes Cereal 1/2 c Shortening
1 c Boiling Water 1 1/2 c Sugar
2 1/2 c Unbleached Flour, Sifted 2 Large Eggs
2 1/2 ts Baking Soda 2 c All-Bran Cereal
1/2 ts Salt 2 c Butter/Sour Milk

Combine 40% Bran Flakes and boiling water in bowl. Let stand 10 minutes. Sift together flour, baking soda and salt; set aside. Cream together shortening and sugar in large mixing bowl until light and fluffy, using electric mixer at medium speed. Add eggs, one at a time, beating well after each addition. Stir in Bran Flakes mixture and all-bran into creamed mixture. Add dry ingredients alternately with butter/sour milk to creamed mixture, mixing just enough to moisten. Spoon batter into well-greased 1 1/2-inch muffin-pan cups, filling 2/3rds full. Bake in 400 degree F. oven 25 minutes or until golden brown. Serve hot with butter and jam. NOTE:Batter can be stored for a few days in the refrigerator. Bake as directed.

Title: Sour Cream Brittle bread
Categories: Cajun, Appetizers, Breads
Servings: 10
2 3/4 c All-purpose flour 1 c Sour cream
1/4 c Sugar 2 tb Creole seasoning
1/2 ts Baking soda 2 tb Kosher salt for sprinkling
1/2 c Butter

Preheat the oven to 400F. Sift together the flour, sugar, salt, and baking soda into a bowl or food processor. Cut in the butter. Add the sour cream and Creole Seasoning (see recipe for Creole Seasoning), and mix to a soft dough. Roll out paper-thin on a floured board. Cut into 1-1/2 inch squares. Sprinkle with kosher salt and place on an ungreased baking sheet. Bake for 5-8 minutes. Turn off the heat and allow the bread to crisp in the oven. Nathalie Dupree describes this recipe in her book "New Southern Cooking" this way; "This crisp, cracker-like bread is good just flavored with salt and sour cream. But add Creole Seasoning and you'll have a hot and spicy appetizer that will leave your guests begging for the recipe. It's nice to keep a big airtight cookie jar full of these for snacking."

Title: Pepper Biscuits
Categories: Cajun, Breads
Servings: 12
2 1/2 c All purpose flour 1/2 ts Baking soda
1 tb Baking powder 3/4 c Shortening

1/2 ts Salt 1 c Buttermilk
1 tb Coarse cracked black pepper
Preheat oven to 450-500F. Sift 2 cups of the flour with the baking powder, salt, pepper, and baking soda into a bowl. Cut in the shortening with a pastry blender or fork, or work it in with your fingers. Add the buttermilk to make a soft dough, mixing just until the dough holds together. Flour your hands. Pull of a piece of dough the size of a biscuit and dip the wet edge into the extra flour. The roll or pat into a biscuit. Place slightly touching, on a lightly greased baking sheet. Bake until golden golden brown. 8-10 minutes.

Title: Southern Biscuit Muffins

Categories: Cajun, Breads
Servings: 12
2 1/2 c All-purpose flour 1/4 ts Sa;t
1/4 c Sugar 1/4 lb Plus 2 Tbsp unsalted butter
1 1/2 tb Baking powder 1 c Cold milk
In a bowl, combine the flour, sugar, baking powder and salt; mix well,breaking up any lumps. Work the butter in by hand until the mixture resembles coarse cornmeal, making sure no lumps are left. Gradually stir in the milk, mixing just until dry ingredients are moistened. DO NOT OVERBEAT. Spoon the batter into 12 greased muffin cups. Bake at 350F until golden brown, about 35 to 40 minutes. The finished muffins should have a thick crust with a cakelike centre.
Louisiana Kitchen

Title: New Orleans Black Muffins

Categories: Cajun, Breads
Servings: 12
3/4 c Hot water 3/4 c Sugar
1/2 c Molasses 3 tb Baking powder
1/4 c Milk 1 ts Baking soda

2 c Whole wheat flour 1 ts Salt
1 c All-purpose flour 1 1/2 c Chopped dry roasted pecans
In a medium-size bowl combine the hot water and molasses, stirring until well blended. Stir in the milk until blended.
In a large bowl sift together the flours, sugar, baking powder, baking soda and salt. With a rubber spatula, fold the liquid mixture and the pecans into the dry ingredients just until flour is thoroughly incorporated; do not over mix. Spoon into 12 greased muffin cups. Bake at 300F until done, 45 minutes to about 1 hour. Remove from pan immediately and serve while hot.

Title: Hushpuppies
Categories: Cajun, Breads
Servings: 30
1 c Cornmeal 1/4 ts White pepper
1/2 c All-purpose flour 1/8 ts Dried oregano leaves
1/2 c Corn flour 1/4 c Vy fine chopped green onions
1 tb Baking powder 1 1/2 ts Minced garlic
3/4 ts Ground cayenne pepper 2 Eggs, beaten
1/2 ts Salt 1 c Milk
1/2 ts Black pepper 2 tb Pork lard
1/2 ts Dried thyme leaves Vegetable for deep frying
NOTE: Corn flour is available at health food stores.
Combine all the dry ingredients in a large bowl, breaking up any lumps. Stir in the green onions and garlic. Add the eggs and blend well. In a small saucepan bring the milk and lard (or other fat) to a boil; remove from heat and add to flour mixture, half at a time, stirring well after each addition. Refrigerate 1 hour. In a large skillet or deep fryer, heat 4 inches of oil to 350F. Drop the batter by tablespoonsfuls into the hot oil. Do not crowd. Cook until dark golden brown on each side and cooked through, about 1 minute per

side. Drain on paper towels. Makes about 30 hushpuppies.

Title: Cheddar Pancakes
Categories: Cheese, Breads
Servings: 6

8 oz Cheddar; Md, Grated 3/4 ts Salt
3/4 c Dairy Sour Cream 1 1/2 ts Thyme
3 Egg Yolks, Lg, Beaten 1/2 ts Mustard; Dry
2 tb Unbleached Flour; PLUS 2 tb Butter
1 ts Unbleached Flour

Set out a heavy skillet. Put the grated Cheddar Cheese in a bowl and add the sour cream and egg yolks, mixing well after each addition. Add the flour salt thyme and dry mustard, which have been mixed well in a separate bowl or cup. Melt the butter in the skillet over low heat and drop the batter by tsp into the skillet. Cook over medium heat until lightly browned on the bottom. Loosen the edges with a spatula, turn and lightly brown the other side. Serve at once with bacon or pork sausage. Makes about 2 dozen 3-inch cakes.

Title: Quick Applesauce Muffins
Categories: Breads, Fruits
Servings: 12

2 c Bisquick 1/4 c Milk
1/4 c Sugar Egg
1 ts Cinnamon 2 tb Cooking oil
1/2 c Applesauce
---------------**TOPPING**---------------------------------
1/4 c Sugar 2 tb Butter or margarine, melted
1/4 ts Cinnamon

Preheat oven to 350 deg F.
Combine Bisquick, 1/4 cup sugar, and 1 teaspoon cinnamon. Add applesauce, milk, egg amd oil, and beat

vigorously for 30 seconds. Fill greased muffin pans 2/3 full and bake 12-15 minutes. Cool slightly and remove from pans. Mix remaining sugar and cinnamon. Dip tops of muffins in melted buter, then in sugar-cinnamon. Makes 12.

Title: Boston Brown Bread
Categories: Breads, Main dish
Servings: 10
1/2 c Rye meal or Plain flour 1/2 ts Salt
1/2 c Corn Meal 3/8 c Molasses
1/2 c Coarse whole wheat flour 1 c Sour milk
1 ts Baking Soda 1/2 c Seedless Raisins
Mix dry ingredients and stir in molasses and sour milk. (To make sour milk, add 1 T Vinegar to 1 cup sweet milk). Grease two #2 tin cans and place rings of waxed paper in bottoms. Divide batter evenly between the two cans, and cover with aluminum foil. Place in covered kettle of boiling water, bring water half way up sides of cans, and boil for two hours. When ready to serve, unmold by running knife around inside of can and shaking out onto plate. Cut thinly and serve with Boston Baked Beans.

Title: Shirley's Nut Bread
Categories: Breads
Servings: 10
2 c Boiling water 2 Eggs
1 c Raisins 2 ts Vanilla
2 ts Baking soda 4 c Flour
1 c Oleo (2 sticks) 3/4 c Chopped nuts
2 c Sugar
Boil 2 cups water, add 1 c. raisins and 2 t. baking soda. Let cool. In a large bowl, mix 2 sticks of oleo, 2 c. sugar, 2 eggs and 2 t. vanilla. Alternately add 4 c. flour and butter mixture to the raisin mixture. Add nuts. Bake at 325,,for l hour in

greased loaf pans. Makes two loaves. Great with butter or sprinkled with powdered sugar.

Title: DIRTY RICE
Categories: Breads, Cajun
Servings: 2

2 tb Chicken fat 1 ts Black pepper
1/2 lb Chicken gizzards 2 ts Paprika
1/4 lb Ground pork 1 ts Dry mustard
1 Bay leaves 1 ts Cumin
1 Yellow onions 1/2 ts Thyme
1 1/2 Celery stalks 1/2 ts Oregano
1/2 Bell peppers, green 2 tb Butter
1 Garlic cloves 2 c Pork stock
1 ts Tabasco sauce 1/2 lb Chicken livers
1 ts Salt 1 c Rice

Mince onion, bell pepper, celery and garlic. Grind livers and gizzards. Place fat, gizzards, pork and bay leaves in large heavy skillet over high heat; cook until meat is thoroughly browned, about 6 minutes, stirring occasionally. Stir in the onion, celery, bell pepper, garlic, Tabasco, salt, pepper, paprika, mustard, cumin, thyme, and oregano; stir thoroughly, scraping pan bottom well. Add the butter and stir until melted. Reduce heat to medium and cook about 8 minutes, stirring constantly and scraping pan bottom well. Add the stock or water and stir until any mixture sticking to the pan bottom comes loose; cook about 8 minutes over high heat, stirring once. Then stir in the chicken livers and cook about 2 minutes. Add the rice and stir thoroughly; cover pan and turn heat to very low; cook about 5 minutes. Remove from heat and leave covered until rice is tender, about 10 minutes. Remove bay leaves and serve immediately.

Title: Apricot Almond Buns

Categories: Breads, Fruits
Servings: 14

4 3/4 c Flour - all purpose 3 tb Margarine
1 c Brown sugar -firm packed 2 Eggs
1/2 ts Salt 1/4 c Margarine - melted
2 pk Yeast 1 c Apricots, chopped dried
1/2 c Milk 1/2 c Almonds, slivered
1/2 c Water

In a large bowl, mix 1 cup flour, 1/2 cup brown sugar, salt and undissolved yeast. Heat milk, water and 3 tbs margarine to 120F -130F. Add to dry ingredients; beat 2 minutes at medium speed of mixer. Add eggs and 1 cup flour; beat at high speed 2 minutes. Stir in enough remaining flour to make soft dough. Knead 8 to 10 minutes. Set in greased bowl; grease top.Cover; let rise until doubled, about 1 hour. Punch dough down. Divide in half; roll each to a 14 x 9 inch rectangle. Brush with melted margarine; sprinkle with remaining brown sugar, apricots and almonds. Roll each up from long side; seal seams. Cute each roll into 7 slices. Make 2 cuts in side of each slice, 2/3 the way through. Fan sections; set on greased baking sheet. Cover; let rise until doubled. Bake at 375F 15 to 20 minutes.

Title: Oatmeal Bread

Categories: Breads
Servings: 4

3 1/2 c Water 2 tb Salt
1/2 c Margarine 4 Eggs
1/2 c Honey 1/2 c Wheat germ
5 1/2 c White flour 1/2 c Cornmeal
4 c Rolled oats 4 1/2 c Wheat flour
4 pk Yeast

Heat water, margarine, and honey to 120f (48c). Add white

flour, oats, yeast, salt, and eggs. Beat in mixer for 3 minutes. Add remaining ingredients, beat at higher speed 3-4 minutes until stiff dough. Knead on floured board til smooth & not sticky. Place in greased bowl, turn over, cover, and let rise 45 minutes til doubled. Punch down, cut into even portions, roll out evenly to 3/8" thickness. Roll like a jelly roll, pinch down ends, fold ends under, & place in greased pans. Cover and let rise 1 hour til doubled. Bake at 375f for 40 minutes, cool on wire racks, serve. Makes 4 large loaves.

Title: Piney Woods Hush Puppies
Categories: Breads, Texas
Servings: 48
2 1/2 c Yellow Corn Meal 1 tb Baking Powder
1 ts Soda 1 Egg, beaten
1 ts Salt 2 c Buttermilk
2 tb Granulated Sugar 1 1/2 c Cooking Oil (about)
2 tb All-Purpose Flour

Mix all dry ingredients; beat milk and egg together and combine with dry ingredients; batter should hold its shape when picked up in spoon. If it is too soft, add more cornmeal. Drop by molded Tablespoon into 350"F fat and cook about 1 1/2 minutes; turn and cook on second side 1 minute. Allow oil to heat a few seconds after removing a batch. Delicious freshly cooked and hot; however, leftover hush puppies freeze well. When ready to serve frozen hush puppies, place on oven rack in preheated 250"F until very hot and crisp. Makes about 48 hush puppies 2" round. Hints on frying: Using a small diameter heavy saucepan allows using a minimum oil; a 5 or 6 inch pan with oil 1 1/2 inches deep and heated to 350"F will cook three hush puppies in about 2 1/2 minutes. When batter consistency is correct and oil is at 350"F, hush puppies will become firm, round shapes almost as soon as they enter the hot oil. If they are cooked in oil that is too hot, they will not cook in the center. Serving suggestions: Especially good served with fried catfish, trout, shrimp, oysters, chicken or chicken-fried steak. Recipes from Texas

Title: Smackin Cracklin Cornbread
Categories: Breads
Servings: 8
2 c Self-rising corn meal 1 1/2 c Buttermilk
1 ts Sugar 1 tb Flour
1/4 ts Salt 2 ts Melted butter
1 1/2 c Crackers 1 1/2 c Cracklins
Mix all ingredients well. Form into two pones. Put additional shortening or drippings on top. Bake at 450 degrees for 20 minutes. You may use a divided iron skillet or cornstick pan. Actually, you can use a regular on skillet if that's all you have.

Title: The Peace Maker
Categories: Main dish, Seafood, Breads
Servings: 6
1 c Rice 1 French bread loaf
36 Oysters 1 Butter, seasoning
Boil the rice and keep hot and dry. Cut off the top crust of the bread. Hollow out the inside. Fry the oysters. Butter the inside of the loaf well and place in the oven to brown. Fill with the hot fried oysters. The top of the loaf of bread may be buttered, toasted and placed on the oysters to retain the heat, although the oysters stay more crispy if served uncovered. Serve on a platter with hot boiled rice which is seasoned, dotted with butter, and garnished with minced parsley and paprika. Yield: 6 servings. Note: A finely minced clove of garlic may be used to flavor the butter. From Rice, 200 Delightful Ways to Serve It

Title: Banana And Mango Bread
Categories: Breads
Servings: 2
1 c Butter 1/4 ts Grated Fresh Nutmeg
1 1/4 c Packed Brown Sugar 1 1/2 c Mashed Ripe Bananas
3 Eggs 1 Small Ripe Mango
3 c Self-raising flour 1 c Golden Raisins
1/2 ts Salt 1/2 c Chopped Walnuts
1/2 ts Cinnamon

„The recipe says to use self-raising cake/pastry flour and the small ripe mango should be peeled and pureed. In a bowl, cream the butter with sugar until fluffy; beat in eggs, one at a time, until incorporated. In another bowl, combine self-raising flour with salt, cinnamon and nutmeg. Combine mashed bananas with mango puree. Mix the dry ingredients and banana mixture, alternately, into the creamed mixture until batter is just combined; fold in raisins and nuts. Pour batter into 2 greased 8 1/2 by 4 1/2 inch loaf pans. Bake at 350 degrees for 50 - 60 minutes or until cake tester inserted in the centre tests done. Leave in pan for 10 minutes; remove form loaf pans and let cool on racks. Makes 2 loaves.

Title: Cherry cheddar bread
Categories: Breads
Servings: 1
2 1/2 c Flour 1 1/4 c Milk
1/2 c Sugar 1 Egg, beaten
1/2 c Brown sugar, packed 3 tb Oil
3 ts Baking powder 1 1/4 c Sweet cherries, frozen
1 ts Salt 1 1/4 c Cheddar cheese, shredded

Combine flour, sugar, brown sugar, baking powder and salt. Combine milk, egg and oil; pour over dry ingredients and stir just enough to dampen. Gently fold in cherries and cheese. Pour into greased 9 1/4 X 5 1/4 X 2 ¾ inch loaf pan. Bake at 350F 55-65 minutes or until wooden pick inserted near center comes out clean. Cool on rack 10 minutes; remove from pan. Cool completely before serving. Serve at room temperature, or toasted.

Title: Hot Cross Buns

Categories: Breads
Servings: 24
4 1/2 c All-Purpose Flour 1/4 c Melted Butter
1/3 c Granulated Sugar 2 Eggs, beaten
2 tb Quick Rise Instant Yeast 1 c Raisins or part currants
1 ts Salt 1/2 c Mixed Candied Peel
2 ts Cinnamon 1 1/2 c Icing Sugar
1/2 ts Grated Nutmeg 2 tb Milk
2 c Warm Water

In a large mixing bowl, combine the flour, sugar, yeast, lemon rind, salt cinnamon and nutmeg. Stir in warm water and butter, then beaten eggs. Using a wooden spoon, vigorously stir dough until smooth and elastic. Stir in raisins and candied peel. Scrape down sides of bowl, cover with a clean dry towel and stand for 10 minutes. Grease 24 medium to large-sized muffin cups and spoon in batter -- no more than 2/3 full. Brush tops with melted butter. Cover and let rise in a warm place until almost double, about 20 - 30 minutes. Bake in an oven preheated to 375 degrees for about 20 minutes or until tops are browned. Let cool on wire racks until warm, about 10 – 15 minutes. Combine icing sugar with milk until smooth; place in a piping bag or spoon on top of buns to make crosses. Makes 24 buns.

Title: MISSISSIPPI CORNBREAD ROBERT

Categories: Breads

Servings: 6
2 c Stoneground white cornmeal 2 Large eggs
1 ts Baking soda 2 c Buttermilk
1 ts Salt 1/3 c Bacon drippings or Crisco

Preheat oven to 450 degrees F. Place bacon drippings or Crisco in 9-inch cast iron skillet. Heat skillet in oven until fat is smoking hot, while preparing batter. (This should take no more than 5-10 minutes.) Thoroughly combine cornmeal, baking soda, and salt in medium bowl. Add eggs and buttermilk all at once. Blend thoroughly, using wire whisk. Slowly pour all but 1 tablespoon of hot fat into batter, continuing to beat quickly with whisk to incorporate fat. Turn skillet around to coat sides and bottom thoroughly with remaining fat. Pour batter into skillet. Bake on top rack of oven for 25-30 minutes, or until top of cornbread is firm. Turn cornbread onto plate and slip back into skillet upside-down. Return to oven for 5 minutes. Turn out onto rack, cut into 6 wedges and serve immediately.

Title: Poppy Seed Bread
Categories: Breads
Servings: 3
1 Box of yellow cake mix 1/2 c Cooking sherry
4 Eggs 1 Small vanilla inst. pudding
1 c Oil 1/4 c Poppy seed
8 oz Sour cream

Combine all and mix well. Put in 3 small floured pans. Cook 325 degrees 1 hour.

Title: Amy's Cornbread
Categories: Breads
Servings: 4
1 pk Frozen brocoli 1 Med. Onion 2 c Grated chedder sharp

cheese 1 Box jiffy cornbread mix Bake in glass pan for 25-30 minutes at 400 degree.

Title: Deb's Breakfast Cake

Categories: Breads

Servings: 10

1 pk Forzen rich's rolls 1/2 c Brown sugar
1 Stick of butter 1/2 c Pecans
1 pk Small vanilla pudding

Place frozen rolls in bundt pan. Melt butter and pour over rolls. Mix pudding, brown sugar and nuts togehter. Sprinkle mixture over rolls. Cover pan with paper towel or waxed paper and let rise overnight.Bake 350 degree oven for 30 minutes.

_Title: Monkey Bread

Categories: Breads

Servings: 6

1/2 c Pecans 3 cn Biscuits
1 ts Cinnamon 1 Stick of butter
1/2 c Sugar 1 c Brown sugar

Place pecans in bottom of Bundt pan. Combine cinnamon and sugar. Cut each biscuit into quarters and roll in sugar mixture. Stack biscuits in pan.Combine butter and brown sugar. Pour over biscuits. Bake 30-40 minutes at 350.

Bibliografische Information der Deutschen Nationalbibliothek: Die Deutsche Nationalbibliothek verzeichnet diese Publikation in der Deutschen Nationalbibliografie; detaillierte bibliografische Daten sind im Internet über dnb.dnb.de abrufbar.

Herstellung und Verlag:
BoD - Books on Demand, Norderstedt
ISBN 978-3-7412-5272-3

© 2016 H.von Bugenhagen